HASKALAH

Key Words in Jewish Studies

Series Editors
Deborah Dash Moore, University of Michigan
Macdonald Moore, Vassar College
Andrew Bush, Vassar College

I. Andrew Bush, *Jewish Studies*
II. Barbara E. Mann, *Space and Place in Jewish Studies*
III. Olga Litvak, *Haskalah: The Romantic Movement in Judaism*

HASKALAH

The Romantic Movement in Judaism

OLGA LITVAK

RUTGERS UNIVERSITY PRESS
New Brunswick, New Jersey, and London

Library of Congress Cataloging-in-Publication Data

Litvak, Olga.
   Haskalah : the romantic movement in Judaism / Olga Litvak.
      p. cm. — (Key words in Jewish studies ; v. 3)
   Includes bibliographical references and index.
   ISBN 978–0–8135–5436–5 (hardcover : alk. paper) — ISBN 978–0–8135–5435–8 (pbk. : alk. paper) — ISBN 978–0–8135–5437–2 (e-book)
   1. Haskalah. 2. Judaism—History—18th century. 3. Judaism—History—19th century. I. Title.
   BM194.L58 2012
   296.09′033—dc23

                                                            2012005543

A British Cataloging-in-Publication record for this book is available from the British Library.

Copyright © 2012 by Olga Litvak

All rights reserved

No part of this book may be reproduced or utilized in any form or by any means, electronic or mechanical, or by any information storage and retrieval system, without written permission from the publisher. Please contact Rutgers University Press, 106 Somerset Street, New Brunswick, NJ 08901. The only exception to this prohibition is "fair use" as defined by U.S. copyright law.

Visit our website: http://rutgerspress.rutgers.edu

Manufactured in the United States of America

FOR MY PARENTS

Diffused over enlightened Europe, an order of men has arisen, who, uninfluenced by the interests or the passions which give an impulse to the other classes of society, are connected by the secret links of congenial pursuits, and, insensibly to themselves, are combining in the same common labors, and participating in the same divided glory. . . . A new spirit seems to bring them nearer to each other; and, as if literary Europe were intent to form but one people out of the populace of mankind, they offer their reciprocal labors to each other . . . and that knowledge which, like a small river, takes its source from one spot, at length mingles with the ocean-stream common to them all. But those who stand connected with this literary community are not always sensible of their kindred alliance.

—Isaac D'Israeli, *The Literary Character* (1846)

Contents

Foreword — ix
Preface — xi
Acknowledgments — xv
Note on Transliteration — xvii

Part I Terms of Debate

1. Wrong Time, Wrong Place — 3
2. Beyond the Enlightenment — 23

Part II State of the Question

3. Haskalah and History — 49
4. Haskalah and Modern Jewish Thought — 65

Part III In a New Key

5. Exile — 81
6. New Creation — 89
7. Faith — 113
8. Paradise — 131
9. Fall — 157
10. The End of Enlightenment — 181

Notes — 191
Index — 221

Foreword

The Rutgers book series Key Words in Jewish Studies seeks to introduce students and scholars alike to vigorous developments in the field by exploring its terms. These words and phrases reference important concepts, issues, practices, events, and circumstances. But terms also refer to standards, even to preconditions; they patrol the boundaries of the field of Jewish studies. This series aims to transform outsiders into insiders and let insiders gain new perspectives on usages, some of which shift even as we apply them.

Key words mutate through repetition, suppression, amplification, and competitive sharing. Jewish studies finds itself attending to such processes in the context of an academic milieu where terms are frequently repurposed. Diaspora offers an example of an ancient word, one with a specific Jewish resonance, which has traveled into new regions and usage. Such terms migrate from the religious milieu of Jewish learning to the secular environment of universities, from Jewish community discussion to arenas of academic discourse, from political debates to intellectual arguments and back again. As these key words travel, they acquire additional meanings even as they occasionally shed long-established connotations. On occasion, key words can become so politicized that they serve as accusations. The sociopolitical concept of assimilation, for example, when turned into a term—assimilationist—describing an advocate of the process among Jews, became an epithet hurled by political opponents struggling for the mantle of authority in Jewish communities.

When approached dispassionately, key words provide analytical leverage to expand debate in Jewish studies. Some key words will be familiar from long use, and yet they may have gained new valences, attracting or repelling other terms in contemporary discussion. But there are prominent terms in Jewish culture whose keys lie in a particular understanding of prior usage. Terms of the past may bolster claims to continuity in the present while newly minted language sometimes disguises deep connections reaching back into history. Attention must be paid as well to the transmigration of key words among Jewish languages—especially Hebrew, Yiddish, and Ladino—and among languages used by Jews, knitting connections even while highlighting distinctions.

An exploration of the current state of Jewish studies through its key words highlights some interconnections often only glimpsed and holds out the prospect of a reorganization of Jewish knowledge. Key words act as magnets and attract a nexus of ideas and arguments as well as related terms into their orbits. This series plunges into several of these intersecting constellations, providing a path from past to present.

The volumes in the series share a common organization. They open with a first section, Terms of Debate, which defines the key word as it has developed over the course of Jewish history. Allied concepts and traditional terms appear here as well. The second section, State of the Question, analyzes contemporary debates in scholarship and popular venues, especially for those key words that have crossed over into popular culture. The final section, In a New Key, explicitly addresses contemporary culture and future possibilities for understanding the key word.

To decipher key words is to learn the varied languages of Jewish studies at points of intersection between academic disciplines and wider spheres of culture. The series, then, does not seek to consolidate and narrow a particular critical lexicon. Its purpose is to question, not to canonize, and to invite readers to sample the debate and ferment of an exciting field of study.

Andrew Bush
Deborah Dash Moore
Macdonald Moore
Series Editors

Preface

This book is part of the Keywords in Jewish Studies series; I have taken the point of my contribution to this collective scholarly enterprise very much to heart. It is meant to serve as a point of entry into the study of the Haskalah, to introduce students, teachers, and scholars to a subject, an idea, and a movement that lies at the intersection between Jewish history and Jewish literature. The tasks set by the editors of the series—to explain a concept that is central to Jewish studies, to assess its role in stimulating scholarly debate, and to anticipate questions that lie beyond the horizon of current research—have prompted me to articulate a new interpretation and develop a fresh approach to a topic, the significance of which has, in my opinion, been almost wholly misunderstood.

The nature of the series informs the structure of the book as well as the presentation of the argument and the choice of sources. Every possible care has been taken to help the uninitiated reader navigate both through the historiography and the primary texts, without sacrificing (I can only hope) nuance, imagination, and intellectual rigor. In the first section, "Terms of Debate," I unpack the standard usage of the term "Haskalah" as the Jewish offspring of the European Enlightenment. As the subtitle of the book indicates, I think this genetic connection is misconceived. The first section makes clear why. The second section, "State of the Question," considers the current scholarship on the Haskalah. My presentation is not meant to be comprehensive. I interrogate the principal themes that inform Haskalah research as it stands today. In the course of doing so, I explore the kinds of tensions within the field that have provoked scholars to challenge the consensus approach to the Haskalah as the Jewish ideology of emancipation.

The last section, "In a New Key," rereads some of the most interesting primary texts produced by the Haskalah through the analytical lens that I adopt in this book. Most of these texts are works of fiction that normally do not make it into histories of the Haskalah; if they are read at all, they are read by literary critics. Scholarship has carefully segregated the Hebrew and Yiddish literature written by maskilim from other kinds of sources, such as philosophy, journalism, polemics, and petitions to the state, that are treated as more authoritative. I think this is a mistake. The Haskalah was a literary movement but that does not mean that its literature is exclusively the business of literary scholars. The division of labor between those who study the literature and those who study the history of the Haskalah seems arbitrary and wrongheaded, especially in light of the way other kinds of Jewish literature have been mainstays of the writing of Jewish history for as long as the field has existed. Talmudic Judaism was a literary movement too; whatever else it later became, rabbinic culture was first a revolution in writing. As, for that matter, was Jewish mysticism. To be sure, Haskalah poetry and prose belong with modern Jewish literature, just as the Mishnah belongs with the literature of Jewish antiquity and the *Zohar* with that of the Jewish Middle Ages; but, for all that, they are each an integral part of the history of Judaism.

While Haskalah literature remains just literature, the fantasies of a small group of Jews who lived in third-century Palestine are filed under the "history of religion." Is this because the world of the rabbis is more believable than the fantasies of Jews in nineteenth-century Eastern Europe? I, for one, find the novels of Peretz Smolenskin more credible than the stories of R. Akiva. Or is it because more people read the latter than the former? But the history of Judaism celebrates books that were meant to be read by the few rather than the many. Moreover, a larger number of people probably read *A Donkey's Burial* than the *Guide for the Perplexed,* although most of them probably wouldn't admit it. Or is it because the latter made people do things while the former ostensibly left no trace on people's behavior? This too is a debatable proposition, especially if we consider thinking the beginning of doing. The point is not to make the facile disciplinary distinction a basis for classifying what is historical and what isn't, but to ask why one text might make us want to do things and another makes us wish we had the courage not to do them. Some texts become historical, but none of them start out that way. It is important to understand, rather than assume, such differences. Or, finally, is it because the people who put themselves in charge of building libraries and devising filing systems were sure that they knew which stories were true and which were mere fiction? If that's the case, than it is surely the responsibility of historians to put the books out of order.

My own choice of source material was not dictated by the specious divide between the history of the Haskalah and its literature. It was, in most instances, driven by the current state of Jewish publishing. I chose works that would be accessible to English-speaking readers. As it happens, most of the relevant stuff that has been translated is confined to literature (which, without putting too fine a point on it, tells us something about the continuing cultural resonance of what historians have dismissed as merely decorative or illustrative). My immediate goal was to encourage all teachers of Jewish history, even those of us who are fortunate enough to be able to read the originals, to integrate the Haskalah more fully into their curricula. In order to do this, we must have a key to the texts that are readily available and that our students can read for themselves. The argument in this book is that a new history of the Haskalah does not stand or fall by the discovery of new archival sources or by the recovery of unknown philosophical masterpieces. A new history of the Haskalah is hidden in plain view. It is available to anyone who is prepared to take Abraham Mapu's *Love of Zion* as seriously as we have been taught to take the tales of R. Nahman of Bratslav.

Acknowledgments

For their support of the project and their critical feedback, I am grateful to the editors of the Keywords in Jewish Studies series, Deborah Dash Moore, Macdonald Moore, and Andrew Bush. My thanks to Leora Batnitzky, Willi Goetschel, Gershon Hundert, Marcus Moseley, Derek Penslar, Moshe Rosman, Naomi Seidman, and Shaul Stampfer for conversations that proved always helpful and frequently eye-opening and, particularly, to Rachel Manekin for sharing her expertise on Galicia as well as her unpublished work. A special thanks to John Gager for his empathetic and trenchant critique of my reading of Paul.

Clark University offered a congenial and receptive environment in which to write. Amy Richter, the chair of the history department, and Debórah Dwork, the director of the Strassler Center for Holocaust and Genocide Studies, provided much-needed encouragement and expert advice. I was able to complete the final version of the book thanks to a Starr Fellowship from Harvard's Center for Jewish Studies, where I also had the opportunity to present my work on Judah Leib Gordon. I am grateful to all the members of the Starr Seminar for their searching questions and comments.

Several colleagues and friends took time and thought from their own work to read through various drafts of the manuscript, sometimes in multiple incarnations. For all of their help and support, my profound thanks to Amir Banbaji, Elisheva Carlebach, Kristen Cosby, Yaacob Dweck, Chae Ran Freeze, Jay Harris, Paul Litvak, Alice Nakhimovsky, and Alyssa Quint. The generosity and candor of anonymous reviewers dispelled lingering doubts. At Rutgers University Press, Marlie Wasserman and an expert production staff brought ship to shore with speed and care.

This book is dedicated with affection and gratitude to my father, the romantic, and my mother, the enlightener. And, as always, to Abby, my delight and my darling girl, for no reason at all.

Note on Transliteration

In transliterating Hebrew and Russian, I have followed the Library of Congress rules, except that I have eliminated most diacritical marks. Yiddish terms are generally romanized according to the standards of the YIVO Institute for Jewish Research. All translations are my own, except where indicated. The transliteration of Russian-Jewish personal names follows their original Russian, not their current Yiddish or Hebrew, spelling; hence, Abramovich and not Abramovitsh.

PART I
TERMS OF DEBATE

1 Wrong Time, Wrong Place

The historical treatment of the Haskalah is a case study in mistranslation. Scholarly convention uniformly renders this Hebrew word as "enlightenment," a definition that inevitably invites comparison with the European movement of the same name. Nearly every book or article dealing with the subject assumes and then proceeds to expound upon this ostensible kinship. The consensus view of the Haskalah from the perspective of the European Enlightenment is more or less taken for granted as an article of scholarly faith, even in Israel where there is no need for translation from the Hebrew. To be sure, historians disagree about the significance of a "Jewish Enlightenment" in shaping modern Jewish experience and expression. Yet the very fact that current usage equates "haskalah" with "enlightenment" prescribes a normative course of research and folds the history of a "Jewish" Enlightenment into the history of its European counterpart. While historians of the Haskalah continue to debate the fine points of the comparison, they remain riveted to the standard translation, trying to perform the conceptual equivalent of sticking a square peg into a round hole.

But the term "haskalah" has its own Jewish genealogy; the persistence of the word into the modern period is not, in itself, a good enough reason to argue that the Haskalah represents a case of Enlightenment "in national context" or an example of "religious Enlightenment."[1] The word "maskil" (which, like "haskalah," has a venerable Jewish pedigree, as we shall see) does not have to be translated as "enlightener" or "rationalist." In its modern sense," maskil" corresponds more precisely to the word "intellectual," derived from the root word *sekhel*, which means "intellect" rather than "reason." To refer to a maskil as an intellectual is still not necessarily to tie the Haskalah to the Enlightenment. There were intellectuals in ancient Greece and in twentieth-century France—and no maskilim in either place.[2]

The connection, whether causal, contextual, or comparative, between the Haskalah and the Enlightenment is not self-evident. For one thing, the chronology is off by at least a century. While the Haskalah developed into a literary and philosophical movement between the 1780s and the 1870s, the European Enlightenment began with the Scientific Revolution in the seventeenth century and culminated in the French Revolution in

1789. By the time the first maskilim had begun to make a discernible impact on Jewish thought, the underlying premises of Enlightenment rationalism were already being questioned not just by the defenders of established forms of political and religious authority, but from within the ranks of the Enlightenment itself. The moment of enlightened self-scrutiny, associated with the ideas of J. J. Rousseau and Immanuel Kant, was the real point of crisis that promised to close one era in the history of ideas and shortly to open another.

It was Rousseau who first broke the crucial link between scientific discovery and the moral progress of humanity, a cornerstone of the Enlightenment's implicit trust in the civilizing power of reason." There is in Asia a vast country in which the sciences are a passport to the highest position in the state," Rousseau pointed out. But "if the sciences really purified morals ... if they really inspired courage, then the people of China would assuredly be wise, free and invincible. But as a matter of fact, there is no sin to which they are not prone, no crime which is not common amongst them."[3] Rousseau's "China" is not really China; the reference to the self-satisfaction of a rising political class of savants is a thinly veiled attack on his own contemporaries, the *philosophes*. In contrast to their enlightened optimism, Rousseau expressed his own acute skepticism about the power of reason to lead a person toward virtue. Reason, he said, was more likely to silence the voice of conscience.[4] In fact, the cultivation of the intellect enabled the proliferation of unsatisfiable narcissistic needs and the invention of antisocial desires. In place of philosophizing, Rousseau enjoined spontaneous feeling as the only reliable arbiter of moral choice.

Rousseau contrasted the spontaneous action of human sentiments with rationalization, the sole purpose of which was to justify the gratification of selfish caprice and degenerate appetite. "All morality," he wrote in the second *Discourse* (1754)," is based on pity, which is prior to reflective thought."[5] The only way for a jaded, modern adult to return to the moral purity of the child was, ironically, to recapture a state of uncorrupted innocence, in other words, to perform with conviction the role of perfect artlessness. "Art," wrote Kant of Rousseau's system of modern education, "when it reaches perfection, once more becomes nature—and this is the ultimate goal of man's moral destiny."[6] Rousseau insisted that absolute sincerity, pursued without regard of its consequences for the well-being of other people, was the ultimate expression of heroic individualism, "for it is better to cause a scandal than to be a person of no account."[7]

Rousseau's discovery of the prerogatives of subjectivity dovetailed with Kant's radical reassessment of Enlightenment empiricism. One of the singular achievements of the age of Enlightenment was the development of scientific methods dependent on observation and experiment rather than on speculation for definitive knowledge of the sensible world. Building on Descartes's paradoxical idea that doubt of everything except the human capacity for reflection provided the only ground of metaphysical certainty, Enlightenment philosophy adopted a mechanistic approach to the problem of perception. Descartes envisioned the human being as a "thing that thinks," a reasoning machine stimulated by the power of physical sensation. Reason was the internal mechanism that ordered the barrage of external, sensory impressions into principles of personal conduct and good government, akin in their stability to the laws of nature. Impressions were particular and highly irregular, but the rule of reason was universal in its mathematical precision. Following Descartes, Spinoza argued that rational thought effectively closed the gap between nature as a passive object of empirical inspection and nature as a self-governing, rational force. According to Spinoza, the reasonableness of nature was itself resident in the uniquely human capacity to generalize and draw logical conclusions from the evidence of the senses. The assumption that reason's aim was chiefly to regulate the faculty of perception formed an underlying premise of empirical science.

Kant rejected the instrumentalization of reason as misleading and unsatisfying.[8] He deplored the inability of early modern science to prove—rather than dogmatically assert—the existence of the intelligible world outside of human perception. Kant argued that all metaphysical abstractions, including such elemental organizing ideas as time and space, were "a priori intuitions," based in "immediate and non-conceptual awareness" rather than in the experience of the way that reality "out there" actually worked.[9] The sensible world appeared to people in the guise of "representations," the formation of which, Kant said, depended on "inner human activity," not direct apprehension by the sensory organs. Both "objects of inner sense (our own inner mental states) and objects of outer sense" which Descartes and the empiricists "represented as distinct from our own inner states" are *"in us . . . not* things as they are in themselves, independently of our cognitive access to them."[10] Certain basic laws in the function of the universe such as cause and effect conform to our "representations," because our own notion of order is grounded in the same natural laws as the physical world that we inhabit. But transcendent truths that lie beyond the scope of experience in the world—such as God, freedom, and immortality—remain empirically unverifiable and depend entirely on the autonomous "self-construction" of reason. In this realm, man remains perfectly free, subject not to the iron-clad laws of the physical world but only to the integral moral law of the "categorical imperative," derived from reason alone.

According to Kant, "our conception of ourselves as doing things *because* there is reason to do them, manifest in our making of *ought* judgments ... commits us to the existence of a causality other than that of nature—a causality of reason—and consequently to a conception of ourselves as transcendentally free, as entities whose wills are not determined merely by empirical causes."[11] In contrast to the followers of Spinoza, Kant understood rationality not as a quality embedded in the ready-made order of nature, but as the ultimate source of human freedom from necessity. The mind enables the faculty of choice between *is* and *ought*; all other living things exist entirely under the inexorable rule of natural instinct and biological determinism.

Kant's groundbreaking manifesto, published in 1784, in response to the question "What Is Enlightenment?" presented a provocative defense of intellectual autonomy, without precedent in Enlightenment philosophy.[12] In this essay, Kant argued that enlightenment consists in "mankind's exit from his self-imposed immaturity" through the use of "one's own understanding." His credo "Dare to know!" has become a commonplace in the history of Enlightenment and his essay treated as a summation of one hundred years of progressive thought. Yet his motto ran against the grain of Enlightenment rationalism. In Kantian terms, "enlightenment" refers to the "activity of critique" rather than to systematic acquisition and efficient deployment of ready-made knowledge.[13] The achievements of enlightenment, before Kant, inhered in the systematization of information, a capacity impressively exhibited in such famous Enlightenment compilations as the *Encyclopédie* and Samuel Johnson's *Dictionary*. Kant's principled rejection of all intellectual authority, including, presumably, the accumulation of philosophical and scientific learning available in books and embodied in professional expertise, places the individual use of reason beyond the pale of civilization. Kant admitted the political and personal imperative of "obedience" to authority but offered a picture of enlightenment that was both liberating and fundamentally antisocial, potentially inimical to the rules of scientific consensus that governed Europe's republic of letters.

More than that, Kant's insistence on a limitless capacity for free thought exempted human beings from any system of determination, including even the laws of nature that, like political laws, tended to work upon the body with the functionality of a "machine." Indeed, political *bodies*, like their non-metaphorical counterparts, represented the "obstruction of things," not, as readers of Spinoza had been asserting for a hundred years, aspects of the same material "substance" that ensured the essential harmoniousness of the cosmos and the stability of responsible government.[14] In its emphasis on the heroic capacity of human beings to transcend their deep-seated biologically determined inclination to obey, Kant's philosophical system was more subjectivist than even Rousseau's. The mandate of critical thought threatened the common truths of Enlightenment no less than the well-established precepts of religion and the dictates of conventional morality. Whatever conclusions man did not reach exclusively through the use of his own reason, even if they had the appearance of scientific axioms (which made them more, not less, deceptive than any other disciplinary truths), retained the dubious status of dogma.

The anthology in which Kant's essay appeared did not simply recycle a set of generally acceptable proposition. The other essays, many of them equivocal if not downright hostile toward Enlightenment rationalism, pointed in the direction of radical self-criticism that Kant had introduced in his own contribution. The question itself—"What Is Enlightenment?"—effectively dispensed with a century's worth of assertions on the subject and presumed the need to leave reason itself open to the same scrutiny as that to which Voltaire had so ruthlessly exposed the teachings of the church. Kant marked the end of an "enlightened age" and the beginning of the "age of enlightenment." A sense of achievement attendant on the assurance of living in a universe of expanding certainty gave way to the idea that enlightenment, by definition, demanded constant self-examination, its truth claims always unresolved and its tasks left perpetually unfinished.

Kant's paradoxical formulation put the idea of scientific progress into question and forced every subsequent thinker into a position of radical independence from the past. Like Rousseau, Kant depicted humanity in a constant state of rebirth, unburdened by the weight of tradition but thrown into an uncertain future. Both associated "enlightenment" with remorseless self-analysis rather than the attainment of perfection, a process that, for Spinoza, resolved in the infinite tranquility of "blessedness."[15] Perfectibility, argued Rousseau in the second *Discourse*, was humanity's destiny and its perpetual curse, not a source of blessing and inner peace.

Nineteenth-century European thought inherited both the Enlightenment's promise of the good life and the critical project initiated by Rousseau and Kant. Beset by a palpable sense of contradiction that made Rousseau and Kant the chief contrarians of the Enlightenment, the nineteenth century engaged in a search for synthesis and in the struggle to reconcile multiple truths: mind and body, freedom and necessity, rational judgment and emotional response, artistic creativity and scientific rigor, the desire for autonomy and the need for society, human individuality and mass conformity, liberty and law. The Enlightenment's vision of the universe as a determined, well-ordered mechanism had become, as Kant suggested, an offense to human dignity, at best a comforting fiction, at worst a blueprint for a prison of man's own making.

Kant and Rousseau left the eighteenth century in shambles. This is the point at which the history of the Haskalah begins. The Jewish movement was part of the same paradigm shift that had shaken the confidence of the Enlightenment. Effects of the "Copernican revolution" in metaphysics initiated by Kant began to seep into every aspect of European intellectual culture and to transform the meaning of religious experience, the content of imaginative literature, and the understanding of human behavior. Maskilim inclined far more to the work of Rousseau and Kant than to the giants of seventeenth- and early eighteenth-century European thought, including Spinoza, who was not only a pivotal figure in Enlightenment science but also a Jewish thinker.[16] Among the first generation of Jewish intellectuals there was a number of distinguished Kantians, including Marcus Herz, Solomon Maimon, Lazarus Bendavid, and Saul Ascher.[17] More generally the philosophical vocabulary that distinguished the Haskalah from previous attempts to integrate reason and revelation—for which there was already ample precedent in ancient and medieval Jewish philosophy—lent itself strikingly to Kantian terminology. For instance, the word that maskilim normally used to refer to "independent judgment" (Heb. *hakirah*) in contrast to "tradition" (Heb. *kabbalah*) was similar in meaning to Kant's idea of critique. Maskilim referred to themselves as "inquirers" or "critics" (Heb. *hokrim*), not as "men of letters," which was the more common Enlightenment term for those who devoted themselves to the acquisition of scientific learning.[18] The affinities with post-Kantian thought only deepened over the course of the century. Nahman Krochmal's *Guide for the Perplexed of Our Time* (1851)—the philosophical credo of the Haskalah—wrestled with the implications of Kantian idealism for the future of Judaism.[19] The most profound challenge to the post-Kantian framework of the Haskalah came from the resurgence of Enlightenment materialism, first in Karl Marx's economic history, and subsequently in the empirical methods of "positivism" developed by the French founder of sociology, Auguste Comte.

Jewish intellectuals owed no less to Rousseau than they did to Kant. Their invention of modern Jewish autobiography was directly inspired by his *Confessions*.[20] Their theories of education drew on Rousseau's ideal of a return to nature as a cure for Jewish book culture.[21] Their obsession with social hypocrisy and false piety may be traced to Rousseau's strident insistence on sincerity.[22] Less easy to pin down was the general feeling of restlessness among maskilim, far more characteristic of the age of critique than of an age marked by confident belief that human beings were well on the way to "establishing some kind of science that would make people happy, free, virtuous and just."²³ There was, to be sure, a Jewish Enlightenment but it was an early modern phenomenon and it was *not* the Haskalah.

The Enlightenment found its partisans everywhere in Europe, but nowhere as many as in the North Atlantic world. Commercial and political connections that bound the Dutch, the British, and their colonial possessions together enabled and encouraged the circulation of Enlightenment ideas. Some historians go so far as to argue "that there was no Enlightenment without the Atlantic." The Atlantic, they contend, was "embodied and traversed in the trade and colonization, the discoveries and debates, the discourses and concepts that together became known as the Enlightenment."²⁴ Such a position presents a sharp contrast to master narratives that typify the Enlightenment as essentially "French" or "British" or even as "European."²⁵ The "Atlanticist perspective" moves beyond regional "exceptionalism" to consider the Enlightenment as a "network of . . . possibilities" enabled by the "interaction of people, ideas, and commodities from Europe, Africa and the Americas" within a space that "allowed for exchange, mutual influence and conflict between the peoples of four continents."²⁶

The beginning of Europe's age of revolutions has likewise been relocated to the Atlantic.²⁷ The French Revolution followed the American; moreover, says Jonathan Israel, the formative political moment of the Enlightenment was England's long-lasting "Glorious Revolution" in 1688–89, which "imparted a revolutionary impulse to Scotland and Ireland, and also to the American colonies and the West Indies."²⁸ The earliest French speakers who participated in the work of Enlightenment were Protestant exiles from Catholic France who found a refuge from state and church in the trading cities of the North Atlantic. After 1688, the leaders of the Huguenot diaspora (many of them readers of Spinoza) began to look to the Glorious Revolution as a precedent for the "constitutional remodeling of France."²⁹

Scholars of Atlantic history point to a cluster of factors that promoted the circulation of Enlightenment between the Dutch Republic, England, and the Americas: the internationalization of trade and increasing complexity of transnational instruments of exchange, the breakdown of confessional uniformity, the spread of literacy, and a legacy of resistance against absolutism and religious persecution.³⁰ Capitalism fostered greater tolerance in public sociability and fed a seemingly infinite demand for new information. Colonial trade transformed European port cities such as London, Amsterdam, and Marseilles into early modern cosmopolitan hubs. Producers of urban wealth became consumers of a vibrant vernacular print culture. Protestant Biblicism contributed to the secularization of reading habits and to a new emphasis on individualism. The power of money began to compete with the dominance of landed wealth, ecclesiastical preferment, and royal patronage. At the same time, emergent forms of human and ecological exploitation were well served by Enlightenment materialism and sustained by empirical arguments from rational calculation. In fact, the dynamism of the North Atlantic exemplified the heroic achievements of Enlightenment as well as its prodigious moral and social costs. On one side of the ledger lay democracy, religious diversity, and scientific discovery; on the other, the harrowing spectacle of exploitation, slavery, racism, and the despoliation of the environment.[31]

Like their Protestant counterparts from France, Iberian Jewish refugees, harassed by agents of the Inquisition, migrated to the Atlantic world.[32] Recent converts to Christianity, Iberian Jewish merchants who called themselves "men of the Portuguese nation" established new communities in Amsterdam, London, New York, and other Atlantic port cities where they could safely return to Judaism, ply their trade, and achieve a measure of collective and personal security.[33] Marked by the trauma of dislocation, social life in the Sephardic diaspora was subject to acute internal tensions. "No problem ... was more critical ... than that of balancing two clusters of ideas about the collective self, one associated with the Jewish religion and peoplehood, the other with 'the Nation,'" the basis of which was "ethnic" and grounded in collective memory of common Iberian origins.[34] On the one hand, Portuguese exiles were freer and less provincial than most of their Jewish contemporaries. Because so many of them had spent a significant amount of time living as Christians, they enjoyed a far greater familiarity with contemporary literature in non-Jewish languages, particularly Castilian Spanish, than most of their learned Jewish contemporaries, while their knowledge of Jewish law and lore was frequently minimal, often inflected by residual Christian theology.[35]

Throughout the premodern Jewish world, most Jewish communities were formed under the auspices of the Christian state. Communal powers of enforcement were underwritten by royal, noble, or ecclesiastical authority. In contrast, "ethnic" communities of "Portuguese" merchants exhibited the organizational patterns of secular "commercial groups" and were treated so by the state and the other urban corporations with whom they shared the tax burden.[36] Membership was voluntary. Sanctions were imposed by common consent and enforced only by the power of mutual agreement. In some sense, the organizational style of the "Portuguese nation" presented as a social contract in miniature rather than a holy congregation, secured by charters and modeled on the medieval town or bishopric.

In the absence of legal empowerment, Sephardic communities struggled to preserve collective discipline and to enforce some measure of conformity. Committed to their own Iberian memory-culture, Iberian exiles took great pride in the distinctions of wealth and lineage. Iberian-Jewish society remained tightly knit and fiercely patriarchal, bound together by financial interests and filial loyalty. Intellectual dissent was treated as a form of egregious social deviance.[37] But attempts at policing personal behavior were only effective insofar as individuals were unprepared to suffer collective ostracism as well as potential exclusion from the privileges of synagogue membership, costs that could be considerable but in some cases borne with a remarkable degree of equanimity. Shows of communal intransigence in particularly dramatic cases of excommunication—such as Spinoza's in 1656—masked a latent structural weakness of Iberian "ethnicity" to uphold the bonds of religious loyalty.

The Iberian diaspora both nurtured and repressed what Jonathan Israel calls a "pre-1740 Sephardic-Jewish Enlightenment."[38] Many Sephardic exiles had spent years living as Catholics. The need to maintain dual confessional allegiance, Christian in public and Jewish in private, often left people suspicious toward all innocent professions of faith.[39] "Fluid religious identity" was highly characteristic of Sephardic transplants "throughout much of the seventeenth century," writes Francesca Trivellato in her recent book about the Sephardic diaspora in Livorno.[40] Rabbinic responsa registered a widespread tendency toward laxity in ritual observance among Western European Sephardim as well as the proliferation of intellectual heterodoxy.[41] Spinoza's foundational role in the "radical Enlightenment" was certainly exceptional; but his ideas took shape against the background of a Jewish culture already deeply scarred by religious doubt and riven by the search for spiritual relief.[42] Some Sephardim sought it in mystical speculation, others in philosophy. Both traditions were deeply rooted in medieval Sephardic experience and imbued with increasing contemporary significance in the aftermath of conversion, displacement, and return to Judaism.[43] Throughout the Western European diaspora, Sephardic Jews seeking Enlightenment could look back onto a long engagement with rationalism that continued to exert a powerful influence on post-expulsion Sephardic writing.[44]

Direct contact between Enlightenment ideas and Sephardic culture was not confined to Spinoza's hometown of Amsterdam. Nor were all Sephardic Jews who read Enlightenment literature radicals prepared to flout rabbinic authority and violate Jewish law. On the contrary, just like the Enlightenment itself, its Sephardic constituency produced only a few public dissenters like Spinoza, and a much larger, more moderate mainstream. David Ruderman, for instance, has identified a "Jewish

Enlightenment in an English key" that had its origins in the Sephardic ambience of early modern London.[45] Ruderman attempts to insert his study of the intersection between Jewish religious thought and Enlightenment philosophy in eighteenth-century England into the history of the Haskalah; but his book makes a much stronger argument for differentiating more systematically between the former and the latter. Ruderman shows that Sephardic luminaries such as David Nieto, who served as rabbi of London's Bevis Marks Synagogue in the beginning of the eighteenth century, were deeply engaged with Enlightenment science and biblical criticism. Sephardic controversialists argued with contemporary Enlightenment scholarship about the meaning of Jewish texts and the nature of Jewish belief. They helped to found a distinctive Anglo-Jewish culture that was, by the end of the eighteenth century, similar in its religious and political attitudes to the "moderate Enlightenment" in Britain and North America. In her research on the Sephardic diaspora in Bordeaux, Frances Malino similarly found that early modern Sephardim embraced a distinctly French style of revolutionary patriotism that drew on the vocabulary of the Enlightenment.[46]

Whatever intellectual connections may exist between the Jewish Enlightenment in the early modern Sephardic diaspora and the Haskalah, they are not the product of a shared milieu. The Haskalah did not develop anywhere near the North Atlantic epicenter of the Enlightenment, but in Eastern Europe, a region where the diffusion of Enlightenment ideas became associated with the expansion of state power, not with revolutionary politics, scientific discovery, or the decline of religious belief. Substantial differences in political culture, confessional organization, social structure, and economic life distinguished the great land mass east of Berlin and west of the Ural mountains from the Atlantic world and determined the future of the Enlightenment in the east of Europe.

Early modern Eastern Europe was ruled by one of two competing systems of government: absolutism and noble republicanism. In Russia, the autocracy, held by the Romanov dynasty since the early seventeenth century, claimed unlimited power over its subjects. The Russian nobility remained beholden to the person of the tsar, charged by God with patrimonial and religious responsibility for the entire realm. Even for the aristocracy, there were no juridically guaranteed rights, only privileges granted and withdrawn at the monarch's pleasure in return for service.[47] Central Europe was divided between the Kingdom of Prussia, headed by a branch of the Hohenzollern family, and the Holy Roman Empire, under the Austrian Habsburgs. In both instances, the ruling house was practically synonymous with the state. The administration of empire rested in the hands of a royally appointed bureaucracy ultimately accountable only to the king.⁴⁸ In the Polish-Lithuanian Commonwealth, by contrast, the nobility, which composed nearly 10 percent of the entire population, successfully competed with royal power. Headed by a small number of Polish and Lithuanian magnate families in control of the greater part of the country's land and wealth, the aristocracy considered itself the Polish political nation. Every nobleman, rich or poor, was theoretically equal to every other nobleman; but the independence of the nobility, which weakened the sovereignty of the Polish crown, was based in the concept of aristocratic honor that also excluded every other estate.⁴⁹

Confessionally, too, Eastern Europe did not encourage people to make connections between religious difference and the possibility of popular sovereignty. Although the Russian and Habsburg empires had to contend with more religious diversity than any other European regime, confessional identity, enshrined in law, was much less politically charged than in the North Atlantic. The regnant church—Catholic in the Habsburg lands, Russian Orthodox in the Romanov empire, and Lutheran in Prussia—was, for all intents and purposes, subservient to the state.⁵⁰ In tolerant Poland, the nobility jealously guarded its own political prerogatives and continually checked the autonomy of the clergy.⁵¹ Religious education produced obedient political subjects and did not encourage speculation on the possibility of separation between church and state.

Like religion, social status was fixed by statute. Sociability barely cut across estate lines that divided the servile majority from a tiny non-servile elite. Throughout the period, Eastern European state structure strengthened existing social and confessional hierarchies.⁵² Even the peculiar domestic intimacy that existed between servant and master tended to confirm rather than subvert social rank. In Russia, where virtually the whole of the vast agrarian population in the interior consisted of serfs, who were either the personal property of the nobility or the official property of the state, status remained a constant and painful preoccupation. In medieval Muscovy, social identity had been notoriously opaque; but by the end of the eighteenth century, Russian society was subordinated to the estate system and to the Table of Ranks, instituted by Peter I in 1722 in order to transform Russia's landed nobility into a gentry service class. The Table of Ranks destroyed the last vestiges of aristocratic independence in Russia and for more than a century divested liberal professions—medicine, law, education—of corporate autonomy and prestige apart from the attainment of rank.⁵³

Economic development in Eastern Europe likewise supported the dominance of the state. In the imperial domains, the state sponsored manufacturing and commerce, primarily in the interests of financing the military.⁵⁴ There were few independent entrepreneurs who could dispense with state patronage. Big money was to be made in government concessions, tax farming, and monopolies rather than in international trade. Most native merchants held little liquid capital and traded locally in agricultural goods.[55] The growth of Berlin, St. Petersburg, and Vienna exemplified not the independence and civic-mindness of urban community but the impressive capacity of the state to generate revenue and engage in massive feats of social and political engineering. Both the human geography and the architectural landscape of the three Eastern European capitals reflected the importance of the state; Berlin, Vienna, and St. Petersburg developed in the shadow of the imperial court.[56] Their magnificence presented a stark contrast to the large number of Eastern European towns that blended right into their rural surroundings. Older cities such as Prague, Kiev, and even Moscow did not benefit from large-scale state investment and were often doomed to staid provincialism despite their venerable history and impressive size.[57] In Poland, where city-building was a pet project of the nobility, urban development was equally slow and inconsistent.[58] Most of the moneyed elite preferred to live abroad anyway. Nowhere in eighteenth-century Eastern Europe did urban life promote the creation of a new reading and writing public that was financially and socially independent of the state. Eastern European *philosophes* came mostly from the ranks of the reforming bureaucracy, engaged in "enlightenment" on behalf of the state.

Indeed, Enlightenment ideas first traveled to Eastern Europe by way of government policy. The accession of Peter I (r. 1682–1725) to the Romanov throne opened a new era in Russian history. The "artisan-tsar" undertook to turn an Orthodox client-state into an efficient bureaucratic and military machine run by a Western-educated service nobility.[59] The court society that Peter installed in his new capital of St. Petersburg was fashionably French-speaking. However, the Petrine version of Enlightenment rationalism was indebted to German cameralist theory, the cornerstone of which was centralization of executive power and the replacement of "clerks" with an efficient and expert administration.[60] The "revolution of Peter the Great" created modern Russian society that was meant to serve as an instrument of the state. The upper ranks provided military personnel and staffed a civilian bureaucracy, charged with ensuring the orderly supply of provender and men to an enormous standing army. In order to educate his new elites, Peter expanded the network of printing presses (one of which began, in 1703, to print Russia's first newspaper) and founded several secular institutions of higher learning, including the St. Petersburg Academy of Sciences.

Peter became the first political apostle of "enlightened absolutism" in Eastern Europe. The idea entered into the fabric of Russian imperial ideology. Every one of Peter's successors had to contend with the heroic image of the "reforming tsar" and to affirm a commitment to the Petrine project of state-sponsored improvements.[61] Catherine II (r. 1762–1796), whose dynastic claim to the throne was shaky since she was a Romanov only by marriage and came to power following a palace coup, adopted Peter as her own spiritual father. Under Catherine (like Peter, known as "the Great"), Russia witnessed a revival of enlightened absolutism.[62] Catherine flirted with French men of letters—including Denis Diderot, who spent several years in Russia, and Voltaire, whom she commissioned to write a biography of Peter—and attempted wide-ranging legislative and administrative reform, inspired by her fitful reading of Montesquieu and Beccaria. Like Peter, she supported limited efforts at expanding education and publishing, but she suppressed any views that subverted autocratic government. Catherine bitterly resented what she described as the presumption of public opinion trying to "teach her how to govern" and clamped down hard on even the mildest reproof of her person or her policies (even though she encouraged attacks on the notorious foibles of the nobility).[63] Throughout Catherine's reign, the commitment to enlightenment served imperial expansion and autocratic legitimation.[64] Although she patronized the leading figures of the French Enlightenment, Catherine consistently referred to the backwardness of the Russian populace in her defense of enlightened absolutism, stressing the importance of censorship and political surveillance in the protection of the realm against its internal enemies.

By the second half of the eighteenth century, enlightened absolutism was well entrenched as a model of effective government not only in Russia but in Prussia and in the Habsburg Empire. Frederick II, who called himself the "first servant of the state," recruited a new administrative elite, expanded the Prussian army into a formidable force, sponsored compulsory public education, and turned Berlin into a center of enlightened sociability.[65] Joseph II made similar legislative efforts to transform the administrative patchwork of the Habsburg Empire into a model of bureaucratic uniformity, economic productivity, social transparency, and religious forbearance.[66] The high point of the enlightened reordering of Eastern Europe were the partitions of Poland. Between 1772 and 1795, Frederick, Catherine, and Joseph jointly dismembered the noble republic and turned the former lands of the Polish-Lithuanian Commonwealth into a laboratory of modern state-building, the final political frontier of the Enlightenment in Eastern Europe.[67] However, between the Pugachev rebellion and the French Revolution, "enlightened absolutism" increasingly became associated with the resurgence of royal conservatism. The deaths of Frederick (in 1786), Joseph (in 1790), and Catherine (in 1796) left some uncertainty about the future of further state-sponsored reform. The bloodshed of the Terror, followed by the Napoleonic Wars, in which monarchical Austria, Prussia, and Russia joined in a "Holy Alliance" against republican France, discredited "constitutional experiments" and raised suspicions about the risks of popular education and freedom of expression. In Eastern Europe, the age of revolutions heralded an era of religious quietism and political reaction.[68]

Nevertheless, the Eastern European legacy of enlightened absolutism had endowed the state with enormous prestige as the agent of progress. Throughout the first half of the nineteenth century, Russian educated society continued, for the most part, to identify state-building with enlightenment. Schooled in Western Europe but enmeshed in the Russian culture of serfdom, Russian people of rank idealized the principle of undivided sovereignty even though they resented bureaucratic encroachment on noble privilege as an affront to their dignity.[69] Their ambivalence toward the legacy of the reforming state became especially acute during the reign of Nicholas I (r. 1825–1855), the tsar who began his reign with the brutal suppression of the Decembrist revolt, instigated by noble republicans from within the elite.[70] Known after 1848 as the "gendarme of Europe," Nicholas I embodied the principle of authoritarianism that infiltrated every aspect of Russian social and political life. Yet the ideal of enlightened absolutism was more important to Nicholas than it had been even to his grandmother, Catherine.

Nicholas, who saw himself as a nineteenth-century incarnation of Peter the Great, actively supported a new cadre of reforming bureaucrats, charged with efficiency, probity, and accountability by the autocrat himself, but completely beholden to the principle of duty and the hierarchy of official rank.[71] The Nicholaevan program of "enlightenment by the police" reverted to the Petrine notion of a wise and all-seeing tsar concerned with the public good as the only legitimate and peaceable alternative to the dangerous path of political liberalization. In fact, it was Nicholas's various attempts to deal with the intractable problem of serfdom that finally led to abolition at the start of the reign of his heir, Alexander II (r. 1856–1881). Russian civil society, which flowered under the rule of this "tsar-liberator," was likewise forged in Nicholaevan institutions of higher learning. During the first half of his reign, Alexander's pursuit of reform from above kept alive the possibility of an enlightened absolutism in the minds of Eastern European intellectuals, more ambivalent than ever about the prospects and costs of a revolution from below.

But from a North Atlantic perspective, revolution might have been the whole point of the Enlightenment. By the time Nicholas I came to the throne, eighteenth-century patriots and obstreperous colonial subjects on both sides of the Atlantic had redrawn the political map of Western Europe and the Americas on the basis of a "new revolutionary consciousness" that "generated a powerful revulsion against 'aristocracy,' traditional ideas, and ecclesiastical authority," as well as against "'enlightened despotism' and forms of absolutism assuming a superficial veneer of Enlightenment, such as evolved in ... Russia, Austria, Spain and Prussia."[72] The Atlantic revolutions that began in North America in 1776 and ended in the 1830s with the Latin American wars of independence may have been fired by local grievances, but they deployed the secular language of popular sovereignty and natural rights that originated in the Enlightenment.[73]

Unlike the "men of the Portuguese nation" who were not only immediate observers but frequently participants in these events, maskilim lived in the long Eastern European shadow of enlightened absolutism. For them, the formative political moment was not revolution but partition—the imposition of Russian, Prussian, and Habsburg rule over the borderlands of the Polish-Lithuanian Commonwealth between 1772 and 1795. Like Eastern European educated society in general, the Haskalah developed into a movement under the protection of the absolutist state. Russian maskilim became notorious for their warm relationship with the government of Nicholas I, a regime that Jewish popular memory associated chiefly with the conscription of Jewish minors into the pre-reform army where two-thirds of them converted to Russian Orthodoxy. Maskilim showed little interest and even less faith in the Enlightenment's "constitutional experiments" as the best way to resolve the tension between freedom and responsibility. They remained largely indifferent to eighteenth-century innovations in political theory and they wrote nothing about the political reordering of society, the abiding preoccupation of the *philosophes* and their counterparts throughout the North Atlantic. Their much-maligned affinity for state-sponsored projects of social engineering and their identification with reforming elites in St. Petersburg and Vienna involved an entirely different set of assumptions about the essence of all political arrangements than those which informed the Enlightenment's idea of natural rights. These assumptions emerge with particular clarity in Kant's critical assessment of social contract theory.

In one of his most widely known essays, "Perpetual Peace" (1795), Kant pointed out that self-government was not exactly a tribute to human virtue.[74] Even a "nation of devils," Kant said, would be capable of organizing itself into a state and enacting laws that would prevent people from killing and robbing each other. Collective survival would be assured as long as their "constitution was so designed that, although the citizens

[were] opposed to one another in their private attitudes, these opposing views may inhibit one another in such a way that the public conduct of the citizens [would] be the same as if they did not have such evil attitudes." The making of the kind of mutually beneficial agreements that Enlightenment politics idealized as conducive to progress and the cornerstone of the good society did "not involve the moral improvement of man." Democratic government might very well be little more than a bond of honor among potential thieves and murderers.

In full view of the French Revolution, Kant resigned himself to the fact that people's "selfish inclinations" lent themselves naturally to the making of "constitutions," but that did not make "citizens" any more virtuous. The "moral attitudes" of the governed did not automatically "produce a good political constitution." In fact, just the opposite: only through good laws, enacted by a "moral politician," could "people be expected to attain a good level of moral culture." The politics of interest—in which legislation was the direct political expression of popular self-representation—was not the same thing as a politics of virtue, conducted by "public right" according to moral principles. There was here a potential conflict between "public right" (Kant's version of Rousseau's "general will"), which Kant insisted could not be contravened or resisted, and the "private rights"—the personal liberties that social contract theory enshrined as natural and inviolable.[75] But the tension was only apparent because Kant was operating with a different understanding of freedom, one that was fully consistent with "enlightened absolutism" and the imperative to subordinate the political freedom of the individual to the "public right" claimed by the community.

Kant defined freedom as moral autonomy. "What Is Enlightenment?" presented a counterintuitive interpretation of the relationship between personal liberty and public duty that was both a trenchant critique of the Enlightenment's concept of the rights and duties attached to citizenship and a perceptive analysis of what intellectuals had to endure under absolutist rule. Underpinning democratic constitutions throughout the Atlantic world, social contract theory distinguished between the public responsibilities of the citizen and the private inclinations—freedoms—of the individual. The doctrine of natural rights equated freedom with relief from state interference in one's personal life. But Kant reversed this conventional meaning of the terms "public" and "private." He said that one's freedom in the public domain lay beyond the reach of state authority; but in the private sphere, the individual was obliged to adhere to state authority implicitly. "I understand," Kant explained, "under the public use of his own reason, that use which anyone makes of it *as a scholar* [Ger. *Gelehrter*] before the entire public of the *reading world*. The private use I designate as that use which one makes of his reason in a certain *civil post* or office which is entrusted to him.... Here, one is certainly not allowed to argue; rather one must obey."[76] The private individual always acts as an instrument of a "certain mechanism," that is, as a member of society and as a cog in the state machine. In private life, every individual is continually engaged in some form of "mechanical" service to others; human survival depends on this system of mutual obligation. The widest compass of service lies in obedience to the "commonwealth," represented in the "public right" of the state to command all private persons to act in the best interests of the social whole.

Kant's striking inversion reveals that the political understanding of private freedom is, in some fundamental sense, a political myth, since the very existence of the private individual depends on his using and being used by others, on being continually reduced to the condition of a "machine." The liberal principle of political autonomy rests on the illusion of an impregnable private sphere, where the arm of the state does not reach. The ideal of freedom implicit in the claim that a man's home is his castle is based on a tenuous legal fiction, propounded by the "constitution" of the state itself, always in danger of being hijacked by private persons in defense of their own "natural rights" against the rapacious appetites of their own neighbors. In this political picture, the state functions as an arbiter of private interests; without the intervention of the "commonwealth," private life is not only perilous (something which Kant surely learned from Hobbes) but impossible. But the dispassionate deployment of one's reason "as a scholar"—an intellectual, one might say—is something else. Here, one enters into a realm that transcends the constraints of material necessity, the political network of mutual obligations, and the entire system of implicit or explicit coercion maintained by the state. This realm is "public" because it lies beyond the influence of private interests and competing desires entirely. It is free, because independent scholarly judgment is (literally) disinterested. As soon as the autonomous power of reason is bound to a commitment outside of itself, it becomes merely "private" and personal; it immediately loses its public character and its truth-value. The condition of a *Gelehrter* thus approximates the perfected state of moral autonomy, toward which every person ought to aspire.

The paradoxical position of a public "scholar" who wears the private uniform of a loyal state servitor is one that Kant, as a philosopher and a subject of Frederick the Great, knew intimately well. Actually, the tension that he describes between the sacrosanct privileges of the public sphere and the absence of personal freedom neatly captures the contradictions of "enlightened absolutism." Frederick's Berlin was a haven of uninhibited philosophical and literary inquiry. Yet the basic right of living there at all was highly restricted. Jews could reside in one of the freest cities in Europe only under the special protection of the crown in exchange for financial services. The same was true of imperial St. Petersburg, a city that became an ambivalent symbol of enlightened cosmopolitanism and autocratic fiat.

The position of the *Gelehrter* under "enlightened absolutism" bred the double consciousness that was the real subject of Kant's essay. A "faculty of philosophy" maintained and employed by the state lay itself constantly open to the charge that the assertion of merely philosophical privilege was an admission of real political impotence.[77] Heine, who could sniff out cant at a hundred paces, diagnosed the inveterately ironic mood of modern German intellectuals as a symptom of an acute sense of political deprivation that they could not bear to admit but refused entirely to deny. The recourse to irony enabled them to survive the oppression they felt otherwise powerless to resist: "We talk a good deal," Heine conceded, "about . . . humorous irony" as if it were an expression of "special excellence."

> But it is only a sign of our lack of political freedom, and as Cervantes had to take refuge in humorous irony at the time of the Inquisition in order to intimate his ideas without leaving a weak spot exposed for the serfs of the Holy Office to seize upon, so Goethe also used to say in a tone of humorous irony what he, as a minister of state and courtier, did not dare to say outright. . . . Especially writers who languish under censorship and all kinds of restrictions on freedom of thought and yet can never disavow their heartfelt opinion have to resort to the ironic and humorous manner. It is the only solution left for honesty, and in this disguise such honesty is revealed most movingly.[78]

Most intellectuals who lived east of the Rhine were, like Goethe, obliged to a state system that continually held out the promise of enlightenment without the "inconvenience" of political emancipation.[79] Deprived of the individual liberties that the North Atlantic world increasingly took for granted, they were primed to embrace a Kantian commitment to intellectual integrity as a "high degree" of freedom that, as Kant himself admitted, was "almost paradoxical." "A high degree of civic freedom," he said, "appears advantageous to the *spiritual* freedom of a people, and yet it places before it insuperable restrictions; a lesser degree of civil freedom, in contrast, creates the room for spiritual freedom to spread to its full capacity." "Civil freedom" while seeming to offer more opportunities for "enlightenment" actually binds the political subject closer to the state and perpetuates an insidious form of intellectual blindness. Insofar as it obscures the true nature of the instrumental and exploitative relationship between the government and the governed, "civil freedom" gets in the way of critique, which is the starting point of "enlightenment."

"Enlightened absolutism" made the nature of all political necessity self-evidently clear and enabled intellectuals to perceive their own abjection. In this argument, the relationship between enlightenment and emancipation was the reverse of the assumption that citizenship rendered people free. Only the free life of the mind could transcend the unlimited capacity of state and society to reduce human bodies to the condition of "machines." Nurturing the "vocation for *free thinking*—... works back upon the character of the people (who thereby become more and more capable of *acting freely*) and finally even on the principles of government, which finds it to its advantage to treat man, who is now *more than a machine*, in accord with his dignity."[80] People who could not free themselves from their own "self-imposed immaturity" would never be emancipated by law. "Constitutions" that were informed by the "selfish inclinations" (as Kant had put it in "Perpetual Peace") of the governed rather than the moral principles of government created only private "citizens" who would be functionally incapable of telling the difference between individual autonomy and personal license; the triumph of the latter, as Rousseau has first suggested, was a vicious and debilitating form of private enslavement.

Kant's dialectical position became a critical reference point for maskilim, first in their bitter polemic against "pseudo-enlightenment" as an alibi for the pursuit of selfishness and the abdication of social responsibility and then, eventually, in the nationalist charge that political emancipation was "slavery within freedom."[81] This manifest tension between the Enlightenment's promise of citizenship and the Kantian ideal of freedom requires rethinking not only the beginning but also the end of the Haskalah. Although historians disagree about the former (a point to which we shall return), no one seems to have a problem with the standard claim that the Haskalah came to a near-apocalyptic halt in 1881, when a wave of pogroms against Russian Jewish property convinced Jewish "enlighteners" that their quest for emancipation was hopeless. At this point, so the history books tell us, maskilim wised up and invented Zionism. Several things are wrong with this picture. First of all, the Eastern European Jewish struggle for emancipation did not end with the so-called end of the Haskalah. Neither the product of maskilic initiative nor the fulfillment of maskilic aspirations, the Russian-Jewish campaign for emancipation began in earnest in the era of the Great Reforms (1861–1878) and did not end until it was finally won in February 1917, when the Provisional Government enacted Russia's first comprehensive set of laws on civil rights. Second, the causal relationship between the end of the Haskalah and the beginning, fitful though it was, of Jewish emancipation in Russia is exactly the reverse of the way in which it is normally presented. It was the impact of partial emancipation during the last decade of the reign of Alexander II that threw maskilim into a profound state of confusion and despair about the future of Judaism. Jewish nationalism was not a response to the "failure" of Jewish liberalism in Russia, because the Haskalah (in Russia and everywhere else) was not a species of liberalism; Jewish nationalism developed well within the discourse of the Haskalah itself, as a response to the political challenges of emancipation. Indeed, the symbolic handoff between maskilim and Zionists actually predated the pogroms by a decade. The line dividing the era of the "Jewish Enlightenment" from the "national period" in Jewish history is more apparent than real, because Jewish nationalism did not break with the Haskalah. Zionists took over the maskilic project of Jewish renewal and, as frequently happens, disavowed their connection to their own intellectual origins.

The current of emancipation anxiety that runs like a red thread through the discourse of the Haskalah persists in the Zionist indictment of "assimilation." Concerns about the "false enlightenment" of secular, emancipated Jews still feature regularly not only in modern Jewish historiography but in debates about the collective future of the Jewish people. Insofar as "haskalah" refers to a cluster of political attitudes and cultural values exemplified but not monopolized by Eastern European Jewish intellectuals, the "haskalah" is not even the sole possession of nineteenth-century Eastern Europe.[82] Rumors of the abrupt end of the Haskalah have thus been greatly exaggerated. The persistence of maskilic concepts can be detected in twentieth-century Jewish politics, literature, and religious thought. For example, the idea of Jewish regeneration sponsored by a reforming state remains a foundational premise of Israeli political culture. But so is maskilic skepticism about the prospects of Jewish "enlightenment by the police"—or by any means other than independent thought. The Kantian premise that the project of "Jewish Enlightenment" will never be finished (accompanied by the nagging sense that this may not be such a terrible thing) takes the history of the Haskalah beyond the Enlightenment.

2 Beyond the Enlightenment

In defiance of basic chronological and geographical discrepancies, Haskalah scholarship persists in trying to wedge the history of a nineteenth-century Eastern European movement into the history of eighteenth-century Western Europe. New books that advance bold interpretive claims about the Haskalah barely venture beyond Berlin in the 1790s. Despite the recent appearance of local studies that focus on the Haskalah in Galicia and Russia (see below, chapter 4), the mindset of the "Jewish Enlightenment" is still positioned within the framework of late seventeenth- and early eighteenth-century German rationalism and treated as an offshoot of the dogmatic philosophy of Leibniz and Wolff. Meanwhile, the last comprehensive study of the Haskalah in nineteenth-century Eastern Europe was published a century ago.[1]

In order to make the "Jewish Enlightenment" fit more solidly into eighteenth-century intellectual history, scholarship has begun to place its beginnings as far back as the 1720s.[2] The investment in backdating demonstrates just how difficult it is to integrate the Haskalah into the history of the age of Enlightenment without having to explain why Enlightenment ideas should have reached European Jews one hundred years after they reached European Christians and why a Jewish Enlightenment developed in places that were on the periphery of the Enlightenment world and not in places like America and France, where Jewish entry into the fray of democratic politics actually had a discernible impact on the process of Jewish emancipation. The temporal lag turns the Haskalah into a belated Western European "correction" of the "anomalies" of Eastern European Judaism and fails to address all of the ways in which the Haskalah represents a characteristic development of Eastern European culture. The geographic and chronological displacement of the Haskalah creates the impression that maskilim, typically misdiagnosed as "radicals," were completely out of touch with their own reality, deluded for thinking that the values of Enlightenment could have any real relevance to the concerns of the Eastern European Jewish masses and utopian in their expectations that Enlightenment ideas would melt a political glacier like the Russian autocracy. The forced comparison with Enlightenment, which is meant to integrate the Jewish experience more fully into the study of European modernity, both wrenches the Haskalah out of context *and* relegates it to the margins of Jewish thought.

This book starts with the premise that referring to the Haskalah as a "Jewish Enlightenment" is misleading and ahistorical. Even if one restricts an account of the Haskalah to its beginnings in late eighteenth-century Berlin, the analogy with the Enlightenment remains deeply problematic. First, the passage of cultural time does not correspond neatly to the passing of centuries. The eighteenth century may have ended in 1799, but the age of reason had reached a philosophical point of no return at least twenty years earlier. The anthology in which Kant had asked his seminal question, subjected the "ideas and aspirations of the Enlightenment ... to a scrutiny so thorough [that] it is only a slight exaggeration to suggest that subsequent critics have raised few points that were not already considered" by their predecessors in the 1780s.[3]

The Haskalah was not a belated Jewish embrace of the Enlightenment's assertion of rational certainty. It was inspired by the same radical doubts that defined the Kantian "age of criticism" when the very idea of a rational universe had come unstuck from its moorings in reality. Throughout the first half of the nineteenth century, maskilim were engaged in the attempt to put together a "ready-made world" that was broken. The internal crisis that historians of the Haskalah associate with the irreversible decline of the Jewish Enlightenment during the 1790s marked the beginning of a nineteenth-century movement.

Second, there is the matter of location. The careful distancing of the German origins of the "Berlin Haskalah" from its subsequent development in Habsburg Galicia and Romanov Russia obscures the fact that when the Haskalah began, Berlin *was* Eastern Europe. "German-speaking Jewry," writes Steven Lowenstein, "was the creation of the emancipation-age." Eighteenth-century Berlin lay well east of the dividing line between "Ashkenaz," where people spoke Western Yiddish and followed their own local customs, and "Polin," the home of what has come to be known as Jewish Eastern Europe.[4] "Poland," so went an early modern Jewish saying, "begins at the Hamburg city gate."[5] More to the point, the first generation of so-called "German" maskilim were all newcomers to the city. Most of them arrived in Berlin from points further east, had a traditional Eastern European Jewish education, and spoke Eastern Yiddish.

The Haskalah did not have to be transplanted to "Poland" after its center shifted away from "Germany" following the Napoleonic Wars (at which time, neither place appeared on any map of Europe). The Haskalah was, from its inception, both transnational and Eastern European, a feature reflected in the composition of the immediate circle of Moses Mendelssohn, known as the founder of the "Jewish Enlightenment." Moreover, maskilim always held Jewish society in Eastern

Europe at the forefront of their concerns; in fact, it was the invention of Eastern Europe in the wake of the Polish partitions that mobilized them into a movement. The German debt that Jewish intellectuals in Habsburg Galicia and in the Pale of Settlement owed to the Prussian origins of the Haskalah was literary and philosophical rather than genetic. Along with the poetry of Goethe and Schiller, they read the novels of Balzac and Eugène Sue—but that did not make them anymore French than it made other Eastern Europeans who had the same tastes.

In this book, I take the position that the Haskalah ought to be located in a different context, one that is more consistent with its immediate provenance. Let me put the argument as plainly as possible: when I started writing about the Haskalah, like everyone else, I assumed that I was writing a book about the Enlightenment. By the time I had finished the first draft of this study, I knew that I had written a book about Romanticism. To explore fully the implications of this claim would take several studies in literary criticism, intellectual history, and philosophy. Here, I can only undertake to point out the most salient lines of convergence.

The history of Romanticism overlaps both in time and place with the history of the Haskalah. If the intellectual center of Enlightenment was the North Atlantic between 1650 and 1750, the core ideas of Romanticism developed in the German-speaking world between 1750 and 1830. Romanticism provided the impetus for a full-blown cultural revolution in nineteenth-century Eastern Europe.[6] After 1830 and until the advance of scientific "positivism" in the 1860s, the most important exponents of Romantic ideals in literature, history, and social thought lived in the imperial borderlands of the Habsburg and Romanov lands. But the correspondence is not only circumstantial. "In Central and Eastern Europe," argues Ivan Berend in his survey of Eastern Europe's "long nineteenth century" a "great deal of Enlightenment thinking arrived with Romanticism."[7]

The history of the Romantic movement in Eastern Europe substantiates the case made in recent scholarship that despite its reputation for deliberate obscurantism, religious self-absorption, and narrowness of mind, Romanticism was not dedicated to the denial of reason; it was no "enemy" of Enlightenment. Its revolutionary polemic against empiricism, on the one hand, and against abstraction, on the other, was part of the process of critique that had begun with Kant and Rousseau, and was itself within the scope of Enlightenment inquiry about the limitations of human knowledge. "An off-spring of the critical age, and therefore of the Enlightenment, Romanticism saw itself as a sort of grand transformation of letters, the arts, imagination, sensitivity, taste and ideas. In this sense,

Romanticism can be considered, metaphorically, a 'rebellious child'" of the eighteenth century.⁸ More precisely, the nineteenth-century upheaval in religion and literature "fed on the unresolved problems of Kantian thought in ways that reveal a surprising degree of continuity" with the Enlightenment.⁹

Thus, when we talk about the Haskalah we are talking not so much about the absorption of Enlightenment ideas, but their critical reception and imaginative revision. Strictly speaking, the Haskalah is the first post-Enlightenment movement in Jewish history; the tenuous and not always happy marriage between Judaism and modernity continues to manifest the traces of an original Romantic encounter. Like other Romantics, maskilim produced a foundational response to the problem of secularization that inspired the modern ideology of culture and provided a metaphysical argument for nationalism. Reverberations of anxieties about the costs of modernization, first roused among maskilim by the spectacle of revolutionary Terror, can still be heard in various strains of Jewish and non-Jewish post-modernism. Romantic ambivalence toward Enlightenment cosmopolitanism crops up both in Zionist mythology and in post-Zionist angst. These lingering echoes are not fortuitous; they are the result of an important historical conjunction between the Haskalah and Romanticism that has yet to be acknowledged by students of either movement.

To begin with, "haskalah" is itself a romantic concept. Its significance to maskilim has been obscured by the association between the movement attached to the word "haskalah" and the Enlightenment. Uzi Shavit points out that the conventional translation of "haskalah" as "reason" (which implies that the Haskalah refers to the Jewish embrace of Enlightenment rationalism) postdates the Haskalah. "Like the ideology of the Enlightenment," wrote Max Erik in his 1934 history of the Jewish Enlightenment, "the ideology of the Haskalah is rationalistic. The term 'haskalah' is the exact equivalent of the word 'rationalism,' from *ratio* which is the meaning of *sekhel*." Erik was arguing from a rigorously Marxist perspective; but this view prevailed in Zionist scholarship too. The most technically "accurate translation of the word 'haskalah,'" asserted Joseph Klausner in his canonic history of modern Hebrew literature, "is rationalism (*ratio* = *sekhel*), but it also corresponds to the German concept of Enlightenment."¹⁰ In contrast to the regnant assumption, Shavit posits that the connection between "haskalah" and "Enlightenment rationalism" is not self-evident; the word has an alternative genealogy of Jewish resistance to the secular "ideology of the Enlightenment."¹¹

Shavit demonstrates that the founders of the Haskalah did not use the word "haskalah" to refer to their own project, precisely because its roots in the Hebrew word for "reason" carried pejorative connotations. In the work of N. H. Wessely, a close follower of Mendelssohn and the author of the foundational document of the Haskalah, a polemical pamphlet called *Words of Peace and Truth* (see below, chapter 8),

> the word 'haskalah' appears . . . close in meaning to the words 'reflection' . . . and 'investigation,' which is to say that it refers to the searching activity of the human mind. All these words are connected with philosophers and the wise among the gentiles; they are the opposite of [Jewish] 'wisdom' [Heb. *hokhmah*], which comes from God and finds expression in the Torah. What we have before us is a binary structure which clearly distinguishes between the positive and the negative: the divine and the human, divine wisdom and secular reason [Heb. *haskalah*], religion and philosophy, the wisdom of Israel and gentile philosophizing.[12]

Moses Mendelssohn began to employ the word "haskalah" in a more positive sense. Unlike Wessely, he insisted that "haskalah" (reason) constituted a divine gift that "enables man to reach the truth by means of his own ability."[13] For Mendelssohn, "haskalah" was interchangeable with "logic," a word with an eminently respectable Jewish pedigree going back to the work of Maimonides. It was in this connection with Maimonides that "haskalah" became attached to the Kantian ideal of rational autonomy.

In the work of Solomon Maimon (see below, chapter 10)—a sometime member of Mendelssohn's circle and one of the earliest Jewish exponents of Kantian philosophy—the term "haskalah" acquired a kind of dialectical Jewish significance. Maimon wrote a commentary to Maimonides' *Guide for the Perplexed* (1791), in which he traced the Kantian conception of the creative mind to Maimonides' vision of intellectual striving as the transcendent aim of human existence, implicit in rational being itself: "The perfectibility [Heb. *shlemut*] of everything in creation lies in the actualization of its own potential, like the perfectibility of a tree is, for example, the production of fruit. And the perfectibility of man is the cultivation of the intellect [Heb. *haskalah*]."[14]

Maimon's Jewish rereading of "haskalah" as the goal of human development comes close to Mendelssohn's teleological concept of "education" (Ger. *Bildung*) which includes both "enlightenment," or the training of speculative reason, and "cultivation," which is "more oriented toward practical matters . . . toward goodness, refinement and beauty in the arts and social mores."[15] Maimon likewise included "various potentialities" within his ideal of rational perfectibility: "the power of sensation, the imagination, memory, speculative reason and practical understanding."[16] Maskilim, Shavit concludes, continued to use the word "haskalah" in this synthetic sense. Until the 1860s, the word designated a "precise [Hebrew] equivalent of the [German] word *Bildung*."[17] The debate about the meaning of "haskalah" that began in the 1860s, in fact, marked a shift in the history of *the* Haskalah (see below, chapter 9).

Shavit does not discuss the philosophical provenance of the German idea of *Bildung;* this is unfortunate, for it might have helped to sever the ill-founded link between the Haskalah and the Enlightenment once and for all. To be sure, the emphasis on perfectibility through education can be traced to many sources in eighteenth-century German thought. But in the first half of the nineteenth century, German Romantics began to identify "education" not with the transmission of correct and clear conceptions (as Wolff had done) but with a new all-embracing ideal of culture.[18] This move, already evident in the work of Mendelssohn and Maimon, became politically urgent in the aftermath of the French Revolution and the Napoleonic occupation of the Rhineland. *Bildung* would serve to redeem humanity from a "false enlightenment" that had contributed to the violence of the Terror and to instill a sense of spiritual community in place of an absent political sovereignty.

Culture represented wholeness. The German Romantics stressed the importance of self-integration and did not limit education to the training of reason. The chief vehicle of reconciliation between the critical and the imaginative faculties was art. This argument first gained currency in the work of Schiller. The "romantics followed Schiller in seeing art as the chief instrument for the education of mankind and in viewing the artist as the very paragon of humanity."[19] Art, more specifically literature, a term that Romantics used in its widest sense to include philosophy, history, and poetry, would counteract the existential loneliness of unbelief and train the senses so that people would embrace high "principles" in place of their own "interests and passions." "The lesson to be learned" from the violence of the French Revolution, Schiller argued, was that "it is not sufficient to educate the understanding alone. It is also necessary to cultivate feelings and desires, to develop a person's sensibility so that he or she [is] *inclined* to act according to the principles of reason."[20]

It was in the light of Schiller's new educational imperative that Romantics envisioned the vocation of the poet and the Kantian "scholar" [Ger. *Gelehrter*]. A modern priest and prophet, the new Romantic intellectual presented a complete contrast to the image of the *philosophe*, the Enlightenment's urbane and essentially secular ideal of the "man of letters." The Romantic intellectual combined the high spiritual calling of art with a commitment to critical thinking. He was, in other words, the embodiment of *Bildung*, in whom desire and responsibility, freedom and form, feeling and philosophy were all to be reconciled. He was both the guardian and the creator of culture. His work combined a conservative devotion to the past with a radical passion for renovation, a potentially contradictory set of aims reflected in the dynamic understanding of tradition that the Romantics invented and enshrined as the repository of creative genius.

The self-concept of the Romantic intellectual traveled along with German philosophy and poetry. In Eastern Europe, the impossibility of direct political engagement endowed the new educational program with an urgency and significance out of all proportion to the actual number of poets and scholars and to the extent of their influence over the conduct of ordinary people. In any case, the spectacle of revolutionary violence in France went a long way toward discrediting the mobilization of the masses as the best way to improve society and redeem mankind from its own worst instincts. Hope now lay in a modern "clerisy," charged with the "imposition of meaning upon the chaos of experience."[21] In a society given over to "mediocrity" and bourgeois philistinism, the "function of the clerisy was to maintain a cosmos in which literature and history made sense and in which, consequently, human actions and aspirations would still have meaning."[22] Against encroaching materialism and popular frenzy, poets and scholars took it upon themselves to "speak to the world in a transcendental manner."[23]

Romantic intellectuals complained constantly of their isolation and of being misunderstood (this was very different from the eighteenth-century "republic of letters," which emphasized the importance of sociability). On the one hand, this was a characteristically Rousseauian gesture toward the primacy of subjectivity. On the other hand, the alienation of Romantic intellectuals reflected an acute tension between their cultural ambitions and their desire for affective, personal ties. Romantic circles remained tiny, linked by marriage, family, and friendship. Even as they aspired to transfigure the course of modern culture, most of the founders of the Romantic movement wrote primarily for each other. While Romantic intellectuals had "received an education which gave them certain intellectual and emotional ambitions," they were likely to be underemployed, financially dependent, "bookish, and very awkward in society."[24]

At least in part, their characteristic obsession with wholeness derived from a personal sense of social marginality. But the Romantic ideal ran broader and deeper. For all the variety and multiplicity of Romantic thought, its style, its aspirations, and its themes expressed a common yearning for reconciliation and synthesis, for the transcendence of all particular finitudes. The urgency of the quest for infinite peace derived from the acknowledgment, sometimes tragic, sometimes ironic, of an immense human variety, a reality that was in constant flux, a world in a state of "chaos which is perpetually striving for new and marvelous births."[25] Always alive to this essential paradox, "Romantic concepts affirm[ed] the contingency of social relations ... through their very faith in the integrative power of poetry, literary speech, the performance of legal ritual and rhetoric."[26] "Affected with a high coefficient of deterritorialization," Romantic intellectuals oscillated between fantasies of communal intimacy and cosmic visions of renewal.[27] While the invention of the nation-state is most commonly associated with the rise of Romanticism, "there was hardly one to be found among the leading Romantic players." It was empire—British, German, Russian—which contained the "paradoxical combination of heterogeneity and fragmentariness" within a vision of "one ever-expanding whole."[28]

The quest for wholeness took several forms, the most pervasive and popular of which was an imaginative attachment to the past. While the Enlightenment read history as the accumulation of experience (mostly bad), Romantic historicism emphasized organic development and process.[29] In history, the philosophical "education of humanity" (the well-known phrase belongs to Lessing, a German playwright and philosopher of the late eighteenth century) depended on the embrace of cultural variety. Post-Enlightenment metaphysics, associated primarily with Hegel's reading of Kant, descried in history a convergence between the growth of rational autonomy within the individual and the universal triumph of reason. For Walter Scott, the most popular Romantic novelist of the nineteenth century, historical progress meant a reconciliation between social responsibility and personal desire. Many Romantics associated the former with the myth of community, which some located in antiquity and others in medieval Europe, and the latter with the revolutionary struggle for freedom.

Historicism touched off both a conservative and a radical impulse within the complex of Romantic thought. This fruitful tension puts Romanticism beyond conventional political distinctions between left and right, derived from revolutionary political theory.[30] In any case, many Romantics were impatient with liberal constitutional experiments and equally appalled by the violence of radical politics. Most of them lived in places where intellectuals despaired of any political power at all. Romantic thought focused the expansion of culture not as a concomitant to democratic politics but as an alternative to the enfranchisement of the masses, a prospect that most Romantic intellectuals feared and distrusted. In response to the disillusionment with French republicanism, Romanticism produced a potent critique of social contract theory. Romantic readers of Schiller and Shelley saw in poetry, rather than politics, the promise of a revolution in consciousness that would transform the world.

The search for transcendence led Romantic philosophy back to faith, now suffused with a longing for perfection not only in the sphere of morality and ritual but in the extension of the sacred into the spheres of art, literature, and music.[31] It is difficult, in considering the nature of "romantic religion," to separate the worship of the human imagination from the glorification of the divine order of the cosmos. The latter had, in fact, seemed clearer to Newton and Leibniz than to Coleridge and Schiller, who were awed and overwhelmed rather than comforted and reassured by the grandeur of the universe. To some of their critical contemporaries, Romantic intellectuals seemed to be worshipping their own powers of creation rather than God's bountiful gifts. But the Romantics encouraged this patent confusion. Their new cult of literature elevated the poet to the status of prophet. They reread the Bible as the archetypal Romantic text, both history and poetry, both particular and universal, both ancient and endlessly self-renewing.[32] Romanticism, writes the critic Maurice Blanchot, "formulates the ambition of a total book, a sort of perpetually growing Bible."[33] The discovery of the Bible as literature was a radical departure both from religious devotion to the literal truth of the text and from the mode of historical criticism that had characterized Enlightenment attitudes to the limitations of Scripture.

Scholarly inquiry into the sources of the Bible as history gave way to the appreciation of the Bible as a poetic model. The imaginative visions of the prophets could no longer be dismissed as the chimerical ramblings of primitive minds, hopelessly inferior to the orderly, rational cadences of neoclassical verse. The Bible provided the impetus for writing modern poetry that was redemptive and world-shaking as well as elemental and absolute. Romantic Biblicism produced not only a new poetics, but informed the idea of national culture (a conjuncture that appeared first in the work of Herder, a thinker whose career straddled East and West and whose work lay at the interstices between Enlightenment and Romanticism), as well as the Romantic invention of orientalism (which culminated in Renan's historical studies of the origins of Christianity). Like no other single text, the Bible proved integral to the fabric of Romantic culture; the notable Biblicism of the Haskalah is not merely a fortuitous coincidence.

Historians typically reproach maskilim with the fact that their work found little social resonance among the Jewish masses; but such a charge misconstrues the nature of the maskilic project. The Haskalah was a movement of schoolmasters. Like other groups of Romantic intellectuals—the Oxford Tractarians, the Lake poets in England, the

Slavophiles and Westernizers in Russia, the Jena circle in Germany, the Transcendentalists in the United States—to whom they may be fruitfully compared, maskilim saw themselves as engaged in the work of *Bildung*. In their own revival of biblical poetry, they saw what their Russian Romantic contemporaries described as an "aspect of higher knowledge." "The true poets of all nations and of all times," wrote D. V. Venevitinov, a member of a Russian writers' circle called "Lovers of Wisdom," "have always been deep thinkers, philosophers, and, so to speak, the crowning glory of enlightenment."[34] Maskilim were the bearers of a modern Jewish metaphysics and the founders of a new Romantic religion that would provide a cure for the contemporary decline of Judaism, identified both with secularization (a "false enlightenment") and the "degeneracy" of popular piety exemplified by Hasidism. Maskilim were not secular intellectuals or "rationalists." The Haskalah comprised a Jewish "clerisy" dedicated to the preservation and revival of an authentic Jewish tradition. This tradition reposed chiefly in the biblical text. Biblical language, in turn, would provide a form and a means of expression for modern Hebrew culture, in which all the irreconcilables of the Romantic imagination would fuse.

Jewish followers of Mendelssohn were primed to embrace the ideal of the Romantic intellectual that flourished in nineteenth-century Eastern Europe. There were precedents for the Romantic concept of the "maskil" in the Jewish genealogy of this word, which is why the work of Mendelssohn, Maimon, and Wessely (who was a metaphysical Hebrew poet, as well as a linguist, biblical exegete, and educator) seems to anticipate the evolution of the meaning of *Bildung* that postdates them by a generation. The word "maskil," commonly translated as "instructor" or "teacher," "form[ed] a part of the standard wisdom vocabulary of the Hebrew Bible and related works."[35] Rabbinic culture frequently employed "maskil" as an adjective to describe a person possessed of theological and legal erudition or ritual expertise. The competency of "the instructed one" at times extended to esoteric teachings and practical magic. Medieval and early modern texts went further in this direction, applying the epithet specifically to Jewish mystical adepts.[36] Exegetical works, informed by the development of Kabbalah, described a maskil as a "visionary," engaged in an attempt to unlock the sources of "hidden wisdom" in order to "seek God."[37] In the mid-eighteenth century, the Italian Hebrew poet and mystic Moshe Hayyim Luzzatto first used the word "maskil" in a way that brought mystical contemplation into contact with natural philosophy.[38]

Luzzatto considered rational cognition an integral element of religious training which was ultimately aimed at bringing the initiate into intimate contact with the Divine.³⁹ In his treatise on rhetoric he identified poetic inspiration with spiritual illumination and, for the first time, linked the training of rational and imaginative faculties—a preparatory process he called "haskalah"—to the revival of prophecy, a gift he himself claimed to possess.⁴⁰ In Luzzatto's description of the path toward "saintliness," cultivation of cognitive discipline in order to avoid self-deception rose to the status of a profound ethical obligation. The urgent call to "reflection" was fraught with messianic potential as well as the more obvious pitfalls of error and pride.⁴¹

Luzzatto deliberately limited his following to a small coterie of devoted disciples. But by the nineteenth century, his lofty and exclusive spiritual ideal had acquired deeper intellectual traction. Jewish Romantic poets continued to read and publish his work throughout the first half of the nineteenth century.⁴² They foreswore Luzzatto's contemplative temper and vigorously resisted any slippage between rational thought and mystical practices. Still, their cultural aspirations and their self-image evinced traces of Luzzatto's original philosophical synthesis between poetry and revelation.

Luzzatto's unprecedented attempt to endow his Hebrew verse with the status of prophecy challenged the long-standing rabbinic monopoly on Jewish knowledge. His emphasis on reason and imagination as the wellsprings of transcendence placed the unique insight of the poet above the analytical skill of the most ingenious jurist. Unlike a rabbi, beholden to the tradition of legal commentary that screened the biblical text, the poet could take credit for an unmediated relationship to the language of Scripture; Luzzatto claimed to communicate personally with a divinely appointed "messenger" (Heb. *maggid*). His assertion of spiritual election provided a compelling argument for the creative autonomy of the Hebrew poet and challenged the interpretive authority of rabbinic exegesis. Eventually, maskilim turned authorship into a Jewish spiritual vocation in its own right and broke the textual hold of the rabbinic establishment.

Maskilim owed Luzzatto another important debt as well. Although they disavowed his messianic program, a new sense of time imbued their mission with the same degree of urgency that had gotten Luzzatto into trouble with Jewish communal authorities in Italy and elsewhere.⁴³ Luzzatto's messianic aspirations seeped into every aspect of his work, including his poetry. Most significant for maskilim, he imagined redemption as a perfect synthesis between the knowledge of the human sciences and the divine blessedness that reposed in Jewish learning. Their imminent union, guaranteed by God and ushered in by none other than Luzzatto himself, eventually found expression in the allegorical "marriage" between "Righteousness" and "Praise," the subject of a Hebrew drama in verse that Luzzatto wrote in 1743.[44] The new maskilim likewise interpreted their program of *Bildung* in light of the possibility of a merger between the universal expansion of knowledge and the providential course of Jewish history. Following Luzzatto, they translated their own philosophical messianism into a new imaginative idiom.

Thus, the discourse of Jewish Romanticism developed well within the precincts of Jewish religious thought. But it was still a revolution, one that took the form of a much broader nineteenth-century trend in literature and philosophy. Even a cursory glance at the strongest attachments of the Haskalah reveals connections with Romanticism. To begin with, the Haskalah shared the same set of symptomatic interests in history and literature. The aforementioned biblical fetish of nineteenth-century Jewish intellectuals is virtually a cliché, although it has never been analyzed within the compass of Romantic culture. The maskilic emphasis on moral renewal and on the transfiguration of everyday life is likewise traceable to post-Kantian idealism and to active engagement with Romantic metaphysics. Most important, perhaps, the Romantic ideal of transcendence, set against an acute critique of contemporary social mores, typifies the pedagogical sensibility of the maskil and informs the identification of "haskalah" with the primacy of culture attached to *Bildung*.

The conjunction between the Haskalah and Romanticism suggests many questions for future research. I cannot even begin to address them all here. I do, however, want to conclude this chapter with a brief and preliminary reassessment of Mendelssohn and his Haskalah project. I do this not because I subscribe to the school of thought that continues to assign to Mendelssohn a kind of paradigmatic status among modern Jewish intellectuals. I think that the near-exclusive focus on Mendelssohn at the expense of every other thinker and writer associated with the Haskalah has obscured the Romantic connection that might otherwise have been more apparent. Moreover, Mendelssohn's isolation from his younger Eastern European contemporaries has gotten in the way of a nuanced appreciation of Mendelssohn himself, not as the reluctant founder of a "Jewish Enlightenment" but, precisely, as a maskil. This sketch outlines some of the features of Mendelssohn's work that suggest the need for a different approach in defining his position between the Jewish history of the Haskalah and the German history of Romanticism.

Although Mendelssohn's philosophical interests certainly emerged out of the eighteenth century, his approach to Judaism provides a point of departure from Enlightenment rationalism. Mendelssohn introduced a number of key Romantic concepts into Jewish thought. To begin with, literary criticism has long recognized his seminal role in the reformulation of neoclassicist aesthetics. Based on the capacity of art to induce pleasure and to stimulate love of virtue and disgust for vice, neoclassicism had characterized the special provenance of art as the idealized imitation of nature. Neoclassical art was meant to generate interest and enjoyment. Mendelssohn, in his synopsis of the eighteenth-century debate about the nature of artistic endeavor, reformulated this idea in a way that led away from rational instrumentalism. Although he admitted that art can make people "happy or depressed at will," its principal ideal "places no such constraints on the arts." Art "calls only for the creation of a beautiful object." The artist, Mendelssohn argued, "must raise himself above commonplace nature, and as the recreation of beauty is his sole aim, he is always free to concentrate it in his works." Here, Mendelssohn was moving toward an aesthetics of creative expression (poesis) and away from the normative rules of imitation (mimesis). The artist's responsibility, Mendelssohn concluded, was only to himself. His freedom to bring original work into being represented his independence from "commonplace nature" that brought him into direct contact with the "provenient grace of God."[45] In breaking partially with the neoclassical theory of imitation, Mendelssohn made the first important connection to the Romantic concept of the artwork as a transcendent object with an integrity all its own. Moreover, his emphasis on artistic autonomy came close to the way in which the Romantics eventually conceived the prerogatives of original or natural genius, responsible only to itself. This Romantic ideal of originality eventually became attached to Shakespeare, the most protean of poets, whose shifty, mixed imagination had presented a problem for neoclassical aesthetics.[46] Mendelssohn wrote his essay on the general theory of the arts in 1757. His anticipation of Kant and especially Schiller (one of the most important proponents of the Romantic infatuation with Shakespeare) whose arguments about the disinterestedness of art provided a crucial source for Romantic aestheticism is readily apparent.

What is more important for students of the Haskalah is the fact that Mendelssohn translated his departure from neoclassicist norms into Jewish terms. As Jonathan Karp points out in a groundbreaking article, Mendelssohn's investment in the "reform" of Judaism was itself principally "aesthetic." In his analysis of Mendelssohn's short-lived Hebrew journal *Kohelet musar*, Karp demonstrates that for Mendelssohn "morality must be at least in part a function of aesthetic grasp."[47] The concept of an aesthetic dispensation that distinguishes human beings from animals and comes directly from God provided Mendelssohn with a rationale for the pursuit of "plenitude" (Heb. *shlemut*). This moral ideal comes close to *Bildung*; it is distinct both from the traditional pietistic insistence on withdrawal from the world and from the "secular pragmatism" of the eighteenth century.[48]

For Mendelssohn, art anticipated and informed the possibility of transcendence, representing the "human sphere within a divinely constructed, architecturally perfected world."[49] Although Karp situates this formulation of "aesthetic Judaism" within the context of a "religious Enlightenment," his own emphasis on Mendelssohn's attempt to "sacralize . . . everyday life" places *Kohelet musar* much closer to a Romantic "theology of art" than to the secular combination of wit, refinement, and taste propounded in the moral weeklies of the eighteenth century.[50] As a matter of fact, this way of looking at "religious enlightenment" is not too far from the Romantic correction of "secular pragmatism" in the work of Friedrich Schelling, who describes art as an "illumination," an "unveiler . . . of pure truth" and a "direct and necessary expression of the absolute."[51]

Karp's shift of perspective provides an alternative point of view on Mendelssohn's aesthetic investment in biblical Hebrew and, even more strikingly, on his symbolic understanding of Jewish ceremonial, adumbrated in the second part of *Jerusalem*, his seminal treatise on "religious power and Judaism." Although Mendelssohn here conceded that the basic "truths" affirmed by Judaism were fully consistent with the Enlightenment's understanding of "natural religion," he assigned extraordinary importance to ceremonial law as a "living script, rousing the mind and heart, full of meaning, never ceasing to inspire contemplation, and to provide the occasion and opportunity for oral instruction."[52] Mendelssohn differentiated "ceremonies" or "deeds" that "foster a close an intimate union of doctrine (*Lehre*) and life" from "written signs" that were apt to be misread and misunderstood.[53] Writing was, at best, an index of reality, a "dead letter"; but ceremonial law was a symbol of the "spirit of living dialogue" exclusive to the relationship between God and the historic community of Israel.

It is difficult to reconcile Mendelssohn's strikingly "particular" definition of ceremonial law, incumbent upon Jews alone, with an argument that his commitment to Judaism derived from its proximity to the universal truth of natural religion. "The same moral considerations that caused Mendelssohn to deny the revealed character of eternal verities," asserts Alexander Altmann in his reading of the second part of *Jerusalem*, "should have suggested the need for a universal revealed legislation."[54] Altmann's Mendelssohn is a Jewish "enlightener"; therefore, he *ought to have been* a universalist when it came to Jewish law.

In his attempt to force Mendelssohn into line with the standard reading of the Haskalah as Enlightenment, Altmann misses a much better argument that explains rather than represses Mendelssohn's unaccountable Jewish particularism. Mendelssohn's view of ceremonial has nothing to do with natural religion and everything to do with an understanding of law, which is rooted in a Jewish critique of Enlightenment politics. This revision can, I think, be traced back to Rousseau. In *Emile*, Rousseau addresses the contrast between the performative "language of signs" that assured the eternal validity of "covenants" and modern law, which appeals to self-interest but in the end must resort to force:

> I observe that in the modern age men no longer have a hold on one another except by force or self-interest; the ancients, by contrast, acted much more by persuasion and by affections of the soul because they did not neglect the language of signs. All their covenants took place with solemnity in order to make them more inviolable. Before force was established, the gods were the magistrates of mankind. It was in their presence that individuals made their treaties and alliances and uttered their promises. The face of the earth was the book in which their archives were preserved. Stones, trees, heaps of rocks consecrated by these acts and thus made respectable to barbaric men, were the pages of this book, which was constantly open to all eyes. The well of the oath, the well of the living and seeing, the old oak of Mamre, the mound of the witness, these were the crude but august monuments of the sanctity of contracts. None would have dared to attack these monuments with a sacrilegious hand, and the faith of men was more assured by the guarantee of these mute witnesses than it is today by all the vain rigor of the law.[55]

Rousseau contrasts the "vain rigor of the laws" in a modern state with the sublime assurance of "consecrated acts" in premodern society, where all collective treaties and individually held promises are guaranteed by faith in God. Rousseau's model for all "covenants" is explicitly religious or, in the language of modern legal theory, positive. Its strictures have to be accepted as sacred before they can be obeyed; however, once taken on faith, they command an obedience that is absolute. Their authority must be fully internalized as part of the natural order of things. Accordingly, ancient "promises" are always historically particular and embody the spirit of a community without which it disintegrates. In contrast, modern "laws" are only generally binding and therefore profane. The social contract, ostensibly rooted in human nature—which is to say in a society of individuals who are strangers to one another—recognizes no collective principle higher than the "self-interest," which must ultimately resort to force. Modern law can always be broken or revised according to the human desires that it purports to serve. That's why its "rigor" is "vain."

Appropriating Rousseau's distinction between "ancient" and "modern" conceptions of law, Mendelssohn took up modern social contract theory in the first part of *Jerusalem*, leaving discussion of the ancient "Mosaic constitution" to the second part. Mendelssohn formally differentiated the political operation of the "social contract," which is limited by definition and highly contingent in practice, from Jewish law, revealed by God and "consecrated" through the ages by the ritual reenactment of a common historical past. Based in faith, and underwritten by "deeds" rather than words, the Torah is accepted by Jews as eternally and collectively binding. Rousseau's evocation of the ancient "language of signs" echoes in Mendelssohn's understanding of Jewish ritual as a "living script" that engages both the heart and the mind. In both instances, there is no separation between law and life; a Jewish life is, by definition, a life lived by the law. Without "ceremonial," Jews cease to be Jews.

Mendelssohn's concept of the oral tradition likewise recapitulates Rousseau's notion of collective memory as an "archive," its "monuments" a living book "constantly open to all eyes." Both are "always open to instruction," endlessly reread and reinterpreted. But unlike a modern constitution, the "living book" of tradition cannot be abrogated, rewritten, or amended. Rousseau draws explicitly on an analogy with the Hebrew Bible in his examples of the "crude but august monuments" of the ancients.[56] Against the background of this ironic comparison between the good faith of Jewish "barbarians" whom the moralist marshals against the hypocrisy of his own modern Christian contemporaries, Mendelssohn's religious particularism begins to look less like an inconsistency and more like a similarly subtle unmasking of the Enlightenment's self-serving claims on human nature as a justification for coercion.

Mendelssohn's embrace of "ceremonial," in fact, anticipates Romantic reconsideration of the law in the work of nineteenth-century philologist Jacob Grimm and jurist Friedrich Carl von Savigny, who also owed something to Rousseau's pessimistic reading of social contract theory and his prescriptive understanding of the general will. Like Mendelssohn, Grimm contended that law originated not in written agreements, but in the "oral language" of poetry. Transmitted in stories about the past and resistant to the deadening effect of codification, the power of German legal maxims, symbols, and rituals lay "not in dead books and [written] formulas" but "in the mouth and the heart."[57] Law, wrote Savigny in his critique of liberal constitutionalism, is not born of "mere texts" but, like religion, of the spirit. Embedded in the "natural development of communities," law cannot be separated from history and from the "indissoluble organic connection of generation and ages."[58]

The image of an organic merger between religious devotion and political obedience that the Romantics identified with the premodern concept of community was already available to every reader of *Jerusalem*. The Mosaic state, Mendelssohn said, did not come into being by means of a social contract. In the original kingdom of Israel, "civil matters acquired a sacred and religious aspect and, and every civil service was at the same time a true service of God. The community was a community of God, its affairs were God's; the public taxes were an offering to God; and everything down to the least police measure was part of the *divine service*."[59] Although this ideal was set in Jewish antiquity, its traces inhered in ceremonial, a living record of the sacred history of the Jewish people and a covenantal "bond of union" for Jews that transcended mere "civil union" with the gentiles. Significantly, Mendelssohn presented his contrarian reading of Judaism in response to an "empirical"—which is to say, conventional—argument against the persistence of Jewish unreason. Here, then, is a strong case for Mendelssohn, the first Jewish Romantic, directly implicated in the act of enlightened critique.

Finally, there is the *Biur*, Mendelssohn's famous project of biblical translation and commentary, ostensibly moved by enlightened concern to restore the Bible to the Jewish curriculum and to purge Judaism of its dependence on the Talmud. There is, however, another case to be made for the significance of the *Biur*. I think the Biur represents the first step toward a unifying theory of Jewish culture, a precocious example of the Romantic quest for synthesis that so often located its inspiration in the Bible.

Mendelssohn claimed that the *Biur* served the educational needs of his own children, Mendel, Joseph, and Abraham. He had hoped, he said, to create a text that "introduced them to the intent of Scripture" so that "as they grew older they would by themselves achieve the right understanding."[60] Mendelssohn, in other words, wished to create a scriptural text that would accompany his sons through adulthood. Why only sons? Mendelssohn also had three daughters, the eldest of whom (named Brendel, but subsequently known as Dorothea) was, judging by her career, the most intellectually gifted of all her siblings. Why, in other words, did Mendelssohn find it necessary to create a biblical text suited explicitly to the education of Jewish *men*? The answer to this question takes us straight to the Romantic ideology of culture as a form of resistance to the pressures of the literary marketplace and a response to the emergent conviction among German intellectuals that "too many readers were reading too many of the wrong books for the wrong reasons and with altogether the wrong results."[61] Women were especially prone to this modern "reading sickness," but the notorious profligacy of feminine reading habits was held to be generally infectious.

Thanks to the pioneering research of Jean Baumgarten, we are beginning to gain a better appreciation of the eighteenth-century explosion in vernacular print that produced a similarly disconcerting revolution in Jewish reading.[62] By 1750, a non-expert Jewish reader had been at least two hundred years in the making. Early modern attempts on the part of rabbinic authorities to exert control over the literary marketplace assumed the existence of a robust Jewish print culture that potentially undermined the primacy of legal expertise over personal conduct and undercut the rabbinic monopoly on authorship. Of course, Jewish readers throughout history were drawn to books that lay beyond the boundaries of the Jewish curriculum. Rabbinic textuality itself testifies to the subtle interpenetration of Jewish and non-Jewish writing. However, the expansion of the commercial book market produced a distinctive category of lay readers known as "women and men who are like women," that is, people who had no schooling in the Talmud. Their tastes threatened to blur the difference between sacred and secular writing, a distinction that became especially critical to Jewish self-definition in the age of print. For Isaac Cardoso, a seventeenth-century Sephardic polemicist, physician, and courtier, the Jewish rejection of fiction for the truth of Scripture served as a crucial marker of Jewish difference, one of the most conspicuous signs of "Hebrew excellence":

> Books of comedies and amorous novels, with their sweet words and poetic fictions are a strong indication of lasciviousness and a deceitful instrument of perdition, troublers of the soul, violators of purity in which time is wasted, teachers of vanities and vices. Comedies and tragedies were invented by profane nations, not by the holy people Israel, whom the Lord chose to sing His divine praises and not lascivious loves and vicious inventions. . . . And it matters not if one says that they contain also many good things and moral judgments which can reform life and benefit customs, because there are asps hidden among the flowers. . . . It is the sacred books which should be read, for in them is the true doctrine, the most sublime rhetoric and the most supreme delight.[63]

Cardoso's remarks amplify the importance of the ongoing early modern debate about the regulation of popular access to books that contained the "wisdom of the gentiles," as well as controversial philosophical material and mystical teachings. The rise of print induced a need for greater textual control and a nostalgia for Jewish manuscript culture.[64] Print inspired a system of rabbinic self-censorship and raised the stakes on legal specialization. Rabbinic learning became more focused on exegetical versatility and dialectical proficiency. The rabbi became a professional expert reader of the Talmud and its rapidly expanding repertoire of legal commentary.

Despite rabbinic and lay efforts to intervene in the production and distribution of texts, the early modern Jewish book market produced a Jewish literature in the Eastern European vernacular—Yiddish—that consistently traduced the boundaries of rabbinic control and bypassed both external and self-imposed censorship restrictions. Authored by people who were on the margins of the learned elite, this literature was explicitly directed at the non-expert reader. The new vernacular writer often disclaimed the prerogatives of authorship and referred to himself more modestly as an editor, compositor, or publisher. He did not assume a higher spiritual calling and self-consciously marked his work as commercial, driven by the practical needs of his readership. Indeed, much of the new writing was devoted to matters of domestic concern, providing guidance to personal conduct, medical knowledge, information about Jewish customs, prayers, and many other aspects of living a Jewish life. At the same time, vernacular literature also ventured into marketing books for reading pleasure and included early experiments in Jewish fiction, verse drama, biblical paraphrases, and translations of Christian romances.

Vernacular Jewish writers and their readers inhabited a largely unregulated cultural space that remained below the rabbinic radar. Rabbis themselves were not in a hurry to make use of vernacular print except possibly as an instrument of religious discipline. Although they sometimes produced instructional texts that were aimed at a broader readership or even specifically at women, no rabbinic sage was ever tempted to author original legal scholarship in Yiddish or to stake his credentials on writing for an untutored audience of women and men who were like women. No one ever thought of translating the Talmud into Yiddish in order to democratize the established hierarchy of Jewish learning. At the same time, no matter how much it may have tampered with the religious experience and cultural tastes of its expanding readership, Jewish vernacular writing did not unseat rabbis as purveyors of "true doctrine" and Jewish law.

While vernacular literature pushed the boundaries of Jewish textual literacy and contributed to the rise of vernacular piety, it occupied a paradoxical position both at the center of Jewish daily life and on the margins of Jewish textuality. By the end of the eighteenth century, the distance between the Jewish reading public and the talmudic elite had grown into an impassable gulf. The kind of intensive textual immersion required for mastery of talmudic dialectic demanded a lifetime commitment and lay beyond the reach of most people. Rabbinic erudition had become highly professionalized and increasingly confined to a narrow class of full-time scholars, ensconced in the rarefied world of the yeshivah and subsidized by wealthy patrons.

By the time Mendelssohn assumed responsibility for a modern biblical translation, there were at least two Jewish cultures that made up so-called traditional Judaism: one marked male and associated with a full-time commitment to the study of the Talmud and its commentaries, and one marked female and associated with vernacular literature, much of it biblical or biblically inspired.[65] It is altogether too easy to overlook the fact that when Mendelssohn embarked on the *Biur*, most Jewish readers of the Bible in Yiddish-speaking lands (which included not only the vast Polish-Lithuanian repository of new Ashkenaz but also the Habsburg empire, Mendelssohn's native Prussia, smaller German principalities, and the Alsace) were women. What's more, the *Hebrew* Bible was being read primarily in Yiddish.

Biblical translations and paraphrases into Yiddish had been widely available since the last quarter of the seventeenth century. In the decades prior to the publication of the *Biur*, there were a score of new editions of the *Tsene-rene*, popularly known as the "women's Bible." First published sometime in the 1610s (the earliest extant edition is dated 1622), it was reprinted only three times in the seventeenth century; between 1700 and 1775, however, it was reissued at least ten times, primarily in the German-speaking lands. In addition to *Tsene-rene*, the eighteenth century produced an explosion of imaginative literature in Yiddish derived from biblical material, including drama and verse.

But the *Biur* seems to have been most directly aimed at the provoking popularity of *Tsene-rene*. Like the latter, Mendelssohn's Bible provided common-sense commentary that elucidated the plain meaning of the text and only occasionally ventured into homiletical territory. The language of translation—German in Hebrew characters—was a deliberate "correction" of the corrupted Germanic "dialect" also written in Hebrew characters in which the *Tsene-rene* itself was composed. What we have in the *Biur* is not the first German Jewish Bible, but a modern Jewish vernacular Bible, suited to the cultural aspirations of an intellectual elite and free from debasement by the promiscuous tastes of women and untutored men.[66] The *Biur* was Mendelssohn's response to the scandal of vernacular Biblicism, represented by the *Tsene-rene*; it was a precedent-setting text in the romantic "system of defenses against the new power of reading" that motivated the maskilic recovery of the Bible against the eighteenth-century dispersion of Jewish knowledge.[67]

Despite what maskilim repeatedly said, the Bible did not have to be rescued from two hundred years of Jewish neglect. Rather, the biblical text had to be removed from female jurisdiction, where it had flourished throughout the early modern period, and restored to the rigorously masculine poetics of the Jewish revival. The return to Hebrew "excellence" and the attempt to fashion a classical, which is to say, normative, Hebrew vocabulary and syntax, the obsession with grammar, the emergence of literary criticism—all these are evidence of the Romantic attempt to construct a system of literary values in opposition to the realities of Jewish vernacular literacy. Wessely, sounding almost exactly like Cardoso, warned the publishers of the first Jewish literary journal, *Hameasef*, against pandering to the desires of the contemporary reader, particularly for diverting comedy and love lyrics.[68]

The aesthetic revolution inaugurated by the *Biur* set the intellectual agenda for Jewish writers throughout the nineteenth century and informed the ambivalence with which even Jewish populists, beholden to the Romantic concept of Jewish literature, continued to view the modern irruption of mass culture.[69] The textual politics of the *Biur* likewise illuminate the stakes involved in the imaginative assault on women in the works of Jewish Romanticism and the virtual absence of female authorship from nineteenth-century Hebrew and Yiddish literature. The Haskalah frequently coupled its depiction of Hasidim as a signifier of popular culture with problematic images of women. Both represented sources of social pathology associated with the derailment of Jewish faith in human perfectibility. Women were at the nexus of religious hypocrisy and the ungovernable forces of lust and greed. Female piety served as a particularly egregious example of popular folly and the persistence of superstition. Embodied in the figure of the crone and the mother-in-law, female power within the family was symbolically linked to the perversion of religious authority that also accounted for the rise of *tzaddikim*. Female sexuality likewise embodied the decline of moral discipline and the ever-present threat of apostasy. While images of older women were bound up with the problematic language of economic acquisitiveness, young marriageable women signified the frivolous pursuit of luxury and sexuality run amok. Unruly Jewish women represented the dangerous proximity between the marketplace and the brothel.

Historians have exceptional difficulty in reconciling their assertion that maskilim were secular liberals with this escalation of hostility toward women in maskilic texts. Scholarship on "Jewish Enlightenment" does not even attempt to explain why the Haskalah failed to produce a single public attempt to vindicate the rights of Jewish women by women themselves. Shmuel Feiner argues that Hebrew literature excoriated female self-assertion, instead offering up its own "Victorian" ideal of feminine docility and domestic propriety, characteristic of nineteenth-century bourgeois culture.[70] However, it is not at all clear that the ideal of female domesticity ever acquired the kind of widespread intellectual purchase in nineteenth-century Eastern Europe that it did in the English-speaking world—which, nevertheless, produced a robust tradition of imaginative writing by women, some of them Jewish. Maskilic literature did not advocate the reconstruction of the Jewish family along middle-class lines and produced few memorable middle-class heroines. On the contrary, Jewish Romantics exhibited a strong anti-bourgeois streak.

Hostility toward female greed and female sexuality was itself a response to anxiety about the feminization of Judaism and the buying power of the lay Jewish reader, predominantly but not only female, whose tastes were increasingly unaccountable. In fact, maskilim— including Mendelssohn, who was deeply enamored of the late eighteenth-century ideal of male friendship—seemed to have been much more invested in preserving the kinds of exclusive homosocial spaces that traditional society set aside for the learned elite than in freeing the laity (both male and female) from rabbinic control. The *Biur*, a reading Bible designed by men for men, was the first example of this disciplinary commitment. Most Jewish children, male and female alike, learned to read the Bible from women, the Yiddish-speaking source of the popular "disfigurement" of Judaism. Mendelssohn's attempt to remove it from the vernacular jurisdiction of his own children's—more specifically, his sons'—mother effectively underwrote the exclusion of women from the modern Jewish revival.

After Mendelssohn, maskilic fantasy continually returned to the miracle of cultural and biological reproduction without the need for sex and indulged in the utopian dream of a world without women. Not especially exercised by the Victorian ideal of companionate marriage, Jewish Romantics were more inclined to celebrate emotional attachments between men as the highest form of spiritual kinship and the apotheosis of love. The persistent misogyny of Jewish intellectuals was not an incidental byproduct of liberal ambivalence. The reason that women seem so marginal to the world of the Haskalah is that maskilim actively marginalized them. Their philosophical and literary project of Jewish renewal was born in the study house and it was explicitly gendered male.

Socially motivated by the reassertion of masculine privilege over Jewish texts, the Haskalah took on a varied and increasingly promiscuous reading culture that the learned elite could barely control, let alone penetrate. But Jewish Romantics did no better. In a letter to a friend and fellow maskil, David Friedländer ruefully concluded "the [Jewish] nation in its present condition, despite the appearance of culture, taste and learning to be in an irremediably bad state; all of [our] efforts at enlightenment appeared to have been useless. No one reads any of the books written in Hebrew. For whom are they written? I would propose that a sign be placed on all of the Hebrew printing houses, saying 'Here books are printed that are never read.'"[71] A student of Mendelssohn, Friedländer articulated the tension that was already implicit in the work of his teacher, who thought that the effects of "sham enlightenment" were more culturally pernicious than the persistence of "religious prejudice."[72] At least, the latter kept a Hebrew readership alive.

Stuck firmly in the eighteenth century, the scholarship on Mendelssohn depicts him as a Jewish "conservative"; this he may have been, but self-conscious conservatism foreshadows an attitude toward culture that emerged in the full light of day with Romanticism. Mendelssohn is to be considered a maskil not because he sought to dial the clock back to the golden age of Maimonides and Ibn Ezra but because his philosophical "medievalism" anticipates the nineteenth-century invention of tradition, a process that deliberately blurred the difference between historical scholarship and the imaginative construction of a usable past. Mendelssohn himself lived on the edge of a period that German literary scholarship used to call "early Romantic" (Ger. *Frühromantik*), but has since been renamed, more comprehensively, "the age of Goethe" (Ger. *Goethezeit*). There is good reason, argue Nicholas Saul and Richard Littlejohns, to push the origins of Romanticism back to the late-Enlightenment era of "sensibility" and thus to close the artificial gap that divides the classical revival associated with Goethe and Schiller from the nineteenth-century Romantic return to history.[73] In the work of threshold thinkers—of whom Mendelssohn is one—Romantic readers found sources for a "new, anthropologically orientated vision of human fulfillment . . . to be realized through *aesthetic* means."[74]

Mendelssohn was twenty years older than Goethe and thirty years older than Schiller. Viewed against the background of their portion in the development of Romanticism, Mendelssohn the maskil was a generation ahead of Mendelssohn the German philosopher. Scholarship has only now begun to contend with the possibility that the source of Mendelssohn's originality as a *German* thinker lay in his contribution to the creation of modern *Jewish* culture rather than in anything that he wrote as the "Socrates of Berlin," in which capacity he may have remained firmly in the grip of the Enlightenment (although this contention may be similarly open to revision). This tentative post-modern reorientation in Mendelssohn scholarship is indicative of growing discontent with the consensus view of the Haskalah, also evident in the study of modern

Jewish history and literature. As we shall see in the next chapter, the attempt to install a "Jewish Enlightenment" in nineteenth-century Eastern Europe was always a dubious enterprise, subject to vigorous criticism. A tendency to accept a wrong-headed translation as a basis for scholarship overshadows what is, in reality, a highly unstable and contentious field of inquiry.

PART II
STATE OF THE QUESTION

3 Haskalah and History

Historical scholarship on the Haskalah is driven principally by the continual reassessment of the connection between the "Jewish Enlightenment" and the Jewish experience of modernity. The received view assumed a direct and "intimate relationship" between the "Jewish Enlightenment" and the revolutionary "processes of political emancipation and the integration of Jews into the larger society."[1] According to a highly influential argument, presented by Jacob Katz in his *Tradition and Crisis* (originally published in Hebrew in 1958), the Haskalah initiated Jews into secular middle-class culture and launched Jewish intellectuals into the fray of liberal politics. "That the Haskalah movement caused fundamental changes in traditional society," Katz asserted, "is generally accepted by historians and requires no further proof.... The movement's tendency toward secularization demonstrates its radical nature clearly."[2]

According to Katz, Jewish "secularization" emerged against the background of a stable communal structure to which the word "tradition" in his title plainly referred and to which Katz devoted two-thirds of his book. Politically autonomous and efficiently governed by a mutually sustaining combination of lay economic power, rabbinic exhortation, and patriarchal authority, Katz's "traditional" Jewish collective presented a radical contrast to the "enlightened" Jewish ideal of the "neutral society," founded upon a rationalist critique of religion. Unlike the traditional social order, which consisted of "corporations," divided by estate and confession, a "neutral society" was composed of "human beings without any special qualification."[3] Its relationship to the non-Jewish world defined by religious imperatives and the screen of social distance, traditional Jewry, argued Katz, remained culturally self-sufficient, even though Jews were at times prepared to enter into instrumental, mutually beneficial economic arrangements with Christians. The historical high point for the existence of Katz's "ideal type" of traditional Jewish life was "at the end of the Middle Ages" (sixteenth through eighteenth centuries) and its optimal environment, the Polish-Lithuanian Commonwealth.

According to Katz, the Haskalah was one of the two movements that shook the integrity of Jewish tradition and determined the course of Jewish life in the modern word—Hasidism was the other. On the one hand, Katz argued, the personal relationship between the *Hasid* and his *tzaddik* undermined established hierarchies of wealth and learning.

Hasidism elevated the devotion of the ordinary individual above the ascetic ideals of the learned elite and the principle of charismatic leadership above legal expertise. As a result, the "community of Hasidim grew, if not on the ruins of the traditional institutions of society, at least at their expense."[4] On the other hand, the commitment to reason on the part of Jewish "enlighteners" as well as their promotion of secular education and personal autonomy irreparably damaged the sense of Jewish solidarity. Katz concluded that the Haskalah inspired a significant relaxation of communal discipline and "justified, perhaps obligated, the individual to take refuge outside the framework" of Jewish law.[5] Pointedly, he described the "Jewish Enlightenment" as an irreversible ideological "crisis" that touched every aspect of Jewish social life, neatly catalogued in his book under the headings of personal conduct, economic behavior, educational standards and aims, and familial ties.[6]

Katz provided the next generation of historians with what a recent survey of contemporary Haskalah scholarship characterizes as an "utterly logical, orderly, elegant exposition."[7] His sociology of modernity found immediate resonance in Jewish intellectual history. In the late 1960s Michael Meyer's *Origins of the Modern Jew* similarly attributed the "dilemma" of modern Jewish self-consciousness to the impact of the Haskalah. "It is with the age of Enlightenment," Meyer said, "that Jewish identity becomes segmented and hence problematic."[8] Meyer went on to outline the ways in which the experience of Moses Mendelssohn and his disciples demonstrated the historic need for a modern Judaism, attuned to the discordant forces of "external pressures and internal attachments" that have since resonated with every subsequent generation of modern Jews.[9] Like Katz, Meyer attributed the flowering of a "Jewish Enlightenment" in Berlin to a radical conflict between Jewish faith and universal reason and lamented Mendelssohn's "ephemeral" attempt to bridge the gap between the two as historically unrealizable. The tenuous balance between Mendelssohn's "static" view of reason and the "law of Moses" only "held together in momentary unity by the strength of his own person."[10] In Meyer's reading, the intractable tensions between a commitment to Jewish law and an attraction to secular culture were manifest in the personal "tragedies" of Mendelssohn's students and disciples, the archetypal modern Jews. Katz identified a "crisis" across a broad sociological canvas of collective experience and institutional change; Meyer located it specifically in the "dilemma" of Jewish psychology. In both instances, the problem of a Jewish modernity was implicit in the "Jewish Enlightenment."

Historians began to question the marriage between modernization and the Haskalah almost as soon as Meyer and Katz published their work.

Katz's "logical, orderly and elegant" synthesis between new ideas and social change unraveled within a single generation. The demotion of the "Jewish Enlightenment" as philosophically derivative, politically utopian, and generally marginal to modern Jewish experience started in the late 1970s with the publication of Todd Endelman's *The Jews of Georgian England* (1979). Endelman took issue with the connection between the Haskalah and Katz's characterization of Jewish "assimilation." The subtitle of his book *Tradition and Change in a Liberal Society* referred directly to Katz's *Tradition and Crisis*. "The revolution in fundamental attitudes that characterized the Haskalah," Endelman wrote, "was a self-conscious, systematic, intellectual response to the challenge of modernity."

> It was a response, however, that was thoroughly untypical of either European Jewry as a whole or German Jewry in particular. It was the response of the German haute bourgeoisie in Berlin, Königsberg, Hamburg, Copenhagen, and a few other cities and of an equally small group of secularly educated Jews who were employed by the well-to-do as clerks, private tutors, and teachers. The vast majority of European Jews, as they came to alter their customary habits, did not construct an intellectual system to justify the changes they were making or to promote those changes among others more traditional than themselves.[11]

Endelman rejected not only Katz's conclusion that the Haskalah was an instrument of emancipation from Jewish society, but also the axiomatic premise that there was a direct and unambiguous connection between the history of ideas and people's lives. Trained in the Anglo-American school of social history, Endelman was more interested in Jewish "peddlers and hawkers, pickpockets and pugilists" than in rabbis, reformers, and their middle-class patrons. The "peddlers and the hawkers," left out of Jewish history altogether, were surely more numerous than rabbis and arguably constituted the "ancestry" of most twentieth-century Jews. Endelman deplored the tendency of German Jewish historians who followed Katz in treating the "acculturation of the Jews of Western and Central Europe" as if it were a "problem that concerned only the Jewish bourgeoisie." The "Jewish poor, who were the overwhelming majority of European Jewry," neither remained "passive bystanders, unaffected and unmoved by the changes to which their wealthier coreligionists were responding," nor "immune to the attractions of the non-Jewish world."[12]

In contrast to Katz and Meyer, Endelman adopted an agnostic attitude to the process of social change. He did not view modernity as either a psychological or a philosophical "crisis." "From the end of the eighteenth century," Endelman concluded, "many Jews of middle-class origin began to identify themselves more closely with the country in which they had been born and with its inhabitants." But this passage did not necessarily diminish their Jewish loyalty. His own research suggested that people's "sense of identity expanded to include a sense of Englishness as well as a sense of Jewishness." Dual "identification ... came to define modern Jewish self-consciousness everywhere in Western and Central Europe and was the product of ... acculturation and integration" rather than a signifier of a decline in Jewish values.[13] For Katz, the word "and" in *Tradition and Crisis* meant "tradition followed by crisis." For Endelman, the same conjunction in *Tradition and Change* implied the possibility of their coexistence as well as chronological succession. The one did not cancel out the other even though, Endelman conceded, "personal advantages" could vitiate the "survival of the Jewish people in the collective." In a liberal society, the relationship between "tradition and change" was much more complicated than Katz's tendentious juxtaposition implied. "Freedom," Endelman admitted, was "both good for the Jews and bad for the Jews at the same time. This, however, should not be a surprising conclusion. For who today still believes that history advances without ambiguity?"[14]

Endelman displaced the Haskalah from its position as the defining moment in the history of the Jews in "liberal society." Inviting historians to consider the unremarkable effects of gradual change in everyday life from below, Endelman introduced new sources into the study of the Jewish past. His book relied on archival records and newspapers rather than on works of literature and philosophy. Drawing Jews into the orbit of contemporary Western European historiography, Endelman questioned whether there even was a distinctively Jewish path toward modernity; he was the first to separate the philosophical idea of a Jewish history from a secular history of the Jews. According to Endelman, Jews became modern in the course of the same history that transformed the Western European population as a whole. The tide of Jewish "indifference to religious tradition reflected the increasingly secular nature of the western world in the eighteenth century," rather than the specific influence of maskilim or the impact of a revolution in Jewish thought.[15]

Comparative by definition and Whiggish in tone, Endelman's work applied the conceptual framework and research methods of European social history to the study of Jewish modernity. Same but different, Jews began to figure in accounts of Western European modernity not only as victims of antisemitism or as deracinated, intellectually precocious strangers, but as ordinary men and women living alongside their non-Jewish neighbors, subject to the same pressures and open to the same opportunities.[16] The emancipation of modern Jewish historiography from the "crisis" model did not immediately produce a revolution in Haskalah scholarship. But it quickly became apparent that the process of Jewish modernization and the project of "Jewish Enlightenment" could no longer be considered one and the same.

The turn to social history has made it difficult to argue that the Haskalah turned Jews into secular liberals. Themselves swept up in the general "crisis" of the European old regime, Jewish "enlighteners" could take neither credit nor blame for the cataclysmic changes associated with the rise of capitalism, technological development, political revolution, and massive population growth. With respect to these changes, Jews were no different from Christians. There was no reason to presume that Jewish religious leaders would be any more successful in keeping the Jewish tradition insulated from the effects of modernity than were contemporary Catholic and Protestant clergy. Neither, however, was there any reason to expect that Judaism would simply succumb. This idea, now a commonplace in Jewish history writing, is not really so new.

In 1928, Salo Baron published a pungent critique of the then-regnant view that the modern experience of emancipation represented a political boon for the Jews. Baron argued that Jewish emergence from the ostensible cultural and social insularity of the medieval "ghetto" was a necessary consequence of the demise of corporate privilege and the increasing concentration of political authority.[17] That some—and by no means all—Jews were prepared to reinterpret the Jewish tradition in light of this momentous political transformation was a remarkable fact, worthy of historians' attention. But the efforts of Jewish "enlighteners" to defend emancipation (if, indeed, that is what they were doing) ought not to be confused with the history of Europe's own political "enlightenment" and emancipation from the corporate society of the Middle Ages. "Emancipation," wrote Baron, "was even more of a necessity for the modern state than it was for the Jews. . . . Left to themselves, the Jews might for long have clung to their corporate existence. For emancipation meant losses as well as gains for Jewry."[18] Had there never been a "Jewish" Enlightenment, the Jewish tradition upheld by Katz as an ideal would have confronted a fundamental social "crisis" anyway. In his eloquent defense of the "ghetto," an institution with a far longer historical pedigree than the liberal nation-state, Baron made clear that the kinds of changes that produced tectonic shifts in the behavior of large numbers of people lay in the realm of secular causation rather than in ideological factors, the long-term effects of which were notoriously elusive, hard to measure, and often capricious. Postwar Jewish historiography fully bore out Baron's speculative conclusions. New studies of Jewish communities in the modern world divorced "Jewish Enlightenment" from the social consequences of modernization, particularly in places where modern Jews became identified with a rising middle class.[19] However, the ensuing shift in scholarly priorities did not resolve the question of how to write a new history of the Haskalah that would take the findings and the methods of social history more fully into account.

Social historians have considerably attenuated the centrality of German Jewry in the understanding of modern Jewish experience. Likewise, reconceptualizations of "Jewish Enlightenment" undertook, first, to interrogate the transnational character of the movement. Katz and Meyer had emphasized the formative nature of Berlin and had nothing to say about the Haskalah in Russia and Galicia. Most studies of "Jewish Enlightenment" confined the formative period of the movement to Mendelssohn's lifetime and relegated nineteenth-century Eastern European Jewish intellectuals (before the rise of Zionism) to the periphery of modern Jewish thought. Offering his own qualified response to the new emphasis on the local in Jewish social history, Katz undertook to edit a collaborative volume called *Toward Modernity: The European Jewish Model*, the goal of which was to "compare the process of modernization in German Jewry with its counterparts in other countries."[20]

Aimed at demonstrating that almost everywhere the "German model *converged* with the influence of local factors," the book featured essays about the dissemination of ideas associated with the Haskalah. Together, the authors made the point that the process of cultural diffusion from Berlin was a great deal more complicated than Katz's claim of direct influence suggested. In every case, divergence from (rather than convergence with) the "German model" reflected the significance of a different Eastern European setting. In no case was it possible to sustain Katz's original argument that the Haskalah served as the ideology of "assimilation" or that its ideas promoted secularization and encouraged the liberation of the Jewish individual from Jewish society. On the contrary, the essays in the volume depicted maskilim as religious "moderates," committed to preserving Jewish community and developing Jewish education. Hillel Kieval, in his essay on the Haskalah in Prague, put forward an argument that set a new agenda for Haskalah scholarship. "The tone of moderation and traditionalism, so characteristic of the Prague maskilim," Kieval proposed, "was not necessarily unique to this one city" even though "the notion of a conservative Haskalah with quasi-national overtones may indeed have comprised the essence of Prague's contribution to the Jewish Enlightenment."[21] According to Kieval, Prague's maskilim "moderated" the impact of secularization and helped to preserve the city's Jewish institutions from social decline. Their cultivation of modern Jewish culture in Prague helped to create an intellectual framework for the reception of Jewish nationalism at the turn of the century. The "harmonizing tendency" characteristic of German-speaking Jewish intellectuals in Bohemia and Hungary, noted by Kieval and Michael Silber, also extended to the Italian provinces of the Habsburg Empire.[22] In Trieste, a conservative emphasis on "cultural continuity ... reduced the potential for conflict between tradition and modernity," wrote Lois Dubin.[23]

Toward Modernity conveyed the general sense that the Haskalah did not constitute a "crisis" but enabled gradual accommodation to new ideas and adaptation to local circumstances, themes that were fully in tune with the idea of Jewish "acculturation," advanced concurrently by social historians. Furthermore, *Toward Modernity* complicated Katz's argument that Jewish emancipation constituted the chief aim of maskilic projects of educational and social reform.[24] Several of the articles showed that in Habsburg Galicia, Congress Poland, and the Pale of Settlement, maskilic politics were more consistent with the confessional practices of absolutism than with liberal aspirations toward equality. Israel Bartal pointed out that the multi-confessional and multi-ethnic milieu of the Haskalah did not exactly encourage the development of Western-style liberalism. As agents of imperial German culture in an Eastern European province populated by Ukrainians, Poles, and Jews, maskilim in Galicia stood to benefit from state patronage and were reluctant to endorse the creation of a "neutral society," which would deprive them of their special privileges as agents of modernization.[25] Most maskilim, not only in Galicia but in Russia—where "learned Jews" enjoyed state support on a much greater scale and for a considerably longer period of time—were profoundly ambivalent about the personal and social costs of emancipation. Even Mendelssohn's position on the possibility of a "civil union" between Jews and Christians was far more equivocal than Katz's ham-fisted treatment of Haskalah politics in Germany had asserted.

Bartal characterized the "heavenly city of Germany" as an imperial ideal, crucial to the self-image of Galician maskilim as bearers of Enlightenment along the colonial frontier. In fact, the connection between the Haskalah and the politics of empire had been made in Russian Jewish historiography just a few years before the publication of *Toward Modernity*. The first study that located the Haskalah explicitly against Eastern European practices of imperial administration was Michael Stanislawski's *Tsar Nicholas I and the Jews* (1983). Setting aside the link between the Haskalah and Jewish liberalism, Stanislawski integrated Russia's "Jewish Enlightenment" into a study of social engineering from above. He focused his investigation on "how the Haskalah in Russia changed from an amorphous body of ideas into an ideology and a movement," only to find that the transition occurred "in large part as a direct result of the policies and actions of the government."[26] As "employees and allies" of Nicholas's confessional state, Russian maskilim "became a potent force within Russian Jewry and a grave threat to the traditional order."[27] But their "new sense of mission and power" did not encourage an attendant commitment to secularization or to the liberal principles of freedom and equality for all.

The religiously moderate majority of Russian Jewish intellectuals, Stanislawski argued, was prepared to enlist state authority "not to change the tradition but to restore it to its pure state before it was corrupted by the ignorant."[28] Characteristically, the radicals who demonstrated the most "profound dissatisfaction with the government's treatment of the Jews" also experienced an "even more bitter disillusionment with the basic axioms of the Haskalah's political ideology."[29] It made sense that arguments for emancipation did not come from maskilim. Spearheaded by wealthy Jewish merchants and secular Jews in Odessa and St. Petersburg, a nascent struggle for Jewish civil rights in Russia marked a slippage in the status of "learned Jews" educated in government-sponsored institutions and employed by the state. Subsequent research bore out Stanislawski's conclusions and showed that the emancipationist policies of Nicholas's successor, Alexander II, the author of the Great Reforms, fractured the ranks of the Haskalah and promoted the rise of competing elites, composed of Russian-speaking Jewish professionals, university students, and the haute bourgeoisie.[30] These were the groups who carried on the battle for Jewish emancipation and saw it through to its conclusion. Stanislawski's subsequent work on Judah Leib Gordon, the preeminent Hebrew poet of the Haskalah and among the last of the Jewish Romantics who experienced personally the tensions between "official enlightenment" and "selective emancipation," likewise demonstrated that the tentative and short-lived marriage between the Haskalah and Russian Jewish "liberalism" during the era of the Great Reforms was initially beset by "agonizing doubt" and ended in "moral exhaustion."[31]

Following Stanislawski, research undertaken by Nancy Sinkoff, David Fishman, Lois Dubin, and Marcin Wodzinski disclosed the imperial logic of specifically regional experiments in religious and social reform on the Russian and Habsburg frontiers. Dubin argued that the near absence of local opposition to the educational initiatives of Jewish intellectuals in Habsburg Trieste stemmed from the "Mediterranean" character of Triestine Jewry. The cultural and geographic distance of Trieste from the centers of Jewish "orthodoxy" in Eastern Europe nourished an indigenous tradition of openness to secular learning, which rendered Trieste receptive to the reforming aims of the Habsburg bureaucracy.[32] Fishman's case study of Shklov showed that the precocious progress of the Haskalah in one marginal outpost of Jewish Lithuania originated in sponsorship of Russian provincial administrators, eager to impress their reform-minded superiors in distant St. Petersburg. According to Fishman, the position of an obscure town as an incubator of Russian Jewish modernity derived from several distinctive geopolitical convergences, including the separation of the "Mogilev province from Poland—and its annexation by Russia—in 1772, the town's emergence as one of Russia's commercial windows on the west ... and the establishment of Count Semion Zorich's court there in 1778."[33] The presence of Zorich and the other royal favorite, Prince G. A. Potemkin, not only offered new economic opportunities for the city's Jewish merchants but also served to endow the financial support of new scholarship with the status of a noble pursuit.

Sinkoff, turning to a parallel case of noble patronage of "Jewish Enlightenment" in Podolia, demonstrated that the "productivity" of an Eastern European Jewish intellectual often depended directly on the financial and social sponsorship of reforming gentry.[34] Following the Polish Partitions, regional patterns of patronage translated into identification with the imperial bureaucracy throughout the Ukrainian provinces. The "Podolian" maskil Mendel Lefin benefited from his relationship with the local Polish magnate, Adam Czartoryski. Czartoryski, a close friend of Tsar Alexander I (r. 1801–1825), had a stellar career in Russian state service. Lefin saw himself as Czartoryski's partner in the project of imperial reform. Joseph Perl, "arguably Lefin's most eminent disciple in Austrian Galicia," conceived of his own educational goals as an extension of Habsburg state policy.[35] In Congress Poland—the semi-autonomous vestige of the "noble republic" carved out by the partitioning powers and subject to Russian sovereignty—even those maskilim who were invested in Polish culture remained staunchly "monarchist" in their political outlook.[36] Most of them were employed by the state or "associated with government offices."[37] Even in a "constitutional" kingdom, the business of "Jewish enlightenment" was part of imperial administration.

The prospect of state preferment and the possibility of employment by the government in the promotion of Jewish reform raised the stakes on internal conflicts over leadership and endowed social discontent with ideological focus. Political fracture at the turn of the twentieth century had its roots not only in the impact of revolutionary ideas—Zionism, Marxism, diasporism—but in the long history of petty (and not so petty) skirmishing between "learned Jews" and their Hasidic and orthodox opponents for state support and popular acceptance. Eli Lederhendler's 1989 study of the politics of the Haskalah in Russia made the point that "class struggle in the Pale," described by Ezra Mendelsohn in his slightly earlier book about the workers' movement in Jewish Lithuania during the 1880s, originated in the conflict over the nature of Jewish self-government among Jewish intellectuals between the 1840s and the 1870s.[38] Lederhendler argued that the "breach in the continuity of traditional forms" of Jewish self-government "should not . . . be taken for a break in the continuity of Jewish political development. The diffusion of communal responsibility spawned new leadership groups; challenges to the existing communal institutions stimulated new forms of activity; and the loss of the state as guarantor of the community's structural integrity facilitated the discovery of the 'people's will' as the foundation for a new type of political community."[39] In Lederhendler's reading, Eastern European Jewish intellectuals were not prototypical Jewish liberals, content to live and let live and inclined to respect individual rights at the expense of collective responsibilities. Their tendency toward social authoritarianism, their fierce combativeness, their commitment to Jewish "reconstruction," and their idealism anticipated and informed the political style of Eastern European Jewish populism that appeared under various party standards at the turn of the twentieth century. In defiance of Zionist consensus that Jewish nationalism constituted a radical break from maskilic liberalism, Lederhendler effectively proposed that the Jewish politics of "self-emancipation" were not a response to the failure of the Haskalah, but its direct outcome and its most important political legacy.

Archival research subsequently extended Lederhendler's thesis. Rachel Manekin and Marcin Wodzinski showed that in Galicia and Congress Poland, Jewish intellectuals became involved in intramural Jewish politics not to promote the cause of Jewish "assimilation" but to gain control over local Jewish institutions, such as synagogues, schools, and charities.[40] Their "parochial" interests did not lie in democratizing Jewish self-government or in making Jews more liberal and civic-minded, but in transforming the Jewish community into an instrument of cultural renewal. Operating within the framework of imperial social engineering and inspired by Rousseau's romantic politics of virtue, maskilim developed the initial blueprint for a Zionist republic in which a state run by Jewish intellectuals would serve the end of Jewish nation-building.[41]

The comparative decentralization of Germany in the study of the Haskalah has also enabled a new approach to the study of "Jewish Enlightenment" in Berlin itself. No longer saddled with the entire history of Jewish modernity, eighteenth-century Berlin could be viewed through the same lens of local history as any other center of Jewish intellectual activity, such as Dubin's Trieste and Fishman's Shklov. In a sensitive and highly nuanced study of Jewish life in the Prussian capital between the last quarter of the eighteenth century and the post-Napoleonic period, Steven Lowenstein produced a social history of "Mendelssohn and his generation" based on a close reading of statistical information about demography, marriage and conversion patterns, and the distribution of wealth. Lowenstein provided an account of the Berlin Haskalah that divorced the activities of the Mendelssohn circle from the "assimilationist" teleology of *Tradition and Crisis*. Lowenstein explained the dramatic rise of Berlin's "Haskalah milieu" in terms of highly specific economic and political conditions rather than the ideological breakdown of traditional Jewish mores. His "collective biography" of Jewish Berlin yielded a "clearer picture of the process by which Berlin became the first major Jewish community to undergo massive 'modernization.' The role of family relationships, the influences of the choices of one generation on those of the next, the chronological divisions in, and the social influences on the changes and the crisis they produced [could now] be delineated." Still, Lowenstein cautioned, the "results" of his inquiry would not "resolve the ideological debates about the merits of the reform or orthodox party or about the success or failure of either as a bulwark against assimilation."[42] The complicated relationship between "Jewish Enlightenment" and apostasy in early nineteenth-century Berlin grew out of local conditions that obtained only in Berlin and only between the reign of Frederick II and the Napoleonic Wars.

According to Lowenstein, the imminent prospect of emancipation rather than the Haskalah ushered in a "revolutionary stage in the development of Jewish modernity in Berlin," fired an "epidemic" of conversions that polarized the community, and led to the dissolution of the "Jewish Enlightenment."[43] Most important for students of the Haskalah, Lowenstein concluded that the ostensible correlation between the activities of Mendelssohn and his followers and the subsequent "assimilation" of the city's Jewish elite "must be related to specific factors present in that particular time and place" rather than to the ideological intervention of Jewish intellectuals.[44] "Special characteristics of Berlin Jewish society may have led to the explosive events of 1780 and 1830" and produced the local sense of "crisis" that Katz had attributed to maskilic militancy and ascribed to an entire era in Jewish history. Emphasizing the unique position of late eighteenth-century Berlin as a frontier of Jewish modernity, Lowenstein made clear that the trajectory of "tradition and crisis" could not be generalized even to Berlin itself, since the city underwent a religious revival after the Napoleonic Wars. The German Jewish flirtation with secularization proved brief; Lowenstein does not say so, but there were probably more free-thinking, non-observant Jews in mid-nineteenth-century Odessa than in mid-nineteenth-century Berlin.

Lowenstein identified the ostensible "radicalism" of the Berlin Haskalah as a temporary detour from mainstream German Jewish culture, marked by provincial conservatism, the entrenchment of local custom, and durable patterns of religious observance. The discontinuity troubled other historians too. Pushing the origins of the "Jewish Enlightenment" back to the period between 1720 and 1770, David Sorkin attempted to "cast new light" on the ways in which a "later Haskalah alter[ed] or radicaliz[ed]" an "early vision" that he claimed was far more consistent with the conservative temper of German Jewry.[45] Comparing the Haskalah to Protestant pietism and reformed Catholicism, Sorkin consistently underscored the point that the roots of the German Jewish program of "enlightenment" lay in religious renovation rather than in secularization or in the struggle for emancipation.[46] It was this program that continued to set the tone for the development of a German Jewish "subculture" throughout the nineteenth century. Taking up Sorkin's idea that the Haskalah installed the values of Enlightenment *within* (not beyond) modern Judaism, Shmuel Feiner—a tireless defender of the Haskalah against the charge of "assimilation"—has moved further than anyone in emphasizing the "Jewishness" of the "Jewish Enlightenment."

Like other recent treatments of the Haskalah, Feiner's approach betrays the affirmative imprint of Jewish social history. Feiner celebrates the maskilic "revolution" as a successful attempt to manage and contain the disruptive forces of modernization inside a Jewish framework. Feiner claims that the Haskalah promoted the creation of a secular "public sphere" that was both Jewish and free from rabbinic control. Moving away from the idea that the Haskalah promoted or endorsed modernization at the expense of Judaism, Feiner sees Jewish intellectuals as agents of Jewish continuity during a time when the future of a "collective Jewish identity" was no longer secure. Feiner paints a vivid picture of a society afflicted by religious indifference and assailed by the temptations of material culture. Jewish intellectuals, Feiner says, were committed to steering a treacherous course between the "secularization" of a rising Jewish middle class "hungering for the free life outside the ghetto" and the "orthodox rigidity and religious hypocrisy" of the rabbis. Maskilim, concludes Feiner, were "compelled to struggle on two fronts. On the one hand, they escalated their attack on the rabbinical elite, whom they perceived as the enemy of Enlightenment, and on the other, they had to defend the 'true Haskalah' against the 'pseudo-Haskalah,' which both radical and moderate maskilim regarded as a manifestation of substandard secularity."[47] Throughout the history of the movement, maskilim continued to wage a battle for moral and cultural uplift; they were more concerned with emancipation from the rabbis than with emancipation by the state. In an age of Jewish "embourgeoisement," they were outspoken critics of a "false Enlightenment," adopted by middle-class

Jews as an ideological alibi for their precipitate abandonment of Judaism.[48] For all the power of their critique of Talmudic Judaism, maskilim were, from the very beginning, even less enthused with the results of "acculturation," and increasingly appalled by the twin evils of "frivolity and hypocrisy."[49]

Feiner argued that suspicions attached to "pseudo-enlightenment" often implicated women in the spread of "sub-standard secularity." Jewish intellectuals did not meet the "appearance of the modern Jewish woman and the new relations between the sexes with anything like great joy," even though they themselves had been the ones to bring the "woman question" to the attention of the Jewish public.[50] Pointing out the ambivalence of maskilim regarding women's emancipation from patriarchal control, Feiner found still more evidence of intellectual Jewish conservatism in the face of social change. Following Feiner, Tova Cohen argued that what passed for "feminism" in modern Jewish circles did not imply a commitment to enlightened equality or, indeed, any form of political egalitarianism relative to the class and gender divide.[51] New research has gone on to show that interest in women's education came late to the Haskalah, largely as a "pragmatic" concession to the decline of the times, and remained low on the list of Jewish intellectual priorities.[52]

Conservative gender politics informed the maskilic turn to imaginative writing in Hebrew and Yiddish. The Haskalah, argued Naomi Seidman, inherited and adapted the conventional linguistic hierarchy that consigned the vernacular to "women and men who were like women" and restricted writing in the "holy tongue" to the rabbinic elite. Nineteenth-century Jewish intellectuals who aspired to write fiction in Jewish languages never entirely came to terms with the idea of secular authorship, addressed to the unaccountable demands of a "common reader" whom no professional author could afford to displease. "Haskalah literature," Seidman wrote, "spelled not the end but only the beginning of the end of Yiddish's 'female connection.'"[53] Although their subversion of the rabbinic monopoly on Hebrew initiated the "emancipation" of Jewish literature, maskilim could not relegate the normative structure of textual authority to the status of a "vestigial cultural memory" because they remained ambivalent about the prospect of writing for a desiring reader. Only the "enlightenment" of Jewish reading habits could resolve the conflict between stooping to a mass audience for profit, and rising to deliver "searing indictments and impassioned prophecies" in the transcendent language of the Bible that few people could understand, let alone appreciate.[54] Attempts to fashion an understanding and loyal Jewish reader inevitably stumbled on the problem of personal choice and the commodification of literature. Against the contemporary professionalization of authorship and the secularization of Jewish reading tastes and habits in Western Europe, Eastern European maskilim once more emerged as Jewish conservatives, upholding an approach to writing as a religious vocation.[55]

For example, Ayzik Meyer Dik—the most prolific and popular vernacular writer of the Haskalah—adopted the traditional persona of the "domestic preacher" in order to remedy the chaos of Jewish family life, rationalize Jewish economic pursuits, and excoriate popular superstition. David Roskies argues that, despite Dik's commitment to "enlightenment," his real interest and the source of his appeal lay in the entirely traditional function of Jewish vernacular chapbooks—to guide the conscience of the pious Jewish reader.[56] Dan Miron, in his study of "folklore and anti-folklore" in Haskalah literature, detected similar ambiguities in writers' attitudes toward reforming Jewish mass culture. Even as Jewish "enlighteners" deplored Jewish folkways, particularly the ones that they attributed to the influence of Hasidism, the catalogue of popular sins against reason and taste frequently shaded over into "ethnography." Haskalah literature, Miron says, preserved a stylized image of a Jewish "folk" untouched by modernity as an antidote to the corrosive effects of "changes" in contemporary middle-class life that maskilim "propagated and celebrated" but the reality of which "almost always [left] a bitter aftertaste."[57]

Seidman, Roskies, and Miron positioned Yiddish at the nexus of a fraught struggle against the effects of secularization. In Hebrew literature, however, the Haskalah continued to hold up a neoclassical picture of perfection against a friable and corrupted Jewish reality.[58] Bilingualism, says Jeremy Dauber, reflected the impassable gulf between the idealized "heavenly city" of the Haskalah and the "profane" urban milieu in which modern Jews were so deeply enmeshed and which they could not abandon.[59] The intellectual commitment to Hebrew anticipated the national redemption of the "philosopher-poet" from the antitheses of modern Jewish life, rendered in the broken, promiscuous, reactionary idiom of Yiddish.

Beginning with Shimon Halkin, several generations of Hebrew literary critics had argued that the conundrum of an "enlightenment" that was both Jewish and secular was virtually an argument for Zionism. Halkin integrated the unfinished Haskalah project of creating a modern Hebrew literature into the history of modern Jewish culture under the sign of "contradiction" between the philosophical ideal of individual perfectibility and a social program dedicated to the material improvement of Jewish life.

> Insofar as the Haskalah had two aspects—the sublime [Heb. *bat-shamayim*] and the programmatic, dedicated to real change in the life of the

Jewish people—Haskalah literature was likewise not of a piece. This means that matters of universal significance would be expressed in a certain language and in certain specific ways, while practical matters required a different language and different forms of expression. Indeed, the very real difference between the two meanings of [the Hebrew word] "enlightenment" points to a division within the Haskalah. This division was one of the first signs of a crisis. From the start, the Haskalah was divided against itself, and for some time [maskilim] did not recognize the fact.... The division eventually entered into Haskalah literature. In the German period, it is almost imperceptible. In the German period of the Haskalah it is as if everything is still possible.[60]

The "division" between a "programmatic" commitment to the needs of Jewish society and individual aspirations toward "enlightenment" created an irrepressible tension within the literature of the Haskalah. Maskilic bilingualism was not, in Halkin's argument, merely instrumental. It "hinted" at the existence of a structural flaw that only Jewish sovereignty could repair; in a secular Hebrew state, a Jew could afford to be, simply, a human being. The Jewish ideology of maskilim would no longer conflict with the "sublime" potentialities of human nature. The dialectic of a "Jewish Enlightenment" would resolve itself in a higher synthesis of "Hebrew humanism."

But in a recent monograph devoted to Sh. J. Abramovich, a master of both Hebrew and Yiddish prose, the creator of Mendele the book peddler, and one of the most fertile minds of the Haskalah, Amir Banbaji has made a strong case that the "dialectic" of a "Jewish Enlightenment" cannot be retroactively resolved by recourse to the teleology of Zionist history or relegated to Yiddish.[61] Banbaji says that the nationalist appropriation of modern Hebrew deliberately evades the repressive logic of "redemption" that the fractured Hebrew discourse of the Haskalah stubbornly refuses to put out of the way.

The problem with Halkin's dialectical fantasy, Banbaji argues, was always already evident in the maskilic utopia of transfiguration, a genre favored by nineteenth-century Hebrew poets. Hebrew poetry of the Haskalah aspired to effect a synthesis between reason and feeling, the individual and society, knowledge and belief; however, the standard allegorical plot proffered in maskilic poetry depended on the faithful reproduction of irreconcilable differences that could not be harmonized without invoking the deliberate poetic conceit of forced divine intervention. A well-timed "messianic" resolution of the conflict between folly and malice, on the one hand, and thought and virtue, on the other, resolves nothing, signifying the impossibility of evolutionary, progressive change upon which the nationalist reading of Hebrew literature insists.

In *Mendele and the National Project,* Banbaji identifies Abramovich's grotesque human menagerie, rendered in the language of the biblical sublime, as a powerful antidote to the denial of history, implicit in Halkin's Zionist teleology. In Abramovich's work, abject Jewish bodies are not open to remediation through time. Instead, they serve as a horrifying reminder of eternal Jewish "corporeality" that resists and subverts the aesthetic promise of national transcendence. Banbaji's post-Romantic reading of Abramovich makes it possible to reread the Haskalah as having "prepared the cultural infrastructure" both for Jewish nationalism *and* for a conservative Jewish critique of nationalist politics.[62] His work represents the creative culmination of an ongoing effort to reposition the Haskalah within the matrix of Jewish continuity. Countering the view that a "Jewish Enlightenment" provided the ideological leaven for emancipation, historical scholarship has, for over twenty-five years now, been arguing that the "utopian" reforming project of Jewish Enlightenment presents a stubborn form of Jewish resistance to the ineluctable political process that demands the enlightenment of the Jew at the expense of Judaism. Banbaji's revision is similarly implicated in the contemporary appropriation of the Haskalah as a bridge between the fields of Jewish thought and critical theory.

Haskalah and Modern Jewish Thought

In the study of modern Jewish thought, Mendelssohn typically stands in for the Haskalah. For historians of Judaism, Mendelssohn's work is a litmus test for the possibility of a "Jewish Enlightenment," construed as a philosophical experiment rather than a set of new social or literary practices. Mendelssohn's *Jerusalem,* writes Allan Arkush, has "earned a great deal of attention" as the "inaugural work of modern Jewish philosophy. . . . Scholars . . . have treated Mendelssohn as a philosopher whose primary goal in writing this book was to show in a comprehensive manner that there was no contradiction between the truths attainable through unassisted human reason and what had been disclosed by biblical revelation."[1]

Mendelssohn attained his iconic status as the "inaugural" philosopher of Jewish modernity in the work of his biographer, Alexander Altmann. Setting out to dispel the filial piety of the "Mendelssohn myth" prevalent in German Jewish memory and to correct the nationalist reading of Mendelssohn as the father of "assimilation," Altmann represented Mendelssohn as a complex, even contradictory thinker, consumed by a noble, elusive quest for spiritual peace and philosophical truth. "The Jewish tradition," Altmann wrote, "remained at the very core of [Mendelssohn's] being, though the world of European culture tended to overpower him at times. Moses of Dessau, as he signed his name in Hebrew, and Moses Mendelssohn did not always seem to be identical. He lived in two spheres, as it were, and the drama of his life and its achievement is caught within the dialectic of these two realms. Whether he ultimately succeeded in merging them into a unified whole is a moot point."[2]

Altmann saw both the attempt to resolve and the tendency to overlook the contradiction between Mendelssohn's "Jewishness" and his role as the "acknowledged leader of the German philosophy of the latter half of the eighteenth century" as inimical to the pursuit of critical inquiry and false to the "dialectic" of Mendelssohn's own character. He argued that the two parts of *Jerusalem,* the first a passionate defense of freedom of thought, the second a no less passionate defense of the "Mosaic constitution," were held tenuously together only by the author's belief in the "designs of Providence" and the essentially moral "purposes of natural religion."³ In other words, the model synthesis propounded in *Jerusalem* rested on faith in the "pristine purity . . . of heavenly politics," reified in the biblical covenant between God and Israel, not on a positive proof of Judaism's inherent rationality.⁴ The claim to possess such a proof, with its implicit polemical thrust against Christianity, would be self-serving and prejudicial; it affronted Mendelssohn's philosophical attachment to liberty of conscience. The truth of religion, according to Mendelssohn, could not be objectified or generalized, because it resided in particular experience rather than in universal principles. Mendelssohn's Judaism was not, Altmann said, reducible to a Jewish philosophy of Enlightenment. The Torah was a language of Jewish memory and the commandments, a "script" for the continuous reenactment of the formative moment of divine revelation to the Jewish people. In Altmann's depiction, Mendelssohn, committed both to the idea of enlightened impartiality and to the subjective integrity of personal belief, came within an inch of the Kantian revolution.

Altmann showed that the "dialectic" of Mendelssohn's life in two separate spheres both inspired the "Platonic" reach of his vision of Judaism and prescribed its philosophical limitations. Mendelssohn, according to Altmann, was ultimately unable to envision the possibility of a universal moral legislation (see chapter 2). The biographical emphasis on precarious balance—rather than harmonious synthesis—between "two levels of existence" that refused to meet in an "organic unity" gave rise to apposite readings of Mendelssohn's relationship to the "Jewish Enlightenment." Each in its own way privileged one "level" of Mendelssohn's existence at the expense of the other and thereby reduced the force of Altmann's critical reading. On the one hand, Altmann's characterization of Mendelssohn's intractable "dualism" inspired Allan Arkush's attempt to diagnose the acute tensions within the structure of *Jerusalem* as symptomatic of Mendelssohn's failure to answer the claims of "Spinoza and other radical critics of revealed religion."⁵ On the other hand, Altmann's insistence that Mendelssohn's personal experience of the Jewish faith underpinned his perception of Judaism as a religion consistent with the exercise of reason and the pursuit of virtue has led David Sorkin to the cheerful conclusion that such a view rested on a correct assessment of the "reasonable" traditionalism of "medieval Jewish thought" rather than on Mendelssohn's misgivings about the very idea of a religion dictated by rational speculation.⁶

After Altmann, Arkush found it difficult to accept the tradition of German Jewish scholarship that had "taken too rosy a view of the manner in which Mendelssohn managed to balance the conflicting forces in his soul."⁷ Impatient with the waffling that bedeviled scholarly attempts to figure out precisely what constituted Mendelssohn's synthesis between reason and revelation, Arkush contended that Mendelssohn never "develop[ed] a viable and satisfactory philosophy of Judaism." Mendelssohn, Arkush said, was "in the broad sense of the term, a liberal." His "rhetorical" defense of traditional Judaism was "designed to deflect rather than refute the kinds of arguments" against naïve acceptance of scriptural claims that had been advanced in the work of Spinoza.[8] As a liberal, Mendelssohn felt obliged to translate the language of Jewish law into terms that were consistent with the demands of citizenship. All the while, however, Mendelssohn continued to harbor the most serious "doubts . . . concerning the truth of the essential core" of the Jewish faith.[9] In the interests of his polemic against Christianity, Mendelssohn represented "his own theological-political teachings . . . as the perfection or repristination of Judaism." But his most deeply held philosophical convictions were much closer to the carefully guarded skepticism of Locke and Spinoza, who had also decked out the "classics of civility" in the garb of scriptural commentary in order to reassure their orthodox contemporaries. "Through biblical interpretation," Mendelssohn was "trying to fashion a Judaism . . . devoid of illiberal doctrines and theocratic tendencies." Inspired by the Enlightenment's vision of a society bound together by reason and tolerance and uncertain about the ultimate validity of any religious teaching, including his own, Mendelssohn sought to transform the Jewish tradition into a "civil religion."[10]

According to Arkush, Mendelssohn understood that such a task contradicted the assumption that Scripture provided an accurate record of the Jewish covenant with God. He was also fully aware that the principle of freedom of conscience posed an insurmountable challenge to the obligatory nature of Jewish law. However, even if the "God-given character and innate significance" of the commandments could no longer be rationally defended, they might, as Mendelssohn had argued in the second half of *Jerusalem*, yet instill a sense of moral responsibility, instruct Jews in their political obligations, and "serve as a bond unifying the Jewish people" with "other genuine theists" in a world that was "still dominated by highly defective forms of religion."[11] Although hardly a negligible answer to the Christian charge that Judaism encouraged tribalism and precluded Jews from becoming good citizens, Mendelssohn's defense of Jewish "civility" fell far short of proving that the "acceptance of Judaism requires no suspension of human reason."[12] Thus, while Mendelssohn's place in the history of the German Enlightenment could not be gainsaid, the originality of his contribution to the history of Jewish thought appeared to Arkush to be overstated. The modern "synthesis" between faith and reason was a pale shadow of its medieval precedent—Maimonides' classic *Guide for the Perplexed*.

Arkush's trenchant critique of *Jerusalem* presented those who wished to locate Mendelssohn firmly within the history of Jewish philosophy with a stark choice: either to reconsider his position as the founder of a "Jewish Enlightenment" or to revise their understanding of the Haskalah in a way that took Mendelssohn's skeptical strain into account. David Sorkin chose neither of these alternatives. Instead, he argued that Arkush had gotten *Judaism* all wrong. Sorkin did not actually engage with the arguments about Mendelssohn's view of Judaism that Arkush had made on the basis of his analysis of *Jerusalem*. Rather, he presented Mendelssohn's entire program of "religious enlightenment" as a "return" to the essential "reasonableness" of Judaism, consistent with the authentic "personality" of the Jewish religion:

> The Haskalah [Sorkin wrote in the introduction to his own reassessment of Mendelssohn as an exponent of "religious enlightenment"] was the Jewish version of the religious Enlightenment and Mendelssohn its preeminent representative. The Haskalah was an effort to correct the historical anomaly of Judaism out of touch with central aspects of its textual heritage as well as with the larger culture. Throughout most of the Middle Ages in Europe, and especially during most periods of heightened religious creativity, Jews had sustained a balanced view of their own textual heritage as well as beneficial and often intense interaction with the surrounding culture.[13]

Sorkin contrasted the "anomaly" of "baroque" Judaism, "isolated . . . in a world of Talmudic casuistry and Kabbalah, neglecting the Bible, Jewish philosophy and the Hebrew language" and indifferent to "vast changes in the general culture," with the Judaism of "Italian and Sephardic Jews" who required no "corrective" of a "Jewish Enlightenment." This distinction neatly reproduced the nineteenth-century German Jewish critique of "Ashkenazi" (read, Eastern European) Judaism, cast against the image of Sephardic sophistication venerated by German Jews as part of their own usable past.[14]

Throughout his study of *Moses Mendelssohn and the Religious Enlightenment*, Sorkin reverted again and again to a position, popularized by the German Jewish historian Heinrich Graetz, that Mendelssohn presented a program for the reformation of Judaism that was as "rational" as it was consistent with the core of Jewish tradition best exemplified by the luminaries of medieval Andalusia. There is, however, a world of difference between representing a nineteenth-century view of Ashkenazi "isolation" within the context of nineteenth-century Jewish identity politics and presenting such a view as an accurate description of a "historical anomaly" that was actually in need of a German "corrective." Sorkin's characterization of so-called "baroque Judaism," attributed to early modern Polish Jewry, derived entirely from secondary sources, no less subject to the influence of the popular view that still regularly serves up the "Ashkenazic understanding of Judaism" in total isolation from its own environment and from Western culture.[15] Under the circumstances it is difficult to say what the use of the word "baroque" contributes to Sorkin's scholarly reinstatement of a fairly conventional and ill-informed depiction of Eastern European Jews, except that it sets them apart both from modern Jews in Germany and medieval Jews in Spain. Sorkin's felicitous marriage of new Ashkenaz to old Sepharad bypasses entirely the common culture that produced both Hasidism and the Haskalah and entails the startling proposition that the rabbis of early modern Eastern European Jewry was not quite as Jewish as German-Jewish "enlighteners," since the latter relied on a more "authentic" and more ancient precedent ignored by the former. That, of course, is exactly what maskilim (most of whom were themselves from Eastern Europe) had said back in the nineteenth century.

Performing the cultural phenomenon of Romantic Jewish medievalism that he claims to be analyzing, Sorkin remains invested in showing that the father of "Jewish Enlightenment" loyally "followed the Andalusian tradition." Sorkin's monograph on Mendelssohn and the "religious enlightenment" focused on Mendelssohn's Hebrew writings, including his correspondence with other rabbis, his early journal *Kohelet musar*, a selection of biblical commentaries, and annotations of Maimonides' treatise of logic. These sources, Sorkin contends, amply document Mendelssohn's indebtedness to Sephardic culture. Mendelssohn's interest in language, his exegetical strategies, and his biblical purism are all ostensibly traceable to the influence of the Sephardic "synthesis" in which "philosophy and Judaism complemented and explained each other, yet ... [each] retained its integrity and respective sphere." Unlike early modern doubters and skeptics, Mendelssohn felt no compulsion to develop a new "speculative theology that would include a systematic account of Judaism's beliefs or a thorough rationalization of its laws."[16] Medieval Jewish luminaries in "Andalusia" had already done all that; from them, Mendelssohn inherited his own "reasonable" approach to Judaism. At the same time, like his medieval predecessors, Mendelssohn privileged "revelation" for setting "clear limits to the scope of philosophy."[17] Thus, where Arkush had seen an argument for Jewish "civility" dressed up in traditional biblical interpretation, Sorkin saw the deployment of "novel means for conservative ends."

Following Maimonides and Ibn Ezra, Mendelssohn adopted a philosophical vocabulary as an "instrument of self-articulation" even though philosophy had never presented a real challenge to his always already "reasonable" Jewish beliefs. *Jerusalem,* Sorkin asserted, was not and "was not intended to be, a systematic [philosophically driven] account of Jewish belief and observance."[18] Mendelssohn served up his defense of Jewish law as a blueprint for the "heavenly city" of "eighteenth-century politics," in which a divinely ordained and therefore "pristine ancient Judaism represented an ideal of government through education/religion," a polity in which "no conflict existed between individual interest and the commonweal."[19] Although Sorkin did not explicitly refer to Maimonides here, his reading of Mendelssohn's view of the state is distinctly Maimonidean (whether or not it is consistent with Mendelssohn's own political view is, however, another story). It was Maimonides who first argued that the "Mosaic constitution" constitutes/d a perfect model of good government. Insofar as its principal purpose and reason for being (its telos) was the formation of character rather than the distribution of power and the mediation of conflicting interests, the original biblical commonwealth was, for all intents and purposes, an Aristotelian polis.

Sorkin's Mendelssohn is a preeminently a Jewish thinker. His abiding occupation with Jews and Judaism never gives way to the pernicious "dualism" that was, as Sorkin asserted in a subsequent polemic with Arkush, only apparent in Mendelssohn scholarship.[20] According to Sorkin, it was Mendelssohn's own "assimilated" heirs and German historians who refused to consider an image of Mendelssohn that was "too Jewish."[21] For this reason, they were "unwilling to recognize . . . works that showed [him] to be immersed in a world clearly alien to German culture." Altmann and Arkush gave equally short shrift to Mendelssohn's Hebrew writings that, Sorkin asserted, "contain a plethora of evidence" of "ingenious" and "sustained" arguments on subjects such as the historical accuracy of Scripture and the nature of divine revelation, which were meant, one supposes, only for a learned Jewish audience.[22] Although he provided no examples of such arguments, for Sorkin Mendelssohn's identification with Sepharad is by itself sufficient to include him among those eighteenth-century "religious enlighteners" who returned to "neglected texts and historical sources" within their own textual tradition in order to effect an impregnable modern "synthesis" between faith and philosophy.[23]

Sorkin's positioning of Mendelssohn within a comparative context in order to rehabilitate his credentials as the founder of a characteristically Jewish path toward modernity anticipates postcolonial approaches to Mendelssohn not as a representative of Enlightenment universalism but as its most important critic. Both highlight Mendelssohn's Jewish "difference" as a significant contribution to modern European thought. This radically conservative reading vindicates Mendelssohn of overt ideological assimilationism and of an insincere, instrumentalist attitude toward his own tradition. The reconstruction of Mendelssohn's Jewish credentials attests to postmodernist suspicions of secularization, indebted to the theoretical critique of rationalism first advanced in the *Dialectic of Enlightenment*.

Written jointly by two of the founders of the Frankfurt School, Max Horkheimer and Theodor Adorno, during the Second World War, *Dialectic of Enlightenment* was published in 1947; by the late 1980s, it had become a foundational text for postmodernist thought. Adorno and Horkheimer posited a genealogical connection between Enlightenment rationalism and the dehumanization of the individual in modern totalitarian regimes. The Enlightenment, Adorno wrote, worshipped the problem-solving capacity of reason to the point of idolatry. Scientific "positivism" displaced theology as an objective explanation for how the world worked and, in the sphere of politics and morality, became prescriptive. Scientific certainty swept away religious doubt, only to become the most oppressive dogma that mankind had ever known. Brooking no opposition and knowing no god higher than itself, "rationality" could become sufficient justification for extermination. Moreover, because "reason" was ostensibly grounded in universals (it was, literally, embedded in the structure of the universe), its claims overrode any existential appeal to the value of the particular. In this way, reason provided an alibi for Western colonial domination and for the attendant extinction of small peoples in the name of technological efficiency and increased productivity. Throughout the "age of Enlightenment," the Western civilizing project, initiated by the rapacious colonialism of the ancient Greeks, who were its founders, threatened to subject and swallow up the indigenous cultures of its satellites. Horkheimer and Adorno provocatively described Homer's Odysseus, the wily wandering stranger and king in disguise, who tricks and exploits the characters he meets on the return journey to his own native Ithaca, as the progenitor of the "enlightened" bourgeois hero, sweeping the world into his own hand as he prepares for mass slaughter back home.

Horkheimer and Adorno's "dialectic" did not invite a rejection of modern scientific methods or advocate a return to a more innocent age of faith. Rather, the authors stressed the bracing effect of contingency and the importance of intellectual self-restraint against the leveling and reductive power of abstraction. Among scholars of the Enlightenment, their work has encouraged greater sensitivity to the ways in which rationalism both liberates and imprisons the individual.[24] But for modern Jewish thought, the provocative connection between the emancipation of reason and the ultimate form of human subjection—the concentration camp—has a particularly strong resonance. The history of "Jewish Enlightenment" has often been written as if in the shadow of Auschwitz. Hannah Arendt, temperamentally and intellectually close to the Frankfurt School, saw the tragedy of German Jewry in the embrace of Enlightenment universalism by secular German Jews, a misguided attempt at "dialogue" that she and other German Jewish thinkers located in the Haskalah. Traces of Arendt's German Jewish self-critique also appeared in Jacob Katz's thesis that "assimilation" was the end point of the "Jewish Enlightenment." After Arendt, Katz argued that the political hopes of German Jewish "enlighteners" had been misplaced, with terrible consequences. Nevertheless, Katz said (this time in opposition to Arendt, who harbored strong suspicions of Zionism) that their cultural aspirations could be fulfilled on native rather than foreign ground. The German Jewish "utopia of social emancipation," Katz wrote, would be dialectically realized in a Jewish, not in a secular, state.[25]

Jewish postmodernism makes strange bedfellows: Katz's conservative secularization thesis dovetails with a radically post-Zionist critique of "Jewish Enlightenment." Daniel Boyarin, a historian of Jewish antiquity whose work crosses over into critical theory, refers to Jewish "enlighteners" as "colonial compradors." Zionism, Boyarin says, is not a Jewish movement; its political aim of "emancipating" Jews from Judaism recapitulates rather than negates the cultural "assimilationism" of the Haskalah.[26] According to Boyarin, the achievement of Jewish sovereignty in the twentieth century represents a triumph of nineteenth-century liberal values over Judaism, a triumph, that is to say, of the "Jewish Enlightenment" over the "Jewish diaspora." Katz viewed Jewish "self-emancipation" as a response to the failure of the Haskalah. Boyarin now sees the modern Jewish state as an even more tragic symbol of its success. For Katz, Jewish nationalism functions as a cure for the erosion of Jewish loyalty and counteracts the decline of spiritual authority in the modern world. Modern Jewish Orthodoxy is Katz's answer to the question of what constitutes "civil religion" in a modern Jewish state.

For Boyarin, Jewish nationalism is the predictable end result of "Jewish Enlightenment," a vivid demonstration of the way in which all modern Jews (including modern Orthodox Zionists who share Katz's point of view) have internalized hegemonic majoritarian values and now pass them off as authentic Judaism. Boyarin argues that the moral power of Judaism resides in willed powerlessness, a position of "alterity" that he locates in the Talmud, the quintessential product of the diasporic imagination. Jewish "alterity" is ostensibly incompatible with any form of political sovereignty (this claim, as we shall see, sounds oddly like Mendelssohn's argument about the "derivative" and illegitimate nature of Jewish communal autonomy).

The rabbis, authors of Talmudic Judaism, were the original Jewish dissidents who outwitted and survived the pagan might of Rome. In an attempt to redress the Jewish condition of homelessness, first in Europe and then in the Middle East, secular Jewish "enlighteners" have given up the better part of their own ethical heritage, discredited the rabbis, disowned the Talmud in favor of the Bible—a book that advocates the extermination of native peoples so that the Israelites can inherit the land—and, finally, surrendered their conscience to the idea of empire.[27] In contrast to the "colonial compradors" whose legacy he renounces on behalf of Judaism *tout court*, Boyarin adopts the anti-imperial, which is to say the postcolonial stance of the "fat rabbi." An infinitely potent, Rabelaisian figure, both ludicrous and abject, Boyarin's "fat rabbi" is the authentic diaspora Jew who identifies his own marginal person with that of the orphan, the widow, and the stranger. At once male and female, the "fat rabbi" is Boyarin's talmudic alternative both to the "heteronormativity" of enlightened Jews and to Zionist machismo. The bearer of native Jewish wit and wisdom, the "fat rabbi" is the Bakhtinian embodiment of sexual and social liminality. A Jewish trickster and expert dialectician, he persistently evades all forms of collaboration with the gentile conqueror, including the Socratic bullying of Western philosophy.[28]

It might appear as if maskilim couldn't catch a break from anyone who had read the *Dialectic of Enlightenment*. Katz had held Mendelssohn accountable for secularization. That was bad enough. Boyarin subsequently charged him with the "rejection of magically effective ceremonial" (the second part must have been missing from Boyarin's copy of *Jerusalem*) and the exchange of the rich soup of talmudic lore for a watered-down "idea of religion," based exclusively upon abstract "ethical demands."[29] But this is not the whole story.

The *Dialectic of Enlightenment* also lent itself to a postmodern "recuperation" of German Jewish intellectuals as "models of cultural hybridity, and as guides to a specifically modern form of diasporic existence."[30] In the work of Aamir Mufti, the "archetype of the enlightened German Jew" appears as a post-nationalist *avant la lettre*. According to Mufti, Mendelssohn formulated a prescient critique of the "notion of citizenship" from the "position of a *minority*."[31] Mufti reads *Jerusalem* as an "attempt to rethink, from within the Enlightenment project, the structure of relations to state and society which define the Enlightenment citizen subject." Mendelssohn, Mufti suggests, did not accept his position as a "tolerated Jew" within an "enlightened modernity." In his insistence on a native "Jewish Enlightenment," he put into question the secular "terms within which the toleration of minority by majority is conceptualized." Willi Goetschel similarly sees Mendelssohn's unconditional defense of Jewish ceremonial law as a "contested" expression of "Jewish particularity" and the "foundation for an alternative form of universalism" that enables rather than proscribes the political articulation of difference.[32] Jonathan Hess describes Mendelssohn as a subversive "mimic" who appropriates the "universal" vocabulary of civic improvement in order to disclose its underlying anti-Jewish animus. Mendelssohn's "*Jewish* history of religion" recounted in the second part of *Jerusalem* assails the Christian bias of a civilizing project that first reduces Jews to the status of foreign "colonists" and then expects them to cease being Jews altogether.[33] Mendelssohn's own equivocal position as a leading German thinker and a marginal Jew exemplifies, for Hess, the possibility of writing an alternative "history of Enlightenment" which culminates not in the effacement of Judaism but in the exposure of gentile hypocrisy.[34]

In these sympathetic post-modern readings, a *Jewish* Enlightenment becomes a milestone in the account of colonial resistance to the relentless political logic of emancipation that eventually led to the creation of a secular "state of the Jews"—Theodor Herzl's *Der Judenstaat* (lit. "State of the Jews")—which has, once again, made Judaism disappear, except as a placeholder for national conscience. Thus, the Haskalah reenters modern Jewish thought both as a legitimate "moderate" option for Jews who find themselves stranded between reason and faith and as a "dialectical" Jewish answer to the postcolonial question of Zionism.

Like Jewish history, modern Jewish thought has moved toward a more Jewish reading of the Haskalah. Historians have emphasized the importance of Jewish learning, the investment in Jewish history and in Jewish collective life, as well as the engagement with issues of Jewish concern, not as instruments of secularization but as substantive goals, important in their own right. In some instances, the revisionist view goes so far as to suggest that Eastern European Jewish reformers "appropriated" the secular "ideas of enlightened West European non-Jews" in an "effort to disseminate . . . a moderate, religious Haskalah."[35] The "universalism" conventionally attributed to "Jewish enlighteners" has been attenuated if not completely dismissed in favor of a more nuanced picture of conflicting Jewish loyalties. The insistence that Mendelssohn always argued from the subject position of a marginal Jew has endowed his contribution to modern German philosophy with originality and contemporary force. From its new perspective on the father of modern Jewish thought, critical theory has challenged the nationalist consensus that the idea of a "Jewish Enlightenment" was philosophically derivative as well as politically unsound. The Haskalah has reentered the Jewish tradition as a legitimate "cultural option" that offers the possibility of an immanent "transition" to the modern age. Apparently, modernity does not have to be a crisis anymore.

However, the underlying tension between depictions of the Haskalah as a revolt of "secular Jewish intellectuals" against rabbinic authority (Feiner) and a conservative movement, directed against secularization (also Feiner) has not been adequately addressed, let alone resolved. The problem, first detected by the Israeli historian Shmuel Ettinger, is that the Haskalah can be made to carry water for all modern Jewish culture:

> The Haskalah had a substantial impact on Jewish development in the nineteenth and twentieth centuries. . . . Even as it provided an impetus for acculturation and assimilation . . ., it also widened the horizon [of Judaism] to produce all of the trends that prevailed among the Jewish people in the next hundred years: from *Wissenschaft des Judentums*, to neo-Orthodoxy in Germany, to social and intellectual radicalism and the flowering of the socialist movement among Jews in Eastern Europe, and just so to the nationalist movement which, in many respects, represents a direct continuation of the Haskalah movement.[36]

The current trend toward conciliation can explain the inner contradictions of a "Jewish Enlightenment" no better than Katz's crisis model. Neither can fully account for the galvanic effect that the *Biur*, a paradigmatic maskilic text that ostensibly "fortified the workings of rabbinic literature" exercised on the imagination of M. J. Berdichevskii, a devoted reader of Nietzsche and a rebel against all forms of Jewish authority.[37]

> The word *Biur* awakens in each of us youthful memories of the magic power of the age of the Haskalah. In me, it aroused feelings from another world, far removed from the one in which I was born and raised. . . . I noted that every time I uttered the word *Biur,* my father, a strict believer, would contort his face in a grimace—and with good reason. *Paths of Peace* [Heb. *Netivot hashalom,* the formal title of the *Biur*] was actually enormously attractive to me and spurred me on to battle. . . . The original collaborators were almost all faithful to tradition. Their language was bound by tradition, their style rabbinic. . . . But precisely because of that, they were able to kindle a fire in the House of Jacob, bans were imposed, and a powerful ferment was set in motion.[38]

Berdichevskii was certainly on to something. His own paradoxical response to the "traditionalism" of the Haskalah helps us understand why the soft light of the *Biur* ignited such a conflagration. In the process of returning to a medieval Jewish rationalism, Jewish intellectuals enabled radical acts of new creation. Theirs was a rebellion against the Jewish present in the name of an invented Jewish past that was supposed to transfigure the Jewish future. The word *biur* refers to the custom of burning the remaining bits of leavened bread on the eve of Passover, just before Jews reenact the drama of redemption and open the door to the arrival of God's own herald, Elijah the Prophet. Playing on this messianic theme, Berdichevskii imagined Mendelssohn's *Biur* as a small and carefully contained fire that sparked a full-scale intellectual revolt against the Exile.

What Berdichevskii envisioned, what the maskilim themselves had envisioned, what current scholarship on the Haskalah puts at the center of its own search for "another reason" (Gyan Prakash)—a liberating postcolonial alternative to enlightenment by the police—was a transcendent ideal of a perfected Jewish life, redeemed from the unbearable tension between home and the world. This ideal could be imagined; it could be projected onto some other time or some other place, but the exercise was always in the nature of a holiday (like Passover) from reality. Most nineteenth-century Jewish intellectuals understood this. Jewish idealism encouraged a sense of irony. Jewish romantics "hovered" between the divine arrogance of people who believed they could transform human conscience itself and the paralyzing self-doubt of those who are convinced that no one is taking them seriously. From Friedrich Schlegel, maskilim learned that a "writer who can and does talk himself out, who keeps nothing back for himself and likes to tell everything he knows, is to be pitied."[39] Still more to the point, their argument for a "Jewish Enlightenment" contained a critique of the enlightenment of the Jews and their attendant emancipation from Judaism.

The persistent confusion between "Jewish Enlightenment" and the enlightenment of the Jews is traceable at least in part to the translation problem with which we started. The pejorative association of the Haskalah with a programmatic commitment to the "enlightenment of the Jews" "followed," Uzi Shavit says, in the wake of translation: "Initially, the term 'haskalah' had been accepted as the name of a [Jewish movement]. Only afterwards, once it became necessary to find a Hebrew concept to refer to *Aufklärung*, was the word 'haskalah' transferred over . . . to the general European movement."[40] Historical scholarship has, in fact, been struggling to reverse the effects of this "transfer" for a long time. Where it was once difficult for historians to see what was Jewish about the "Jewish Enlightenment," it is now almost impossible to detect the Enlightenment in a movement that apparently goes all the way back to Maimonides. But of course it doesn't.

The "Jewish Enlightenment" is not the Haskalah, but the very idea *is* the work of maskilic imagination, conceived by nineteenth-century Jewish Romantics and championed by David Sorkin and Shmuel Feiner, their present-day intellectual heirs. And, while we are at it, by Daniel Boyarin, who is a maskil too even though he does not know it. For in his disavowal of the enlightenment of the Jews, he is engaging in a critique of "civil union" that had first appeared in Mendelssohn's *Jerusalem*. His imaginative reconstruction of talmudic culture is a prime example of Jewish Romantic historicism. His ongoing struggle to find a form of Judaism that is both true to itself and open to the Other is another version of the Romantic search for synthesis that the maskilim identified with the Jewish messianic tradition and (as we see in the next chapter) with their revolt against Exile. And it is Mendelssohn, the man without a country, the guest at the table, the impossibly crowned "Jewish Socrates of Berlin," with a misshapen body, a gentle self-effacing bearing, and a sardonic, contrarian disposition, who is Boyarin's first modern "fat rabbi." It is not necessary any longer to insist on the contemporary relevance of the Haskalah, because modern Jewish intellectuals continue to speak in the language of Jewish renewal that was first invented by maskilim. This language provides a new key in which to read the sources for the study of the Haskalah.

PART III
IN A NEW KEY

5 Exile

Romantic currents filtered into eighteenth-century Jewish thought with Luzzatto and Mendelssohn. But the Haskalah only crystallized into a movement when the idea of Jewish renewal became an ideology that supplied a novel answer to the question of Exile (Heb. *galut*). Most Eastern European Jewish intellectuals remained unexceptionably pious and deeply immersed in Jewish learning; however, they parted company with orthodox rabbinic opinion on their approach to Exile as a problem in time. A consciousness of living on the edge of a new era in Jewish history imbued the most modest of practical proposals with messianic urgency. In order to appreciate the implications of what it was that maskilim were seeking to understand and explain, the origins of the Romantic movement in Judaism need to be positioned against a century of vigorous debate about the meaning of Exile.

Since the Roman destruction of the Second Temple in 70 C.E., the theological scandal of Exile had not ceased to trouble Jewish minds. It was not dispersion itself that posed a problem (as long as there were Jews in the Land of Israel, there had been a Jewish diaspora too), but the discrepancy between the doctrine of Jewish election and Jewish humiliation at the hands of the gentiles. Over time, the depth of Jewish subjugation proved more and more difficult to reconcile with faith in God's enduring love for Israel.[1] "O Lord, my Lord," lamented an anonymous Jewish author only a decade following the fall of Jerusalem, "from all of the cities that have been built you have consecrated Zion for yourself . . . and from all the multitude of people you have gotten for yourself one people; and on this people whom you have loved, you have bestowed the Law which is approved by all. And now, O Lord, why have you delivered up the one to the many, and dishonored the one root beyond the others and scattered your only one among the multitudes? And why have those who opposed your promises trodden down on those who believed in your covenants?"[2] Judah Halevi, a Castilian Hebrew poet and author of the philosophical classic *The Kuzari* (ca. 1130), exhorted his readers against the complacent acceptance of Exile. How long, Halevi raged, would it be before he would be freed from having to "serve those numerous people whose favor I do not care for, and shall never obtain, though I worked for it all my life?"[3] The ignominy of Jewish subjection to the "multitudes" who "opposed [God's] promises" served as a constant reminder of the paradox of divine election. Despite the well-known traditional tendency to defer messianic expectations and resist messianic activism, the sheer duration of the Exile left a wound that refused to heal. Liturgy and ritual patently encouraged the anticipation of imminent redemption, while rabbis and preachers insisted that Exile constituted a fitting punishment for sin, urged repentance, and counseled patience. Hopes for a miraculous end to the condition of Jewish servility expressed itself in episodic outbreaks of messianic agitation. Irrepressible speculation about the precise date and nature of the end of days often accompanied fantasies of divinely appointed retribution against the wickedness of Edom.[4]

The promise of resurrection and reward in the world to come surely offered some comfort; however, the tension between faith in the promises of a just and merciful God and the experience of Christian, pagan, and Islamic contempt toward His own chosen people produced an irritating sense of cognitive dissonance. Even as liturgical poetry extolled Jewish sacrifice and celebrated Jewish suffering at the hands of persecuting authorities, daily prayers affirmed that the messiah would arrive promptly to avenge the Jewish dead and restore the Temple-state "speedily and in our own days, amen." Periodically vitiated by edicts of expulsion, the contractual basis of Jewish self-rule under crescent and cross informed the conviction that Jewish collective existence under the gentile yoke was only a "temporary hiatus between a glorious past of land, kingdom and Temple and a redemptive messianic future."[5] Royal protection enforced religious and social discipline based in talmudic law and maintained general acceptance of the rabbinic claim that Jews were slaves of kings, not slaves of slaves. But the security of legal privileges, a sufficiency of material comforts, and even enjoyment of good neighborly relations could not disguise the hegemony of those godless "many" whose undeserved political elevation above the chosen "few" presented an object lesson in the dynamics of Exile and inclined Jewish thought toward weary skepticism. "We send [to the gentiles] to say that everything we own is theirs, yet we still do not find favor in their sight," wrote a late fifteenth-century Iberian Jewish preacher, Shem Tob ibn Shem Tob. "We have emissaries in the royal courts and palaces but they are not received. . . . Kings and nobles say that we are their servants, but they do not protect us."[6]

Throughout the Christian Middle Ages, a consciousness of guilt informed Jewish devotional ideals and endowed the cult of Jewish martyrdom with particular spiritual élan. But how many martyrs would have to die at the hands of the impious before God would finally be moved to forgiveness? Sensitive to the doubts that such speculation inevitably engendered, a powerful literature of martyrdom celebrated

Jewish willingness to offer the ultimate sacrifice, even as it acknowledged the difficulties of living with Christianity. "Careful reading of martyrological narrative," writes Jeremy Cohen, "reveals ... characters depicted with ambivalence, characters who at one and the same time embody both the perfection of the deceased martyr-hero and the misgivings of the survivor who submitted to baptism in order to go on living as a Jew."[7] The incorporation of morally ambiguous stories of martyrdom into the liturgy implicitly acknowledged that conversion was a source of constant anxiety. Always, there were people who found the brunt of psychological dissonance and social deprivation too heavy to bear and went over the wall. The dramatic and still controversial history of Jewish apostasy in Christian and Islamic society unfolded not only in the context of violent conflict and active persecution, but also against the background of an exhausting and seemingly interminable day-to-day struggle to come to terms with the contradiction between the doctrine of Jewish election and the experience of legal marginality and "systemic" degradation.[8]

Under the circumstances, theological inoculation against the everpresent temptation to change sides proved remarkably effective. Repeated assurances of divine favor kept mass desertion at bay, but they also helped to push the messianic idea to the forefront of the Jewish imagination. Constant mutual contact shaped a culture of common social practices and customs that chipped away at the theological distance from the Christian and Islamic world. "A single framework of medieval life" produced so many similarities that "differences" between Jews and Christians continue to require explanation.[9] Although Jewish law constantly adjusted to the practical realities of living among non-Jews, rabbinic tradition could never go so far as to normalize the condition of Exile, at the risk of weakening Jewish resistance to the ruling faith. Despite rabbinic efforts to discourage messianic enthusiasm and to discredit messianic claims as dangerous, false, and self-destructive, ritual affirmations of longing for redemption stirred up Jewish hopes and exacerbated tensions between "Exile" and "domicile."[10]

For most medieval Jews, however, it was still "simultaneously possible to be ideologically in exile and existentially at home."[11] But by the eighteenth century, the dialectical "domestication" of Exile became harder and harder to sustain. After the Reformation, theological arguments for Jewish political exclusion from the Christian commonwealth were no longer self-evident. Protestantism forced the recognition of religious difference upon a hostile and resisting Church. Virtuous atheists like Spinoza presented communities of the faithful with an example of a person who lived a moral life and died a tranquil death without any religion at all. The erosion of Catholic unanimity provoked more strident demands for confessional conformity. At the same time, a century of Protestant-Catholic conflict informed the gradual secularization of sovereignty. After the Wars of Religion, "reasons of state" began to be invoked to justify military and fiscal policy without reference to Christian dogma. Social contract theory extended the claims of the state even further, by locating the prerogatives of keeping the peace and protecting life and property in natural law.[12] Restructuring Christian society along the lines suggested by early modern advocates of "reason of state" involved rethinking the legal status of non-conforming Christian minorities and Jews.[13] By the seventeenth century, the standard theological dispensation for Jewish marginality, rooted in the Augustinian "doctrine of witness," gave way to a proliferation of local ordinances and mutually contradictory policies that ranged from ghettoization (in Venice and Rome) to benign neglect (in London and Amsterdam) to royal and noble patronage (in Poland-Lithuania and the German states). The clergy continued to wage a losing battle against the state for jurisdiction over Jewry law, but arguments for and against extending Jewish privileges that explicitly invoked economic benefits and social costs acquired more and more cachet.[14] In this climate of opinion, it could well be argued that Jewish subjection to Christian power was the result of historical circumstances and did not serve any higher purpose.

Early modern Jewish thought faced increasing difficulties in reconciling Jewish theodicy with the changing politics of Jewish settlement in post-Reformation Europe. *Abyss of Despair* (*Yeven metsulah*, 1653), a Hebrew account of the Chmielnicki war (1648) written by Nathan (Nata) Hanover, is an outstanding example of the way in which post-Reformation political culture impinged on the Jewish understanding of *galut*. On the one hand, Hanover offered a shrewd analysis of the economic and political realities of Jewish life on the eastern frontier of the Polish-Lithuanian Commonwealth. He took pains to explain that the Jewish alliance with Polish magnates was a compact of mutual benefit that also placed Jews in the line of Ukrainian attack. Jewish agents of Polish landlords were politically accountable for the part they played in the consolidation of noble estates and in the exploitation of Orthodox peasants. On the other hand, Hanover insisted that Polish Jews were martyrs who submitted unquestioningly to God's will and greeted their political humiliation as an opportunity for heroic self-sacrifice. Hanover delivered a history in the form of a Jewish chronicle: the latter was dedicated to memorializing the exemplary piety of Polish Jewry, but the former effectively evacuated their death of religious significance. In assessing the "background of the religious, ethnic and economic tensions in the Ukraine," concludes Adam Teller in his close reading of

Abyss of Despair, Hanover was "able to reach an astonishing degree of relativity."[15]

The Jewish chronicle that Hanover set out to write did not easily map onto the history of the events that he had to recount. Unlike medieval martyrologies, *Abyss of Despair* did not present stories of temptation, resolved by the triumphant assertion of faith. The crucial element of moral doubt followed by a heroic decision is absent from Hanover's early modern text, which cast Jewish victimhood in the far more equivocal light of a political conflict. The redemptive vision of martyrdom as a fulfillment of biblical prophecy and a Jewish triumph over Christian wickedness competed with a "confusing kaleidoscope of different loyalties, alliances and situations" in which outcomes often depended on rational calculation and the exercise of superior force.[16] Hanover offered the former as consolation to Jewish survivors, but the latter served as an object lesson in Polish weakness, Jewish vulnerability, and Ukrainian cruelty and cunning. Informed by the experience of unchecked violence perpetrated by "masterless men," the spectacle of looting and murder in *Abyss of Despair* made an excellent argument for absolutism.[17]

Hanover moved uneasily between images of God's covenant by which the Jews of Poland were supposed to live and their temporal "covenants"—contracts—with Polish nobles, by which they actually lived and died.[18] The source of the "despair" inscribed into the title of his book may not have been the horrifying spectacle of Jewish martyrdom, the vision of which always already conferred a sense of consolation. The unredeemable pessimism conveyed in the title served to check the sense of moral triumph that suffused Hanover's memorial to the piety of Polish Jewry and alluded to the interpretive "abyss" dividing a view of Jewish abjection as a human tragedy from one in which at the end of a divine comedy of redemption everyone got their just deserts. Unable to resolve this tension, Hanover voids the paradoxical logic of Exile, whereby God reserved the worst punishments for those He loved best.

Abyss of Despair shared the sensibility of earlier historical works such as the *Staff of Judah* (ca. 1550), attributed to Solomon ibn Verga, Azariah de' Rossi's *Light of the Eyes* (1573), and David Gans's *Shoot of David* (1592), which expressed doubts about the explanatory power of rabbinic theology. A willingness to speculate about the proximate causes of Jewish troubles, causes that classical Jewish sources ignored, rendered the language of Exile unstable and ambiguous. Early modern circumspection also raised the disturbing possibility that historical circumstances could not fully account for the distinctiveness of Jewish experience in galut. Historical doubt opened the door to a mystical understanding of Exile. Such understanding transcended temporal reasons altogether. A decade after the publication of *Abyss of Despair*, Hanover himself abandoned history for the teachings of Lurianic Kabbalah. In 1662, he published *Gates of Zion*, a "mystically-informed" prayer book that by the end of the eighteenth century had gone through more than forty editions.[19]

A sixteenth-century pietist and mystical teacher from Ottoman Palestine, Isaac Luria initiated his followers into a new transhistorical vocation. Luria argued that Exile was only superficially a historical problem. The state of galut symbolized a cosmic split that originally took place within the divine. Israel's earthly troubles in Exile reflected the impaired condition of a universe demanding spiritual "rectification" (Heb. *tikkun*). This work, Luria said, constituted the religious responsibility of the Jewish people. Israel's exemplary adherence to the Torah served to restore God's Presence (Heb. *shekhinah*) to its original state of perfection. "In a view brimming with messianic hopefulness, Luria and his disciples believed themselves to be living 'in this final exile,'" a time pregnant with possibility of a second creation.[20] The imminent deliverance of the Jews would raise up the entire world from its fallen state.

Lurianic Kabbalah endowed normative Jewish worship with exorbitant power. The commandments (prayer especially), performed in the proper state of mystical mindfulness, represented a Jewish technology of universal salvation. Jewish observance helped to complete the divine and thereby moved history toward a speedy messianic denouement. Lurianic activism gradually infiltrated other schools of mystical practice and began to exert a powerful influence on Jewish religious life, particularly in Eastern Europe.[21] For both practicing kabbalists and the Jewish laity, Luria offered a compelling spiritual antidote to "profound weariness with the Exile."[22]

Imbued with the same heady sense of cosmic purpose that Luria brought to his contemplative system, Sabbatai Zvi attempted to bring Exile to an end once and for all. The mystical messiah first revealed himself in 1648; from his hometown of Smyrna, tidings of his arrival spread throughout the Jewish world. Sabbatai Zvi attracted a local following. But when his prophet, Nathan of Gaza, began to articulate his messianic aspirations in the resonant symbolic vocabulary of Lurianic Kabbalah—Sabbatai Zvi himself was apparently unfamiliar with Luria's work—level-headed merchants and eminent scholars everywhere began to make preparations for the ingathering of the Exile. By then, many people had come to Luria's conclusion that the world was in its last days.

After Sabbatai Zvi's conversion to Islam, the active movement associated with his name quickly collapsed. A small number of unshakeable loyalists followed him into Islam and formed a marginal and embattled Ottoman sect.[23] Most people, however, could not accept the idea of an apostate messiah, admitted that they had been mistaken, and went back to business as usual.[24] High expectations followed by disappointment left behind a powerful theological backlash against messianic rhetoric and against the popularization of Kabbalah. Mystically inclined heresy hunters called for repentance and demanded greater confessional vigilance over esoteric texts as well stricter adherence to rabbinic authority. The proper path to redemption, they insisted, lay through withdrawal from a world indelibly tainted by sin and guilt (of which the Sabbatian delusion was a symptom). Post-Sabbatian mystical study, reserved for an elite that alone was capable of heroic feats of ascetic detachment, focused on the unbearable distance between divine perfection and human culpability.[25] Rabbinic opinion began to attach legal significance to the concept of "antiquity" in matters of interpretation and customary observance and proscribed religious innovation as a sign of moral decay, fraught with evil consequences.[26] Yet, for all their efforts to quash the memory of the Sabbatian revival, the rabbinate itself was divided between "believers" and former believers in the mystical elation that the movement brought up to the surface of Jewish consciousness.[27]

The Sabbatian controversies of the eighteenth century exacerbated rather than relieved the sense of uncertainty of the future of Exile. Moderate Sabbatianism remained a viable intellectual option, long after the mystical messiah himself was discredited as a fraud. What moderate Sabbatians really believed is difficult to say, however; historical evidence of their notorious "secrets" is scattershot and comes filtered through the polemical reports of their opponents. One important point of contention may have involved a speculative approach to observance of talmudic law. In addition, the notorious Sabbatian emphasis on paradox may have undermined the transparency of moral categories and elevated religious intent above ritual, social, and sexual discipline. Any insistence on the absolute separation between spirit and matter, between Jews and non-Jews, between the human and the divine, between good and evil became potentially insupportable. For this reason, rabbinic opinion construed Sabbatians as "hidden" subversives who lived under a different dispensation where all was permitted. Even those "believers" whose public conduct was irreproachable carried a "heightened awareness of imminent messianic denouement" that constantly threatened to turn every law, human and divine, upside down.[28]

By the second half of the eighteenth century, the Sabbatian movement was gone; but "non-Sabbatian Sabbatianism" had introduced an expectation of messianic immediacy into early modern Judaism.[29] Efforts to cordon off Jewish custom and belief from Sabbatian influence proved largely ineffective. While late manifestations of Sabbatian radicalism attracted a minuscule following, traces of moderately Sabbatian hopes proved more difficult to extirpate. Unresolved messianic tensions suffused both Hasidism and the Haskalah. To be sure, neither movement was fully prepared to acknowledge its debt to the Sabbatian revolt against Exile; but both derived their sense of urgency from the same mood of anticipation that characterized non-Sabbatian Sabbatianism.

Of course, maskilim rejected mystical messianism as an ill-conceived detour from the path toward redemption. Neither did they set out to dispel Jewish belief in God's providential care for the people of Israel or to annul His commandments. But they were educated in a religious environment in which the normative concept of Exile could not be taken for granted anymore. In the post-Sabbatian climate of dashed expectations and rabbinic reaction, they could detect a disturbing current of metaphysical resignation and a rising tide of indifference toward the responsibilities of divine election. "Our Jewish contemporaries," expostulated the tireless heresy fighter Rabbi Jacob Emden in 1745, "are no longer mindful of the fact that they are in *galut;* they mingle with non-Jews, adopting their customs and are a great disgrace. 'The holy seed mixes with the peoples of the earth.'"[30] Driven by this kind of pervasive concern with the exhaustion of rabbinic theodicy, Jewish Romanticism supplanted the punitive logic of Exile with an ideal of spiritual plenitude, a tantalizing promise that Sabbatianism held out but tragically failed to fulfill.

6 New Creation

Maskilic discourse developed within the framework of the Jewish mythology of Exile; but it was the partition of Poland and the reconfiguration of political authority in Eastern Europe between the 1780s and the 1830s that provided the immediate context for a new vision of cultural and intellectual renewal. In order to understand why the politics of partition inspired such extravagant hopes, it is important to appreciate the impact of the precipitous decline of state authority on Jewish communal life in Poland-Lithuania during the second half of the eighteenth century. As the fortunes of the Polish magnates rose, royal power declined. While the dominance of the nobility offered unexpected opportunities for enrichment and for the expansion of certain sectors of the Jewish economy, there are good reasons to think that the erosion of monarchical sovereignty was a growing concern for Polish-Lithuanian Jewry. To begin with, there was the ever-present issue of personal safety. The conflict between Orthodox peasants and their Polish Catholics masters, which had exploded in the Chmielnicki rebellion in 1648, was never really resolved, and intermittent hostilities continued throughout the following century. Roving armed looters, known as *haidamaks,* periodically harassed urban residents in eastern Ukraine. Jewish wealth, often earned under noble patronage, offered a convenient and provocative target. In the absence of consistent efforts at policing the eastern borderlands, Jews remained vulnerable to periodic extortion and violence. It proved increasingly difficult to explain the "pillaging" of the haidamaks by reference to the religious tradition. Victims of robbery were hard-pressed to console themselves with the spiritual rewards of martyrdom. Contemporary Jewish sources registered the haidamak threat as a breakdown in law and order. Ber of Bolechow, an eighteenth-century memoirist who was both unflinchingly pious and eminently practical, described the raid of Ukrainian "ruffians" on his hometown in grim detail. Despite several nods to the martyrological tradition, he reported that local Jewish opinion held the conspicuous absence of the Polish "steward" from the castle of Bolechow responsible for leaving everyone (Jews *and* gentiles) equally exposed to banditry.[1]

Second, the crisis of Polish sovereignty diminished the scope of the established system of Jewish communal autonomy. The effectiveness of regional councils had weakened considerably in the eighteenth century. Intra-communal authority had ceased to function by 1764. At the same time, individuals who had a privileged relationship to noble families amassed incredible wealth and wielded great personal power. The endemic impoverishment of the crown and the political independence of the nobility led to the imposition of extortionate taxes. Jewish communities were beset by growing arrears. Under the pressure of increasing debt, they were forced to rely on the resources of wealthy laypeople who were in a position to flout communal injunctions and ordinances. Preachers railed against moral decay. Attempting to shore up collective discipline, they stoked the fire of religious discontent.

Finally, there was the rising tide of anti-Jewish animus, likewise inflamed by contemporary debates about the dominant role of the magnates in Polish political affairs. In the second half of the eighteenth century, their de facto control of the Polish throne and their virtual monopoly on international trade began to be deeply resented by the rest of the nobility that claimed the same rights and privileges but could not compete with magnate status and financial power. Other constituencies of the Commonwealth—especially the growing urban population and the Catholic Church (the next largest collective land owner in Poland, after the noble elite)—also began to contest their authority. This conflict spilled over into a debate about the presence of the Jews in Polish-Lithuanian society, associated with the personal rule of the magnates. Competing conceptions of the Polish political nation, embedded in the Catholic faith rather than in noble republicanism, challenged the cosmopolitan and tolerant "state without stakes" dominated by the great lords. Anti-Jewish hostility took the form of blood libel charges, public challenges, and theological attacks. Even more disturbing than the virulence of Catholic anti-Judaism, Jewish merchants confronted a chorus of voices calling for their exclusion from Polish commerce. On the eve of the partitions, these conditions bred Jewish nostalgia for effective monarchical control, idealized in myths of the Polish-Jewish royal alliance.

Circumstances that generated anxiety about the future of the Polish state had a direct impact on Jewish attitudes toward partition. The impact of the demise of the Commonwealth was evident in the general Eastern European Jewish tendency to idealize centralization as a guarantor of social peace. Jewish views of enlightened absolutism echoed Hanover's seventeenth-century indictment of Polish misrule. But another crucial issue was the much less common perception that the shift toward an imperial model of government conferred specific and unforeseen benefits on the Jewish population of the partitioned territories. Eastern European Jews had no reason to anticipate improvements in their social and legal situation from their new masters. All three of the partitioning powers had a poor track record when it came to Jewry law. The Romanovs excluded Jews from their realm altogether. Frederick II imposed rigid restrictions on Jewish settlement in Prussia. The Habsburgs likewise sought to control Jewish population growth in the crown lands. Maria Theresa, the pious mother of Joseph II, periodically threatened the largest and most prominent population of Habsburg Jews, concentrated in Prague, with expulsion. In this climate of opinion, the post-partition Jewish policies adopted by Joseph II—and echoed in the more modest reforming efforts of Catherine and Frederick—looked to some people like a miraculous reversal of the recent past. The "well-ordered police state" had arrived providentially to remedy the general ills of Polish "chaos," which by the late eighteenth century had become a byword in European public opinion. To a number of Jewish intellectuals, afflicted by the post-Sabbatian malaise of great expectations, it appeared that this political miracle, this sudden "enlightenment" of powerful gentiles, could only be the mysterious handiwork of the King of Kings, the Rock of Israel, a most merciful and beneficent God.

In 1782, following an official state visit to his newly acquired Polish province, Joseph II initiated a series of reforms, aimed at the administrative integration of Habsburg Jewry. The Josephine project invited Polish Jews to become model subjects of an enlightened emperor. Joseph's plans for legislative reform served notice of an ambitious departure from early modern restrictions on Jewish population growth and economic activity in Bohemia and Moravia. Instead of using the law to marginalize or altogether exclude the presence of Jews from Christian public life, Joseph's first official circular directed at Galician Jewry suggested measures aimed at their "uplift" and "improvement." Joseph's *Toleranzpatent* provided financing for Jewish secular education, encouraged Galician Jews to move out of petty trade into agriculture and handicrafts, and introduced the use of German into Jewish communal and business affairs. Subsequent laws, passed in 1785 and 1789, undermined the collective privileges of Jewish self-government and expanded the right of Jewish residence, enabling Jewish individuals to extricate themselves from the disciplinary structure of the Jewish community. The terms of the *Toleranzpatent* integrated Galician Jews into the same legislative domain as their compatriots in Hungary and in the crown lands, and brought the legal status of Habsburg Jews on a level with that of other non-Catholics.

But, even as the law anticipated the eventual leveling of distinctions between religious minorities, the prescriptive terms of Jewish toleration helped to institutionalize the colonial status of Galician Jewry. Where medieval legislation had recognized a universal theological divide between all Jews and all Christians, the new law constructed a set of fungible social markers that ran right along the Polish frontier. Poor, Yiddish-speaking, and increasingly Hasidic, Galician Jewry, desperately in need of "regeneration," embodied the Eastern European past of Habsburg Jewry. A much smaller, more highly urbanized, and wealthier Jewry of the crown lands apparently represented the future that Galician Jews were supposed to emulate. The Christian charge of Eastern European Jewish "backwardness" touched a very particular Jewish nerve and provoked an immediate response. This response—Naftali Herz Wessely's *Words of Truth and Peace* (Heb. *Divrei shalom ve'emet*, 1782)—became the foundational document of an intellectual revolt against the Exile.

Wessely did not come from Galicia. However, in the last quarter of the eighteenth century, he lived and worked among people who were very concerned with the ambiguous status of Eastern European Jewry, suddenly consigned by the law to the periphery of European civilization, and singularly sensitive to the implications of the *Toleranzpatent*. Situated in the Prussian capital of Berlin, Wessely's closest intellectual intimates included a number of Eastern European Jewish immigrants. Like Wessely, they congregated around Mendelssohn. The development of Berlin in Mendelssohn's own lifetime exemplified the shifting boundaries of Jewish geography that were formally codified in the language of the *Toleranzpatent*. Mendelssohn first came to the city in 1743. At this point in its history, Jewish Berlin was only just emerging from economic, social, and cultural obscurity. The regional capital of a middling German state with an ambitious ruler, Berlin possessed few of the markers of a high-status Jewish community. It had no distinguished medieval tradition of legal scholarship and therefore no rabbinical clout. Before Mendelssohn, Berlin hardly had a Jewish intellectual life at all. There were no local institutions of higher Jewish learning. Prussian Jews who wanted to pursue advanced Talmud study had to go east to Cracow or Prague, as did those who wanted to hire Jewish teachers for their children.

Berlin's Jewish community was itself relatively new, a marginal outpost of Habsburg Jewry; it was founded by a small number of wealthy Viennese families who were invited to settle in Prussia in the 1640s. Berlin's indigenous Jewish high society emerged only in the second quarter of the eighteenth century and consisted of a very ambitious haute bourgeoisie that was practically indentured to the dubious financial schemes favored by Frederick II. Loads of disposable income, earned in questionable transactions on behalf of an enterprising and ruthless monarch, failed to compensate for nagging status anxiety, exacerbated by the proximity of a substantial Jewish underclass that continually drifted into the city from surrounding provinces. Before Mendelssohn got there,

Jewish Berlin hardly registered on any Jewish radar except as an outpost of easy financial pickings. Rich and well-connected Glückel of Hameln (1646–1724) had married off her least promising son to a Berlin family, in despair of a better match in Hamburg, Frankfurt, or Amsterdam. Sure enough, she recorded, improvident, foolish Leib lent "many thousands" to shiftless "Polish" locals—"polacken," Glückel called them—and never saw his money again.[2] Fifty years after Glückel saw fit to turn up her nose at the incorrigible "Polish" morals of Berlin Jews, the character of Eastern European Jewry was still a sensitive subject, nowhere more so than among itinerant Jewish teachers living on the unstable frontier between East and West. Born provincial "polacken" they were also immigrants from the preeminent "center of Torah" in early modern Europe.[3] Ill-disposed to bear the insult that attached to their provincial origins, they aspired to the heights of literary glory and spiritual perfection consistent with their self-image as representatives of the Jewish intellectual elite and instructors to the nation. It is to them that Wessely addressed his *Words of Peace and Truth*.

Wessely cast his tract in the form of an epistle. His title, drawn from Esther 9:30, conveyed a distinctly messianic sense of urgency. At the end of the book of Esther, Haman's threat against the Jews of Shushan is lifted and Mordechai dispatches circulars to "one hundred and twenty seven provinces" of Persia in order to apprise all Jews of their political salvation, wrought through the intervention of a gentile king who miraculously awakens to his responsibilities. These are the "words of peace and truth," sent from an imperial capital to the peripheries, to which Wessely now alluded. Their meaning turned on a question that every subsequent generation of Jewish intellectuals learned, from Wessely, to ask—what time is it?

"Perhaps," Wessely suggested, "the time has now come to remove hatred from the hearts of men, baseless hatred arising out of a conflict rooted not in the present time but in the usages and beliefs of a long time past."

> The present generation has seen the grace of God established in the person of a powerful man and a savior of mankind, his majesty, the great emperor Joseph II, whose wisdom, strength, and wise counsel in war are well known. We have heard of his great and mighty feats against other nations who rose up against him, as well as of his 'words of peace and truth' [the *Toleranzpatent*] that went forth to his entire nation, sorely in need of enlightenment, the basis of which is the love of humanity. In his great goodness, he has not forgotten a poor, forsaken nation, the children of Israel. To us likewise went out words of goodness and consolation.[4]

This passage goes beyond conventional expressions of enthusiasm about a show of royal benevolence. It was not self-evident that the *Toleranzpatent* would be of immediate benefit to Galician Jewry, nor was it clear that it marked a turning point in Habsburg Jewish policy. Wessely was taking a polemical position on the historical significance of Josephine legislation. Pregnant with the sense of its own moment, *Words of Peace and Truth* represents Joseph's Jewish policy as the inaugural act of a new period in Jewish history and articulates the primary article of faith of the Haskalah: that the enlightenment of the gentiles signifies a dramatic, miraculous convergence between Jewish and universal time.

The long period of Exile, Wessely argued, had set Jewish time apart from Christian time. The Christian world operated on its own salvation schedule, according to which the present constituted a hiatus between the resurrection of Jesus and his return. While Christians waited for the completion of the redemption process, Jewish tradition insisted that the world had not yet been redeemed. For Christians, the destruction of the Temple signified a Jewish failure to perceive the significance of Jesus' death and resurrection; leaving Exile required, first of all, a shift in temporal perspective. For Jews, Exile signified the flawed state of the human condition, which obliged them to adhere to their own calendar, governed by the unbreakable rhythm of ritual memory in anticipation of the end-time and the fulfillment of the prophetic promise. According to Wessely, Exile was not a punishment for Jewish sinfulness but the product of an ignominious history of Christian oppression:

> When our people saw that they were being treated harshly, all of creation became disgusting to them. When they saw that they had no share of the good things that other nations enjoyed by the grace of God, in bitterness they abandoned all of the studies that serve civilization.... They said, "What are these to us? Since the other inhabitants of the lands in which we live are our enemies, they will not heed our counsel, our military valor they will not recognize, and further we do not own fields and vineyards. Thus, we shall leave aside all of these worldly pursuits and concern ourselves exclusively with preserving our souls and maintaining our bodies. This is all that remains to us, and even that our enemies dole out in small portions and with great restrictions. We shall therefore lean upon our father in heaven and occupy ourselves only with matters relevant to eternal life, that is, with the laws of God and His Scripture which we have been commanded to keep and which is the basis of the covenant between God and our forefathers and all those who were chosen after them."[5]

For Wessely, the relationship between Christian persecution of Jews and the Jewish withdrawal from Christian history—a self-imposed confinement within their own time—reflected a tension that, according to rabbinic tradition, could be resolved only by God. In the Josephine project of reform, Wessely detected the deft hand of the divine. As in the book of Esther, providence operated unseen and unnamed through the person of a wise emperor. Joseph, Wessely proclaimed, was the "savior of all mankind," who breached the walls of galut: "Joseph, with the exercise of good judgment, has overcome the beliefs and prejudices of the past and emitted forth the light of his justice. His law, which shines like the sun at noonday, turns minds around and mediates between all people with peace and love."[6] Messianic outbreaks among Jews had failed to alter the course of Christian history. Sabbatai Zvi's symbolic inversion of Jewish law was a dangerous delusion. The Hebrew Bible had warned against believing false prophets. However, the providential arrival of Joseph, endowed by God with a "superhuman capacity for doing good," was, Wessely maintained, fully consistent with the biblical current of Jewish time.[7] Committed to only "one religion—that of directing all citizens equally toward the good of the state," Joseph challenged the punitive logic of galut, signified by political marginalization and inveterate religious hostility that Jews had suffered under Christian subjection.[8]

Wessely's political messianism was not a precocious form of Jewish secularization. Nowhere did he even suggest that Jews abandon observance of the commandments; such a thing would imply that divine law was a burden and a temporary misfortune, sustained only by force of historical circumstance. While the "teaching of man" was universally accessible, the "teaching of God" was a Jewish privilege, a divine gift that presented a source of ulterior, intuitive (but certainly not irrational) knowledge. The "law of God and His Scripture which [the Jewish people] have been commanded to keep and which is the basis of the covenant between God and [their] forefathers" could not be a punishment for sin, delivered at the hands of Christians. Jewish persecution was not a necessary signifier of Jewish covenantal obligations but an excrescence of unreasonable and unjustifiable Christian ill will toward Jews. The veneration of martyrdom as the highest expression of piety, rather than a Jewish tragedy and a moral scandal, represented an ethically intolerable view of God as vengeful and punishing. Wessely was sure that that the spread of the "teaching of man" would only deepen the well of scriptural wisdom and strengthen Jewish faith: "God's glory will expand in the mind of man and his awe of the Divine will be increased."[9]

In Wessely's view of Exile, the spectacle of Jewish suffering and forbearance in the face of Christian violence did not serve to make Jews repent of their sins—this purpose had surely been achieved long ago—but to educate the gentiles who were notoriously slow learners. "Truly, it is a wonder and a marvel," Wessely crowed,

> how, despite all of these troubles, [the Jewish people] have survived at all as a unified community and how we have withstood the deluge of miseries and nevertheless retained the ways of humanity. Indeed, it was the divine Torah which helped us. Even though we may have lacked knowledge of the teaching of man, the Torah fashioned manly hearts within us, so that we were spared the failing of cruelty and preserved from doing great evil, may God continue to spare us from such things.[10]

The duration of Exile, still well in evidence in the tenacity of "iron laws . . . that distance us from society and prevent us from being useful to our fellow men" constituted a form of divine provocation to *Christians*, rather than a sign of a Jewish incapacity to participate in the life of civil society. Continuing inequity toward Jews provided a vivid reminder of the disparity between the venerable legacy of Christian barbarism and the tutelary responsibility of the wise king toward all of his subjects. Against the background of the persistence of Jewish degradation in places like Galicia, the *Toleranzpatent* presented a sign of gentile dedication to the principles of common welfare and moral government. What was good for the Jews was good for everyone.

In the meantime, Wessely urged, the new political dispensation demanded the articulation of a Jewish ethos consistent with the basic principle that the "Torah teaches love of humanity and its ways are ways of peace."[11] Wessely's recurrent emphasis on the word "peace" throughout the text and in the title alluded to the providential conjunction between the Jewish time of Moses Mendelssohn and the post-Christian time of Joseph II: "What an excellent thing it is that arrives in due time! Even as we speak, our master and teacher Moses [Mendelssohn], the wise man and scholar, is engaged in publishing a proper translation of the Torah of God into German," Wessely enthused. "Much good will come to the house of Israel from this undertaking."[12] Wessely saw Mendelssohn, the Biblicist, as the harbinger of a new age. Another Moses had arrived to renew scriptural revelation in the form of the *Biur*, which (as we have seen in chapter 4) was actually called *Paths of Peace*.

The appearance of the *Biur*, a new kind of reader's Bible in which rabbinic learning was combined with high literary aspirations, signified glad tidings and identified the spiritual vocation of modern Jewish intellectuals with the creation of a Jewish culture suited to the coming age of grace. Wessely therefore called upon "learned Jews" to return to the biblical wellspring of Jewish creativity and to become modern Jewish authors. This, he promptly did himself: *Words of Peace and Truth* was followed by

Songs of Splendor (Heb. *Shirei tiferet*), a biblical epic about the exodus from Egypt, which alluded to the providential role of Mendelssohn, cast in the role of Moses, the prophet and lawgiver. While Mendelssohn's *Biur* (to which Wessely contributed a volume on Leviticus) was admired from a suitably reverent distance, Wessely's *Songs of Splendor* was read and endlessly imitated by several generations of maskilim in Galicia and Russia.

Wessely's pointed interception of Christian history may be read against Paul's letter to the Romans, a similarly controversial Jewish text that first opened a gap between "Old Israel" and "New," a gap that Wessely's Jewish theory of modernity now proposed to close. It is impossible to know whether Wessely intended to produce a Jewish response to Paul. Evidence of such a connection has less to do with documenting authorial intent than with the way in which Wessely's text replays Paul's "good news" in a modern Jewish key. In any case, Wessely wrote out of a long tradition of Jewish-Christian polemics, to which the Pauline interpretation of the Jewish prophetic promise remained central.

Both epistles share a common sense of messianic urgency. Time is running out; the writer stands poised on the threshold of life-altering transformation. Paul's letter records a new beginning in the history of the world, marked by the coming together of gentile political history and the sacred history of the kingdom of Israel. The death of Jesus enables this miraculous merger; but this event does not mean the same thing for Jews as it does for gentiles. "What is new in the story, the mystery, as Paul calls it, is that the redemption of the Gentiles [through Christ] and the salvation of Israel [by faith in the law of Israel] are intimately intertwined. Their final destinies are interdependent."[13] Wessely too asserts that the painful breach between the Jewish time of Exile and the universal time of gentile history has been healed, now for good, by the transcendence of Christian history. In both instances, writing seems to be motivated by a heightened awareness that the present moment constitutes an "appointed time in the purpose of God," in other words, a providential break in the unmarked chronology of ordinary life.[14] The capacity to recognize the singularity of the moment is a matter of principle and moral commitment, not dispassionate political judgment. It would emerge in the course of the controversy over *Words of Peace and Truth* that the political judgment of the rabbis was more rational than Wessely's urgently Romantic faith.

Contrary to the evidence of the senses, Paul asserts that "New Israel" in Rome inhabits the same history as "Old Israel" in the diaspora. Paul naturally identifies "New Israel" with Romans, but the Greek term that he uses (Gr. *ta ethne*) actually encompasses all "peoples" (i.e., non-Jews).

For Paul, this shared universal history is always already Jewish because the "Gentiles are co-descendants of Abraham."[15] It was his gentile readers who first began to call it Christian, to differentiate it from Jewish time. Wessely, as if he were actually talking to Paul across the divide of centuries, reconstitutes the Roman-Jewish merger on the ground of Joseph's Habsburg domains, also known as the Holy Roman Empire, heir to the political symbolism of Romans, but governed in accordance with the universal—"catholic"—dispensation of the Enlightenment rather than parochial Catholic prejudice. In both instances, the most perspicuous sign of the "appointed time" is the "conversion" or "enlightenment" of the Romans, that is, the political masters. For Paul, "enlightenment" constitutes an awakening to the significance of Jesus' death and resurrection, which now obliges the gentiles to live in righteousness for now they too are included in God's promise to Israel. For Wessely, this "conversion" involves the unexpected embrace of reason and tolerance. In both instances, the end result is the subjection of gentile political advantage to a higher moral—let us call it Jewish—principle. In fact, Wessely and Paul had the same characteristically Jewish suspicion of the boundless entitlements of imperial—let us call it gentile—sovereignty. Writing from the periphery of empire, they reaped the spiritual advantage from a condition of political marginality. In a sense, Paul and Wessely shared a language in which the position of the subaltern signified the capacity to speak truth to power.

The insistence that the moral conversion of the gentiles required a radical act of divine intervention in gentile history did not diminish the Jews. On the contrary, Paul and Wessely spoke from the assumption that the gentile proclivity to sin was pathological, suicidal, and possibly incurable. Jewish wisdom enabled the acceptance and observance of the Law, which both Paul and Wessely understood in ethical terms; Wessely had said that the "diasporic" function of the Torah was to ensure that Jews retain their *humanitas* even when they were excluded from Christian humanity. But for gentiles, the Law "meant death" because although they always knew what the Law required, they were too "foolish" (Rom. 1:22) to act on that knowledge. For Paul, the redemption of idolatrous "Romans" through the self-sacrificing act of the God of Israel served as an object lesson in God's justice. It was the only way to redeem the corrupt gentile world and bring it into concert with the original prophetic vision that Paul, a faithful reader of Jewish Scripture, took for granted.

> Paul presents and defends his gospel under the banner of divine impartiality.... For him this means that any form of boasting, by Jew or Gentile, is excluded for God alone determines the standing of all humans.

At times, Paul does address Jewish boasting . . . but his main concern throughout is with Gentile boasting. To be sure, he says, Gentiles in Christ have been elevated to a status equal to Jews. But given their previously hopeless conditions [of sinfulness] they are in no position to boast. . . . For this status contains not just the promise of salvation but the threat of condemnation, "for every human being who does evil." What has been won can easily be lost.[16]

But the Pauline program failed. "In the long run . . . Gentile Christianity, in the name of Paul, [became] arrogant, proud and boastful against Israel and in the process, completely abandoned Paul's gospel."[17] The "New Israel" misread Paul's mission to the gentiles as a mandate for the exercise of exclusive, "Christian" sovereignty, a deliberate and self-serving confusion of politics and religion that was detected and exposed by Spinoza, another Jew who was well versed in speaking truth to power. Wessely saw Josephine legislation as a historical correction of the misprision that led to the creation of a Christian state and the formation of a persecuting society. For Wessely, this correction flowed from God's providence, not so much on behalf of the gentiles but in order to benefit the only tribe that had a permanent covenant with Him. Paul's mission to the "people" represented a similarly ironic tribute to the faithfulness of Israel. In both instances, universal justification served as a cover story for the assertion of Jewish particularism, implicit in the insinuation that God provided for the moral education of mankind in order to keep His promise to His own best-beloved ancient tribe, chosen for all eternity.

In Paul's view, the miracle of Jesus' death and resurrection as the Christ—given that the end result was the fulfillment of God's promise to the Jews, whose messiah was he, really?—transformed "Romans" into a "New Israel" and drafted the gentiles into the history of the Jewish covenant. This was only supposed to be an opening for a moral revolution that would help to speed the final judgment along. Paul suspended the difference between Jew and gentile only with respect to the final denouement of salvation which he expected very shortly. But when the apocalypse stalled, a new history of Christian Rome displaced the history of Israel. Paul's ironic blurring of categories, a masterful rhetorical gesture aimed at gentiles, since Jews already knew the truth, became permanently transfixed. "While the history of the Jews was decried as the travails of a 'detestable' mob, the history of Israel and of the Hebrews became also the history of Rome."[18] In this scheme of things, Jewish old-timers (an apt characterization if ever there was one) became not only marginal but downright subversive. Their ever-present, self-evident claim to God's promise was a dangerous anachronism that testified to the embarrassing "newness" of "New Israel." It required the most exquisite exegetical contortions to make the case that Christians were morally and spiritually privileged in full view of God's chosen people, armed with their commandments and their Scriptures. No wonder Christian theologians expended such enormous imaginative energy on turning the Hebrew Bible into an "old" testament that, as they tirelessly insisted, was only a pale prequel to their own new and improved gospel. Meanwhile, the continued deferral of the Second Coming, which promised the conversion of the Jews (Paul would have had a good chuckle over this idea: conversion to what, for heaven's sake?), only sharpened the disjuncture between the imperial time-space of Christian "Rome" and the exilic continuum of Jewish "Jerusalem."

To Wessely, the *Toleranzpatent*, which turned the Polish Jews of Habsburg Galicia into an exemplary object of reform, translated the theological doctrine of Jewish election into cultural terms. As had been promised by the biblical prophets, Jews would again become a light onto the nations. The Jewish "teaching of God" brought monotheism into the world; who knew what fresh gifts Jewish mastery of the "teaching of man" would bring to the gentiles? Psychoanalysis? Abstract expressionism? The polio vaccine? Facebook? In any event, Wessely did not doubt that Jews would fully rise to the demands of the present occasion. More significant was the fact that Joseph's repudiation of early modern Jewry law defied Paul's irremediable Jewish pessimism about the moral turpitude of "Romans." These modern "Romans," inspired by the Augustan eminence of Joseph II, could, apparently, teach themselves to govern on the basis of ethical principles rather than the dictates of greed, thinly veiled by a self-serving interpretation of Paul's gospel. And this time around, the education of mankind did not even require the gruesome sacrifice of a nice Jewish boy. Indeed, from the Jewish perspective onto the obscenity of Roman power—Paul's rabbinical contemporaries sometimes referred to the empire as a brothel—the moral awakening of a gentile king, born into a heritage of Catholic intolerance, might very well have looked like an even bigger miracle than the resurrection of Jesus.

Informed by the long, depressing view of Christian "Rome" where faith in the redemptive power of the cross enabled and excused a medieval horror show that made pagan Romans look like pussycats, Wessely's conviction that the "enlightenment" of Joseph II had to be the work of God made good sense. We must remember too that Wessely, like Paul, read the history of the gentiles in light of an unshakeable belief in the scriptural promise to the Jewish people. Jewish history had proven Paul wrong; Jesus' death had failed to awaken the conscience of the "multitudes" and ultimately only made things worse for Israel. That was not the fault of the Jews, only a sign of persistent moral recidivism among the gentiles, which was an offense to God. But finally, the terms of the *Toleranzpatent* rendered the relationship between the progress of humanity and the "improvement" of the Jewish condition clear and transparent.

One additional thing needs to be said about the implications of *Words of Peace and Truth* for the intellectual revolt against Exile. Jewish tradition associated the privations of galut with the undeserved dominion of the unworthy majority over God's own people. Exile signified a moral rather than a political lack. Working well within this tradition, Wessely linked redemption with good government, not with the ingathering of the Jewish diaspora and the reinstatement of Jewish sovereignty, which in its time had not done much better with the temptations of power, and perhaps even a little worse. Jewish kings were not immune to greed and corruption. The biblical historian of the house of David ultimately held Israel's own rulers responsible for the moral collapse of the entire people and their eventual displacement from the promised land. Moral qualms about the exercise of imperial power entered into Scripture after the Exile. I Samuel 8 insisted that the institution of the Israelite monarchy was a concession to popular clamor, and not an original part of God's plan for Jewish society. The biblical understanding of community derived from an ideal of shared moral purpose. Leviticus enjoined Israel to become a "kingdom of priests and a holy people."

In this scheme of things, Exile constituted a problem of time, not space. Wessely, a careful reader of the Bible, knew that Deuteronomy's assurance of a Jewish return to the land of Israel was time-contingent. It would not take place until the appropriate moment, that is, until the people of Israel lived up to their end of the deal. The repossession of the land would follow only upon a return to God:

> And it shall come to pass, *when all these things are come upon thee,* the blessing and the curse, which I have set before thee, and thou shalt bethink thyself among all the nations, whither the LORD thy God hath driven thee, and shalt return unto the LORD thy God, and hearken to His voice according to all that I command thee this day, thou and thy children, with all thy heart, and with all thy soul; that *then* the LORD thy God will turn thy captivity, and have compassion upon thee, and will return and gather thee from all the peoples, whither the LORD thy God hath scattered thee.[19]

The biblical reading of Exile as a metaphysical problem in time meant that the persistence of Jewish life outside the land of Israel was historically neutral. The end of Exile did not require the negation of the Jewish diaspora, scattered to the four corners of the earth even when the Temple still stood. The point is evident in Wessely's imaginative use of the book of Esther to frame his argument.

Esther is the only canonical Jewish text set entirely outside the land of Israel following the cessation of prophecy. In Esther, salvation involves the reinstitution of moral order and the triumph of reason over the caprices of royal power, which was lazy, improvident, and, like Ahasuerus (the king in the book of Esther), highly susceptible to evil counsel. Instead of the repossession of the land and the ingathering of Babylonian Jewry, Esther ends with a striking image of literary dispersion:

> Esther the queen, the daughter of Abihail, and Mordechai the Jew, *wrote down* all the acts of power, to confirm this second letter of Purim. And he *sent letters* unto all the Jews, to the one hundred and twenty seven provinces of the kingdom of Ahasuerus, with *words of peace and truth*, to confirm these days of Purim in their appointed times, according as Mordechai the Jew and Esther the queen had enjoined them, and as they had ordained for themselves and for their seed, the matters of the fast and their outcry. And the commandment of Esther confirmed these matters of Purim; and *it was written in the book*.[20]

The dissemination of "letters" works to create an imagined community, bound by the words of peace and truth spreading to "one hundred and twenty seven provinces." Paul too had relied on the power of letters to fashion a community of memory that transcended, rather than annulled or contested, shifting political boundaries. Empires were free to carve up a world that belonged ultimately to God.

Wessely's letter provided a new paradigm for a literary ingathering by a dialectical means of cultural circulation. Sending forth his epistle, Wessely mobilized the foundational act of the Exile—the transformation of a Temple state into a scriptural community bound by text rather than by geographical proximity or political compact—to produce a vision of new creation which would involve the writing of new books for a new time. Following Wessely, the social organization of Jewish Romantics most often took the form of a literary society or a journal, dedicated to sowing the seeds of a modern Jewish literature that would counteract the geographical effects of dispersion and awaken the Jewish nation to its historic purpose.

Radical in implication and emphatic in tone, *Words of Peace and Truth* elicited an immediate rabbinic reaction. Wessely's practical suggestions about reforming Jewish education and encouraging Jews to take a greater interest in science was not without rabbinic precedent. There were already Jewish schools that curtailed talmudic study in favor of an emphasis on the Bible without incurring the kind of rabbinic opposition that greeted the publication of Wessely's epistle. Moreover, Jewish learning had never fully excluded the kinds of empirical knowledge that Wessely now grouped under the rubric of *torat ha'adam*. Yet *Words of Peace and Truth* provoked the sort of resistance that tends to force people up against walls and into corners. Rabbinic vehemence in the face of Wessely's new sense of time alerted his Jewish readers that there was something vital at stake in his argument and invited them to take sides. In some sense, rabbinic opposition contributed to a still-current but deeply misleading view that the Haskalah was a social movement representing a large and influential segment of Jewish opinion. In reality, maskilim almost never acted or thought as a party. And whatever appeal their work enjoyed outside their own circles, it did not galvanize the Jewish public in the way that current scholarship sometimes suggests.

What, then, did the rabbinic establishment find so objectionable? The initial and most compelling statement of reproof came from Prague's distinguished rabbi, Ezekiel Landau, and his disciple, R. Ezekiel Fleckeles. In a sermon delivered on the Sabbath preceding Passover in March of 1872, aimed explicitly at Wessely, Landau dismissed the claim that any policy change on the part of gentile authorities could be sufficient indication of a break in the long span of the Exile. Jewish history was subject to Divine will, which remained a mystery. Jewish conduct was not resident in heaven, but vested in the hands of communally appointed legal experts. The benevolence of gentile authority could not alter the course of galut. Wessely's expression of hope was tantamount to active messianic speculation. At best, Landau intimated, the reign of Joseph was an improvement on the harsh decrees of his mother. Like Cyrus of Persia, Joseph was a good king. But while Cyrus allowed some Jews to return to the land of Israel and rebuild the Temple, his policies certainly did not put an end to the era of dispersion.

Landau was prepared to obey gentile authority, as required by the talmudic injunction to adhere to the laws of the land, but to confuse the humble acceptance of a change in political circumstances with the advent of a new time was, at best, an error in judgment. How did Wessely know what sort of king would follow Joseph II? His biblical namesake was, after all, forgotten by God and left to rot in prison. At worst, Wessely's claims were arrogant presumption. "Let us not raise ourselves up," Landau warned, "even though we now have a king who is filled with pity and compassion and who sees fit to extend his benevolence unto us. From our own perspective, however, we remain in a land which is not ours and it therefore behooves us to submit to the power of the nations."[21]

> It is true [Landau conceded] that the bitterness of the Egyptian exile was unlike the experience in Persia. . . . This is also the case in our own time

> when our Lord, His Majesty the Emperor, has decided to help us and to raise us from our degradation.... We Jews should not for this reason become insolent and begin to behave with haughtiness and arrogance. We should act respectfully toward the inhabitants of this kingdom. It is their own land while we are only guests. A sense of submissiveness is good when it comes from within. It is enough that His Majesty, the Emperor has extended his protection over us so that no one will use force to harm or degrade us.... Even though God has not forsaken us in our bondage and disposed the king ... favorably toward us, we consider ourselves to be bondsmen.

Worse still was the offensive and faintly perverse suggestion that a Torah scholar, already expert in *torat ha'elohim*, required expertise in *torat ha'adam* to render him useful—as if the Torah were not the sum of all knowledge. The leveling of Jewish textual authority was, for Landau, characteristic of contemporary degeneracy, a sign not of messianic deliverance but of a world turned upside down. Wessely's attempt to breach the walls of Exile looked suspiciously like the heresy of the Sabbatians, who "committed all of the offenses proscribed by the Torah" in the mistaken assumption that the messianic era had arrived. Fleckeles went even further than Landau and explicitly accused Wessely of reading a government decree as if it were a new religious dispensation. Referring to Wessely and to Mendelssohn's circle in its entirety, Fleckeles attacked "those who say it is now permitted [Heb. *hareshut netunah*] to eat unclean things and even pork while reciting the blessing '[Blessed are You, Lord our God, King of the Universe] who has granted us life, sustained us, and enabled us to reach these days' when each man does as he sees fit."[22] Under the circumstances, tolerance and "tranquility" represented a dire threat to the moral integrity of the nation in Exile. It might be better to return to former days when "suffering" (Heb. *tsarot*) rendered the theological necessity of bearing the full weight of the divine yoke with patience and humility, worthy of a divine reward in heaven.

The rabbinic response to Wessely adumbrates the underlying philosophical division between traditionalists and maskilim. The fight was not over secular education; Landau, in the very same sermon that castigated Wessely, actually advised his congregants to take advantage of the new opportunities for economic advancement and send their children to the newly established Habsburg schools for Jews. The problem lay in the revision of the myth of Exile and the shift in the metaphysical status of the non-Jewish world that this revision implied. In 1794, Saul Berlin targeted the self-righteous glorification of Jewish suffering in the rabbinic rhetoric of reproof. His shocking parody of Israel's proverbial love of its own "troubles" remains irresistibly funny and entirely relevant to contemporary Jewish habits of mind.

> For now all that remains to us [Berlin imagined the rabbis saying] is to distance ourselves from them [the gentiles]. Nor shall we ever wish them anything good; and if, thanks to their hatred, the woes that threaten to destroy us should multiply, this is all for the better, for in this way, we shall gain more opportunities to sanctify the Holy Name before their very eyes. For from the day that the Temple was destroyed and the sacrifices were abolished, God, blessed be He, can have no greater pleasure [Heb. *nahat*, Yid. *naches*] than to see us killed and slaughtered like a burnt offering to consecrate His great Name. Our forefathers in former days rejoiced when the hatred of the nations became relentless.... And, may it speedily come to pass that I too, so poor and humble, will be found sufficiently worthy to be murdered or strung up in sanctification of the Lord's Name. Indeed, it behooves any man who calls himself a Jew to desire that the nations should despise us, so that we may attain the status of those righteous ones. And if, because of our many sins, the kings should suspend the evil decrees, and the persecutions and the killings, then we ought to consider this a punishment and ask them to change their minds.[23]

The implications of Berlin's historical optimism for the doctrine of Jewish election proved so anxiety-provoking that Landau's nineteenth-century successors abandoned the traditional flexibility of Jewish legal thinking and prohibited innovation as a matter of principle.[24] Partly as a response to the Romantic defense of Jewish modernity, rabbinic culture became much more attentive to social markers of difference such as language, dress, and names.[25] Modern ultra-Orthodox communities ultimately would be known for self-imposed extremes of social isolation, a confrontational and very public assertion of the "timelessness" of Israel and a visible symbol of the metaphysics of galut. Their insistence that all aspects of Jewish deportment must attempt to recapture Jewish "antiquity" served as one of the chief markers of difference between Jews who may have avowed the same commitment to religious praxis and upheld a common belief in the binding nature of Jewish law but disagreed as to what such commitments ultimately signified about the nature of Jewish difference.

Wessely's reading of Jewish history was not self-evident even within his own circle; Mendelssohn himself challenged the idea that the "enlightenment" of the gentiles was a genuine sign of progress. For him, the timing of Jewish renewal transcended any apparent change in legal or social circumstances. Mendelssohn articulated his doubts in *Jerusalem*, a treatise on "religious power and Judaism," published just after the appearance of *Words of Peace and Truth*. It stands to reason that the essay was, at least in part, motivated by the controversy in which he was potentially implicated.²⁶

Mendelssohn also began by considering the question of historical change. What time is it, Wessely had asked himself. According to Mendelssohn, it was always the same time: the big hand was perpetually stuck at the dawn hour of human progress:

> I, for my part, cannot conceive of the education of the human race as my late friend Lessing imagined it under the influence of I-don't-know-which historian of mankind. One pictures the collective entity of the human race as an individual person and believes that Providence sent it to school here on earth in order to raise it from childhood to manhood. In reality, the human race is—if the metaphor is appropriate—in almost every century, child, adult, and old man at the same time.... Progress is for the individual man, who is destined by Providence to spend part of his eternity here on earth.²⁷

In contrast to Wessely, Mendelssohn held that only individuals were susceptible to the power of education. No political statute could assure the transformation of mankind: "We have good grounds for believing," Mendelssohn had argued several years earlier in his dialogue on the immortality of the soul, "... that this vast universe was brought into existence in order that there might be reasoning beings that could rise step by step, increase little by little in perfection and find, in this ever-growing progress, their joy and felicity."²⁸ No matter how reasonable and just, changes in state law could not guarantee social progress in the long term. The *Toleranzpatent* signified nothing, except, perhaps, the personal inclinations of the lawgiver and the conditions of the society into which he happened to have been born. All ideas of progress were contingent, since "for every people at every level of culture at which it finds itself, a different form of government will be the best."²⁹

Even when the state performed its duty toward its subjects and compelled them to act morally, it was doubtful that the short-term results achieved thereby would "alter conviction," much less influence the minds of people in the long run.³⁰ "Individual man advances, but mankind continually fluctuates within fixed limits, while maintaining, on the whole, about the same degree of morality in all periods—the same amount of religion and irreligion, of virtue and vice, of felicity and misery."³¹ With the birth of every human being, the difficult process of moral education had to begin all over again, "step by step, little by little." Least of all, Mendelssohn said, could one expect "improvement" in the condition of the Jews when Christian prejudice continued to maintain a hold on even the best-intentioned minds of the era? "It will perhaps," Mendelssohn glumly noted, "still take centuries of culture and preparation before men understand that privileges on account of religion are neither lawful, nor, actually useful and that it would therefore be a veritable boon totally to abolish all civil discrimination on account of religion."[32]

Mendelssohn had good cause to be so discouraged. He himself had continually come up against the disjunction between the image of a society governed by the principles of reason and tolerance and the realities of Christian benevolence. Several unpleasant encounters within Berlin's own ecumenical, enlightened circles demonstrated how tenuous the idea of a post-Christian history really was. *Jerusalem* considerably cooled the rhetorical temperature of *Words of Peace and Truth*. But Mendelssohn's theological-political treatise, just like Spinoza's, ultimately addressed something far more disturbing than the stirrings of Jewish Romanticism. If Wessely was guilty of anything, it was only of taking enlightened "Romans" at their word. But "Romans" could not be trusted. *Jerusalem* implicitly contrasted Jewish good faith with Christian bad conscience. Written in the spirit of critique, the book challenged the spurious use of philosophical arguments to justify the continuing abuse of Christian power among people who were busy congratulating themselves on having outgrown the religious prejudices of the past.

Although *Jerusalem* entered into conversation with *Words of Peace and Truth*, its explicit purpose was to answer the challenge of a certain August Friedrich Cranz. Ostensibly in the name of reason, Cranz invited Mendelssohn to reconcile his commitment to freedom of thought with his adherence to Jewish law. Cranz charged that Mendelssohn's philosophical rejection of "all manner of religious compulsion" impugned the existing system of rabbinic authority, heir to the coercive instruments of the original Mosaic constitution.[33] Cranz presented Mendelssohn with a version of an argument that Mendelssohn had refused to answer once before. Some ten years earlier Johann Kaspar Lavater first presented him with the proposition that Judaism and Enlightenment were incompatible. Asserting that Christianity was more in keeping with the universal ethos of natural religion, Lavater publicly enjoined Mendelssohn either to resolve the contradiction between reason and his own ancestral faith or to convert. The idea that the inconsistency between religious authority and the free exercise of the mind might have led Mendelssohn to abjure religion altogether—the real upshot of the argument—did not even occur to Lavater, a slippage that put his own philosophical intent into at least as much doubt as Mendelssohn's.

Writing to Lavater personally, Mendelssohn had objected to his blatant violation of the rules of enlightened civility. "I am fortunate enough," Mendelssohn reminded his interlocutor, "to have as friends many excellent men who are not of my religion. We are sincerely attached to one another, although we guess and assume that in matters of religion our opinions vary widely. I enjoy the pleasure of their company which I find improving and delightful. Never did my heart whisper to me: 'What a shame about their souls!'"[34] No one had the right to interfere with the opinions of another person as to what kind of religious beliefs and observances would best vouchsafe salvation in the next life, as long as the aforesaid beliefs and observances did not violate the liberty of other people in this one. Lavater's aggressive interference with Mendelssohn's express wishes to be left to his own opinions constituted just such a violation. The nature of Mendelssohn's own unswerving commitment to Judaism, like that of every other Jew, was really beside the point, even if Lavater and every other Christian who professed to be enlightened found it incomprehensible, foolish, or hypocritical. "Do our opinions seem incoherent?" Mendelssohn shot back. "There is no need to dispute the matter. We act in accordance with our beliefs, and others are welcome to question the validity of laws, which, by our own admission, do not apply to them. Whether it is proper, friendly, humane of them to cast such scorn on our laws and customs, may be left to their consciences to decide. Since we do not seek to persuade others of our opinion, all dispute is futile."[35]

Lavater's public assault on Mendelssohn's freedom of conscience—which included even the freedom to hold contradictory and "incoherent" beliefs—ultimately threatened the project of Enlightenment to a much greater extent than Mendelssohn's position on whether Christianity or Judaism was more compatible with philosophy. One gets the feeling, from the carefully controlled tone of his letter, that Mendelssohn held back from indulging in the comparison not because he was intimidated by Lavater's Christian zeal. On the contrary, Mendelssohn adopted a posture of restraint out of respect for the same principle of freedom of conscience that ensured Lavater's right to hold on to his own beliefs, which Mendelssohn, if pressed, might have called irrational. "What friend of truth," Mendelssohn teased, "can boast of having found his religion free from all harmful human elaborations? All those of us who seek the truth recognize the corrupting breath of hypocrisy and superstition"—this was obviously a poke at Christianity—"and wish to remove it without detriment to the true and the good. But I am as firmly and unshakably convinced of the *essentials* of my religion as you . . . or any of your associates can be"—another poke—"of yours."[36]

In *Jerusalem*, Mendelssohn went much farther than he had in his exchange with Lavater. By this point, it was probably clear to him that the Lavater incident was not as isolated disturbance of the friendly decorum that prevailed within Mendelssohn's own privileged circle. Now, Mendelssohn saw it as symptomatic of the same categorical confusion between moral persuasion and political power that first afflicted Spinoza and prompted his own challenge of Christian prerogatives back in 1670. Moreover, following Wessely's spirited endorsement of a new age in Jewish policy, Mendelssohn felt obliged to sound a loud note of caution to those readers who found Wessely's arguments congenial and consistent with their own hopes. At the same time, *Jerusalem* undertook to answer the self-professed Christian proponents of Jewish Enlightenment—Cranz, Lavater, and others—who undertook to reform the Jews by dismantling Judaism.

In the first part of *Jerusalem*, Mendelssohn elaborated on his defense of liberty of conscience and expanded on an earlier argument that rabbinic authority had no political dispensation whatsoever. No institution had the power to compel belief, while only the state had the authority to punish acts against public morals. Mendelssohn held this distinction to be absolute, even, he said, at the expense of maintaining historically well-established rabbinic sanctions like excommunication (Heb. *herem*). It might not be immediately obvious why Mendelssohn should have devoted a full half of a work which was about "religious power and Judaism" to rehearsing basic social contract theory. Nothing that he had to say in the first part of the book was original; Mendelssohn referred his own position to John Locke, even though the Jewish indictment of Christian authority owed more to Spinoza.[37] But the matter of the *herem* and the entire discussion of the "non-coercive" character of Judaism in the second part of *Jerusalem* was really an afterthought, a kind of Jewish proof text for the first part. Mendelssohn deconstructed the political theology of the Hebrew Bible largely because he wanted to expose the fallacy attendant on using the Enlightenment as a stalking horse for Christian theology. In the process, he redefined the "Mosaic constitution" in terms that exposed the inevitable duplicity of political agreements and underlined the failure of temporal law to transform a group of individuals into a moral community.

The plain truth is that Mendelssohn did not need the likes of Cranz to enlighten him to the idea that the political terms of the covenant between God and Israel presented a problem for a secular theory of the state. Mendelssohn had read Spinoza; he already knew that the contradiction between religion's capacity to persuade and the state's right to compel, apparently indistinguishable in the "Mosaic constitution," could not be reconciled without trespassing on individual freedom of conscience. But it was absurd to compare the limited sway of the Jewish community over its own members with the sovereignty of the Christian state. The "absolutism" of Mosaic legislation was confined to the biblical text, while the Christian monopoly on state-sponsored violence was rooted in immediate historical experience. Moreover, the practical capacity of the rabbis to enforce their religious rulings derived from Christian power, not from the Torah. Jewish communal autonomy was sustained, first and foremost, by Christian law. Finally, the willingness of the rabbis to exert the full measure of their authority was always limited, as Mendelssohn took pains to stress, by their "superabundant indulgence for human weakness."[38] Informed by Jewish scruples, this legislative "leniency" threw the church's warm embrace of the secular instruments of judicial coercion—otherwise known as torture—into bold relief. It was the height of moral obscenity (*hutzpah*, Mendelssohn might have said) to base a specious argument for conversion of the Jews on the idea of freedom of conscience. While Cranz was content to invoke the authoritarian image of Mosaic law, his exchange with Mendelssohn manifested Jewish vulnerability to Christian pressure and the capacity of Christians constantly to put Jews on the defensive. Behind the dispassionate argument about Enlightenment lurked the memory of countless medieval disputations where the conspicuous presence of the Christian king assured the outcome of a contest in which Jews were always on the losing side.

Mendelssohn highlighted the derivative nature of the "religious power" of Judaism in the introduction to the second section of *Jerusalem*. The question "To what extent should a naturalized colony be permitted to retain its own jurisdiction in ecclesiastical and civil matters in general and the right of excommunication and expulsion in particular?" only *seemed* to concern the Jews. It was really about the source of "religious power" claimed by the Christian state.

> Legal power of the church—the right of excommunication—if a colony is to have these, must have been enfeoffed with them, as it were, by the state or by the mother church. Someone who possesses this right by virtue of the social contract must have ceded or relinquished a part of it to the colony. . . . But what if no one can possess such a right? What if neither the state nor the mother church herself can claim any right to use coercion in religious matters?[39]

The reason that the power of the Jewish "colony" to excommunicate its members was illegitimate was not that it was rooted in Mosaic legislation. It was illegitimate because the original source of this power lay in the conflation of religious power and political sovereignty that established such a privilege in the first place. Mendelssohn was saying that the authority of the synagogue did not merely reflect the authority of the "mother church," abetted by the state. The Jewish "right of excommunication" was practically a Christian invention and a direct extension of Christian power into the recesses of Jewish conscience. The authority of the Jewish "colony" was only apparent, since it had been "ceded" to the Jews by "someone"—the state in cahoots with the mother church—who could always take it back. In effect, the conditional grant of Jewish autonomy underscored the utter powerlessness of the "colony," which existed outside the boundaries of the social contract. What looked like Jewish power was, in reality, the misbegotten product of an unnatural union between the Christian church and the secular state. If the marriage was illegitimate in the first place, surely its misbegotten child—Jewish autonomy—was likewise a bastard.

Where did this argument leave the collective future of the Jews? Mendelssohn drew an exceedingly fine line between "belief" (which Christians attempted to coerce) and religious "instruction" or Torah (which was an expression of the connection between the Jewish people and God). "I believe," Mendelssohn asserted, "that Judaism knows of no revealed religion in the sense in which the Christians understand this term. The Israelites possess a divine legislation—laws, commandments, ordinances, rules of life, instruction in the will of God as to how they should conduct themselves in order to attain temporal and eternal felicity. Propositions and prescriptions were revealed to them by Moses in a miraculous and supernatural manner," but, unlike Christianity, Judaism imposed "no doctrinal opinion, no saving truths, no universal propositions of reason."[40] Jewish teachers bore a responsibility to interpret "divine legislation" in the interests of "temporal and eternal felicity," but no Jewish scholar claimed the same exalted status as the Christian clergy. Insofar as they exercised no political influence through the power of their religious knowledge, all rabbis were really intellectuals forced to wear the uniform of state officials.

Mendelssohn dissociated "laws, commandments, ordinances and rules"—the appurtenances of state power devised and imposed by the divine lawgiver upon His own people—from "universal doctrines" and "saving truths," which the Church alone claimed to possess and dispense but which were really the property of mankind since they were derived from reason. The distinction implied that Jewish autonomy was more of a necessity for Christianity than it was for Judaism; membership in the Jewish community did not depend on the avowal of a specific creed. The emancipation of Judaism from the Christian state would serve to put the religious basis of the political privileges claimed by the church over Christian belief into question. Mendelssohn surely understood that such a step would come with a social cost for the collective discipline that held Jews together.[41] But the liberation of Jews from Jewish authority was a necessary step toward the political dispossession of Christianity.

The alternative was so much the worse. As he knew from personal experience, the assumption of Christian privilege vitiated freedom of conscience for Jews to an intolerable degree. Without unrestricted freedom of conscience, the project of Enlightenment was virtually a dead letter. What was bad for the Jews was bad for everybody.

In the second part of *Jerusalem*, Mendelssohn beat a philosophical retreat from Jewish dependence on the political power of Christianity. He argued that the binding nature of the "commandments and ordinances" was based on the acceptance of the "historical truth" of Sinaitic revelation.[42] The national Jewish covenant had the force of positive law. Echoing the language of Maimonides' famous thirteen principles, Mendelssohn proclaimed that the "historical truths" of the Bible "cannot be accepted in any other manner than on *faith*." Its "laws, precepts, commandments, and rules of life" were "imposed upon the nation and all their descendants as an unalterable duty and obligation" by the undivided authority of God, in his capacity as "Liberator, Founder, and Leader, as King and Head" of the Jewish people.[43] In the absence of rabbinic authority "enfeoffed" by the "mother church" to force people to keep the commandments without true belief, there would be no room for half-hearted commitments.

Powerless to extract religious devotion in any case, a state that continued to empower a church, even a Jewish church, to compel such obedience would fatally compromise people's capacity to accept its authority. As long as it continued, in accordance with Christian doctrine, to support the "religious power" of Judaism to "expel and excommunicate," the government would have on its hands potential "fellow citizens without conscience," hypocrites and liars who could not be trusted to keep faith with any laws.[44] On the other hand, for the state to tamper with Judaism, to presume to reform it or alter it in any way, was equally to trespass onto territory where it had no jurisdiction. If political concord between Christians and Jews could not be "obtained under any other condition than our departing from the laws which we still consider binding on us, then we are sincerely sorry to find it necessary to declare that we must rather do without civil union."[45] Suspicious of political intrusion into the religious life of the Jewish "colony," Mendelssohn reserved judgment on the expectations raised by the *Toleranzpatent*. He was sure that no state law, no matter how well intentioned, had the power to induce a modern Jewish revolution that Wessely practically willed into being. He knew this not because he was a more conservative thinker than Wessely (his defense of Judaism was a more radical response to Enlightenment assumptions about the philosophical limitations of religious belief than anything in *Words of Peace and Truth*), but because his own Romantic turn had preceded the *Toleranzpatent* by some twenty-five years.

7 Faith

Jewish Romanticism developed against the visible contradictions of imperial geography. The partitions introduced an alternative political structure into Polish Jewish life. Prussia annexed its Polish territories outright, absorbed the province of Poznan into its administrative structure, and renamed it Posen (which does not mean that the Polish Jews who lived there instantly became German Jews). But in the Habsburg and Russian domains, the reforming state confronted a much larger and more concentrated Jewish population. Here, the state continued to maintain Jewish communal autonomy in the interests of peace and orderly tax collection. At the same time, representatives of a new bureaucratic and military regime undermined older systems of economic patronage and mutual self-interest that had preserved neighborly relations on the eastern frontiers of the Polish-Lithuanian Commonwealth. Although the power of the great nobility was not wiped out completely, especially in the countryside, rising centers of provincial government drew upwardly mobile enterprising individuals toward expanding cities. Opportunities for financial gain and increasing internal mobility deepened the divide between the Jewish small town, still embedded in the rural economy that was dominated by the manorial system of agricultural production, and a dynamic urban milieu where a more culturally differentiated and demographically diverse Jewish society began to grow. However, the survival of Polish aristocracy, now deprived of political clout by agents of imperial rule, served as an ever-present reminder of the pre-partition past that refused to give way to a state-sponsored future. The unregenerate image of the *shtetl* (the Jewish small town existing in the shadow of the great noble estate) represented the uncanny persistence of medieval Poland in the midst of the nineteenth century.

Maskilim were deeply ambivalent about the costs of socioeconomic reconstruction and cultural change that they were inclined to welcome and that offered new opportunities for employment and education. The lingering presence of Polish Jewry refused to yield to historical reason and haunted modern Jewish faith in the benevolent nature of time. Marked by the familiar architectural topoi of Polish Jewish backwardness—the castle and the marketplace—the residual Polishness of Eastern European Jewry migrated into modern Jewish culture, first and foremost in the diabolical figure of the Hasid.

Jewish intellectuals associated the old "Polish" shtetl with the entrenchment and spread of Hasidic piety, even though the "Hasidic conquest" of Eastern Europe took place in large cities as well as small ones. Maskilim persisted in identifying Hasidism with a perverse sense of Jewish resistance to modernity, despite the fact that the conspicuous success of Hasidism owed just as much as the Haskalah to the political and economic opportunities extended to Polish Jews by their new colonial masters. Prominent patrons of Hasidic piety could be found among the wealthiest beneficiaries of the colonial economy. Why, then, did Hasidism present such a problem to the sensibilities of Jewish intellectuals? It wasn't simply that Hasidism succeeded in attracting a large loyal following while maskilim often felt marginalized within their own communities. Jewish intellectuals took the success of the new movement very personally. In 1832, in a letter to the Warsaw censor of Jewish books, Jacob Tugendhold, Isaac-Baer Levinsohn represented Hasidism as a direct affront to the Haskalah: "How long must we stand by while the sect of the *hasidim*, holding fast to each other in a powerful bond, helping one another, succeed in realizing all of the foolish plans to which they set their minds? And all the while the men of our fellowship [Heb. *anshei shlomeinu*] remain isolated and poor."[1]

Hasidism offered an interpretation of redemption that both mirrored and mocked the prodigious cultural aspirations of Jewish Romanticism. The Hasidic doctrine of "worship through corporeality" imbued ordinary life with extraordinary spiritual significance. Hasidism popularized a new affective mode of personal devotion that transcended status distinctions between learned elites and laypeople. Attachment to the *tzaddik* created new communities of the elect where economic and social tensions were mitigated by a system of moral responsibility and mutual obligation regulated by his charismatic pastoral authority. A new Hasidic literature opened up unexpected professional opportunities for editors and publishers who emerged as powerful cultural mediators and bearers of the sacred into the register of a more popular religious literature. Jewish intellectuals were not nearly so successful in translating their own quest for perfectibility into a communal model (at least not until the rise of nationalism in the late 1870s). Hasidism was a parody of Jewish Romanticism; for this reason, maskilic polemic consistently repressed the intellectual appeal of Hasidic doctrine—which was no less real than the enthusiasm of the masses—and depicted the movement as nothing but a gigantic swindle.

The rapid spread of Hasidism after the partitions rendered the modern view of the Jewish future obscure and increasingly indeterminate. The fear of social and religious chaos that Hasidism seemed to generate among maskilim stemmed from a sense of epistemological confusion about how to read the signs of the times. Hasidism entered into the literature produced by maskilim as a signifier of an ironic awareness that any claim of redemption always ran the risk of being exposed as a self-serving fraud and a pious fiction. Maskilim became deeply invested in unmasking Hasidism as a false and degenerate form of Jewish "sectarianism" that was both inauthentic and corrupt, while insisting that they themselves inhabited a privileged sphere of integrity and truthfulness. But the kind of writing that was supposed to make this distinction explicit and clear inevitably exposed the author's own anxieties about the power of Hasidic "lies" and blurred the line between deceit and legitimate literary artifice.

Scholarship accounts for the modern Jewish turn to fiction writing—which dates to the appearance in 1819, of Joseph Perl's anti-Hasidic novel *Revealer of Secrets* (Heb. *Megaleh tmirin*)—in functional terms. In one version of a common explanation, the earliest literary experiments in nineteenth-century Eastern Europe constituted a deliberate form of "creative betrayal" of traditional Jewish culture in the name of an "ideology inimical to Jewish corporate behavior and aimed at flattening civilization down to a set of universally held principles." In order to "rally their benighted brethren, the first generation of east European Jewish innovators became wolves in shepherds' clothing. Theirs was a treasonous art if ever there was one. They learned to imitate the sacred tale, the sermon, the spoken anecdote so as to laugh them off the stage of history once and for all." Compelled, against their will, to compete with the contemporary popularity of the Hasidic tale, the Hasidic discourse and other forms of the Hasidic art of mass communication, Jewish intellectuals became "predators feeding off the seemingly unusable [Jewish] past." Turning to fiction only to discredit their opponents as charlatans and impostors, they created a secular Jewish literature almost in spite of themselves.[2]

For all its seductive simplicity, this argument obscures the ways in which fiction compromised *any* claims of narrative authority, not just those of the "sacred tale, the sermon and the spoken anecdote." The "treasonous art" of the Haskalah did not simply yield itself up to the direct transmission of anything like "universally held principles." The contingencies of fiction discredited *any* normative statement about the world. Moreover, the artful reproduction of Hasidic falsehoods as an antidote to the highly specific problem of Hasidic hypocrisy implicated maskilim in the same decline of epistemological certainty that, they claimed, Hasidic agents embraced and exploited. The moral line between "creative betrayal" and self-deception was painfully thin. Perl composed *Revealer of Secrets* in the heat of his own struggle against Hasidism. However, the appeal of the book subverted his narrative assault on Hasidic piety and brought the author up against the same charge of pandering to popular credulity and greed that he leveled at his Hasidic opponents. Perl was well aware of this tension. In the prologue to the unpublished Yiddish edition of *Revealer of Secrets,* his alter ego acknowledged the contradiction that modern criticism of maskilic literature tends to smooth out:

> Do you think that the one who wrote *Revealer of Secrets* just wanted to write stories to entertain the public? It seems to me that when the author copied the letters [that constitute the novel], more than once there were tears in his eyes and it was with a bitter heart that he copied them because he saw our gloomy condition—that one cannot address people nowadays in a serious vein as one could in the past. Because of our many sins, we are deaf to serious talk and our eyes are closed. . . . The author of *Revealer of Secrets* knows his brothers. He did not intend just to write stories; he intended something different. He sees we are critically ill and we will not take any medicine, so he mixed the medicine with sugar for us. But what good is it? The public, I see, laps up the sugar and the medicine they don't touch!³

Perl's vernacular narrator contrasts the numinous power of "serious talk" with the uncertainty of writing for a fallen world where meaning has been irretrievably severed from means of expression. In such a world, Perl's double ruefully acknowledges, it has become possible to eat the sugar and to leave the medicine alone. His admission reproaches the contemporary Jewish consumer with an infantile taste for the cultural equivalent of junk food and attributes such "sickness" to modern failure, rather than to the wasted legacy of the Jewish tradition.

Perl had written *Revealer of Secrets* because he believed that "writing stories" would ultimately serve to disclose the truth about Hasidism, but the "secret" that his book revealed was that its author no longer trusted the capacity of language to communicate the truth about anything at all. *Revealer of Secrets* had come to announce that "serious talk" could not compete with make-believe. Inscribed into the novel itself, Perl's ambivalent relationship to authorship reflected the contemporary dispersion of Jewish knowledge, which the novel's work of subversion was powerless to remedy. The ambiguities of fiction did not just allow for the possibility of misreading; they practically invited it. As a matter of fact, Perl could not be sure that Hasidic readers would not take *Revealer of Secrets* for an actual correspondence, thus completely missing its "medicinal" parodic message. No matter how well intentioned, such fictions contributed to the pervasive historical slippage between reality and appearance that no utterance could fix.

Revealer of Secrets makes a wonderful shambles of its own stated purpose. It aims to tell the absolute, unvarnished truth about Hasidism. Yet it leaves the narrative field entirely to the two protagonists, instantly exposed as inveterate cheats and shameless schemers who would lie as soon as they would breathe. Presented as an internal Hasidic correspondence that has somehow fallen into the hands of an imaginary "invisible" editor called Ovadiah ben Petahiah (identified by means of a series of cunning literary allusions with Perl himself), the story is effectively dispersed among a series of authors whose voices the reader is meant to overhear and who cannot be trusted. The irony that putatively attaches to the presentation of Hasidic opinions and schemes spreads like an infection to the rest of the narrative. There is no Archimedean point of reference in the story to relieve the sense of uncertainty that inevitably attaches to gossip, an unstable form of communication that the novel (any novel) naturally privileges.

Significantly, the material object around which the correspondence revolves is a lost "book" (Ger. and Yid. *Buch*) that unmasks the machinations—the secrets—of a certain *tzaddik* to the imperial authorities. Perl deliberately uses the German word *Buch* (rather than the Hebrew word *sefer*) to allude to the secular critique of Hasidic textuality that is the therapeutic goal of his own project. The "Buch" that everyone is looking for turns out to be the book called *Revealer of Secrets*. This self-referential slippage is a wonderful example of romantic irony at play with the figural capacities of language, close in spirit and style to E.T.A. Hoffmann's double-voiced, reflexively self-deconstructing *Kater Murr* (1819–1821), an outstanding Romantic novel that makes similar use of the lost book motif. Naturally, the *Buch* in Perl's story is destined never to be found. Its elusive movement from hand to hand alludes to the dispersion of meaning that rebounds onto Perl's own invisible controlling persona whose running "editorial" commentary is persistently drowned out (lost) within the cacophony of other voices. The metaphor of the disappearing *Buch* refers to the irrecoverable loss of narrative authority involved in writing *Revealer of Secrets* in the first place. The gap between Perl's illusion of omniscience and the coexistence of multiple conflicting stories represents the difference between the transcendent ideal of knowledge and the inescapable reality that knowledge always arrives in contradictory forms, mediated by the informers who provide it. The only book that can be written about Hasidism is doomed to contain a series of fictions, none of which can be verified.

What sort of unspeakable truths are revealed in *Revealer of Secrets?* Does their disclosure ultimately serve the cause of dispelling the pernicious climate of Hasidic lies? Certainly Perl intends that it should. But the chronic sense of uncertainty inherent in the epistolary form of *Revealer of Secrets* also undermines any stable categories of value at the level of theme. Perl sets out to contrast intellectual integrity, embodied in the figure of Mordechai Gold, with Hasidic wiles, associated with the holy man, the object of idolatrous worship on the part of the correspondents, Reb Zaynvl and Reb Zelig, who are busily conspiring on his behalf. Since neither Gold nor his archenemy actually appear in the story to speak for themselves, both good and evil are made out to be competing projections of the various letter-writers. The reputation of the *tzaddik* motivates the action that involves, among other things, bribery, deception, sexual pandering, theft, and slander.

Against the background of Perl's vertiginous plotting, the maskil remains a passive figure. To be sure, he is prepared to intervene with the gentile "prince" in order to foil the plans of the scheming hasidim, but he doesn't initiate anything. This is very curious, given the fact that real maskilim, including the notable arch-enemy of Hasidism, the Habsburg Jewish censor and school inspector Herz Homberg as well as Perl himself, were indefatigable social activists who deliberately provoked the rabbinic leadership precisely by their energetic intervention in the life of Galician Jews. Mordechai Gold, by contrast, is a holdover from the Polish Jewish past. Unlike Perl and Homberg, the imaginary maskil is an old-fashioned merchant with ties to the Polish nobility rather than a writer, educator, and civil servant. Gold alludes to his author's desire to disown precisely the most modern aspects of the social identity of the Jewish intellectual. As Perl well knew, to enter into battle against Hasidism is to risk getting one's hands dirty.

The tension between the spritely representation of Hasidic vice and the archaic inertia of modern Jewish virtue creates an asymmetry that the plot never fully resolves. There is an attenuated, melancholy quality attached to Perl's own fantasy-double that reflects palely the boundless glee with which he attacks the depiction of the creative shenanigans of his Hasidic antiheroes. Perl magnifies the scope of Hasidic domination to Quixotic proportions: "How many grave battles have we had since we started our holy fellowship! How many slanderers and accusers have we had! How many adversaries have risen up against us! How many composed books against our group! How many of them traveled from community to community to preach against us openly! But we, by the merit of the tsaddikim, took revenge against some of them and some of them died and our group endures and in every generation our people increase."⁴ And there is another thing: Mordechai Gold's loneliness (his only company seems to be the "prince" and there are no other maskilim mentioned in the story) is entirely unrelieved by family. Gold is a childless widower whose second marriage likewise remains without issue. Endowed with the miraculous power to ensure biological fecundity, the "holy rebbe," by contrast, possesses a certain gift "particularly as it concerns children. This is a trifle for him."⁵ The success of his intercession, mystical or otherwise, has borne fruit not once or twice but "thousands upon thousands of times." Meanwhile, Mordechai Gold is, for all intents and purposes, impotent and prematurely aged.⁶ At the end of the story, he takes over the upbringing of the eldest of Zaynvl's many sons, borrowing, as it were, from the inexhaustible store of Hasidic vitality.⁷

On his own, Mordechai Gold can hardly be said to embody Jewish hopes for the future. The ending suggests that the Haskalah cannot "reproduce" without its rival movement. At the very least, the role that Perl assigns to Hasidism in the unfolding of God's plan is highly ambiguous. If *Revealer of Secrets* can be read as a commentary on the new teleology of redemption, then the Hasidic plot to turn Jewish history against the current of time paradoxically functions as a catalyst, a kind of secular—amoral—force of self-preservation that will stop at nothing to assure its own increase and thereby, inadvertently, push time toward its apocalyptic resolution. Naturally, at the book's end Zaynvl, the one surviving troublemaker, ends up in the Land of Israel. Zelig, his fellow conspirator and double, expires in an apoplectic fit. Even the death of a hasid is a combustible force.

The indomitable energy of Perl's hasidim expresses itself chiefly in greed and lust, qualities notably lacking in the highly restrained, self-effacing personality of Mordechai Gold. There is a connection between sex and money here. Perl stresses that Gold is an old-fashioned leaseholder rather than a capitalist. His wealth is tied not to entrepreneurial initiative but to a privileged relationship with the local landowner, to hard coin (Gold) that maintains its value but cannot generate profit. The hasidim, by contrast, are constantly borrowing on credit. They are also frenetic, voracious consumers, and not only of material objects, a seemingly endless supply of which is literally engendered by their mystical master and circulated among his followers. Their boundless appetites for things extend also to pleasures of the body. Meanwhile, everything about Mordechai Gold, including the "cravat around his neck," points to pinched, repressive self-consciousness: "His speech is measured and he knows arithmetic. . . . He can't stand a stain on his clothes a. . . and he doesn't drink vodka or smoke a pipe."⁸ *Revealer of Secrets* is a book that dispenses with a narrative center in favor of nothing but a concatenation of free-floating assertions, any of which might be held against the person responsible for them. In this narrative context, the disparity between the plenitude of the Hasidic personality and the self-limiting ethos of the Haskalah invites a counter-intuitive reading of desire that unsettles the status of *Revealer of Secrets* as a straightforward primer of anti-Hasidic invective. Perhaps the unbearable envy of apparently guiltless self-indulgence is Perl's "secret," the thing that cannot be thought, let alone spoken, by any maskil except under the cover of jest.

In the event, *Revealer of Secrets* discloses a range of modern Jewish anxieties not merely about the persistence of false belief and superstition. Perl's depiction of Hasidic id functions as a foil for the Jewish superego of Mordechai Gold, a figure similarly born of fantasy rather than historical reality. Perl's carnivalization of Hasidism bespeaks the same concerns about the secularization of desire without the restraining hand of reason that had first surfaced in the alignment of the lecherous religious hypocrite with the figure of the hyper-sexualized, materialistic young woman in the crisis plays *Frivolity and Hypocrisy*, written in 1794 by Aaron Halle-Wolfssohn, a student of Mendelssohn, and *Reb Henokh or What's to Be Done?* (Yid. *Reb Henokh oder vos tut me damit?*), written in 1798 by Isaac Euchel, a maskil from Königsberg. In all three instances, the authors mirrored modern Jewish corruption in their use of idiomatic—read secular, contemporary—Jewish language. The literary recourse to Yiddish was not, therefore, merely instrumental. Like the turn toward fiction it proved essential to the disclosure of the "secrets" closely guarded by Jewish intellectuals, sometimes even from themselves.

The history of the Haskalah's obsession with Hasidism, both as its absolute Other and as the shadow of its own hidden Self, both as an object of disgust and the source of envy, both repellent and seductive, culminated in the creation of the "two Kuni-Lemls" by the founder of the Yiddish theater, the Russian maskil, Abraham Goldfaden. Just as Perl had done, Goldfaden deployed the unbuttoned figure of the "fanatic" Kuni-Leml to undress his modern Jewish hero.[9] Disguised in the borrowed clothes of the former, Goldfaden's Max can permit himself to repulse the nice middle-class girl he is supposed to love and marry in order to flirt with the dumb and sexy slut he really wants. Justified by the low, didactic register of vernacular farce, Goldfaden invoked Hasidic vice in order to reproduce the contagion of sexual and economic license that modern Jewish writing (like Perl's) was supposed to cure.

What is especially striking about Perl's precedent-setting anti-Hasidic comedy is that the exposure of false religion seems ultimately concerned not so much with releasing the Jewish individual from the dead hand of Jewish tradition as with the consequences of materialism. Hasidic vice reveals that modernity involves too little rather than too much religion. History appears to be governed entirely by the untrammeled exercise of human appetite. The ambiguous ending implicates Mordechai Gold in the irrepressible spectacle of Hasidic carnality. His passivity in the face of Hasidism reflects contemporary anxiety about the secularization of Jewish communal structures in post-partition Eastern Europe, a policy move that subverted the purpose of maskilic social activism. Just five years after the publication of *Revealer of Secrets,* the Habsburg government finally recognized the legal standing of Hasidic prayer gatherings, effectively abdicating its providential role as the bearer of divine reason.[10] The unanticipated "tolerance" of state law for alternative forms of Jewish worship undermined the institutional struggle against Hasidism waged by Jewish intellectuals in Galicia; but it was also a blow to the faith of maskilim. Apparently, Habsburg officials did not care about the religious content of Hasidism, only about whether it encouraged criminal conduct among its adherents. The state's indifference to internal Jewish squabbles left Galician Jews free to make their own choices between Hasidism and the Haskalah. The secularization of religious policy required maskilim to engage Hasidism democratically, that is, by appealing to the unaccountable proclivities of the Jewish masses rather than to reasonable and well-disposed state officials.

The legitimation of Hasidism in Galicia not only failed to moderate the tone of Jewish Romanticism but raised it to a new apocalyptic pitch. Suspended between faith and despair, the discourse of the Haskalah veered between inflated messianic exaltation and a darker mood, marked by unrelieved moments of gloom and explosions of ferocious aggression. Wessely and Euchel after him had attached epochal significance to the providential appearance of Mendelssohn. But nothing in *Words of Peace and Truth* prepared the reader for the gospel according to Prague's Judah Jeiteles, whose diction practically glowed in the dark. In a sermon (Jeiteles was, among other things, a preacher) published in 1830 in the Galician journal with the suggestive title *First Fruits of the Times* (Heb. *Bikureiha'itim*), Jeiteles suggested turning Mendelssohn's birthday into an annual day of worship and thanksgiving for every generation to come so that Jews could offer their gratitude to God for blessing them with a new "redeemer."

> For this day a child was born unto us to increase wisdom among the people of Jeshurun and who would become the father of all the children of Jacob, the prince of peace. . . . This is the day that God brought light unto us and cast off the darkness . . . opening the eyes of the blind who had strayed from the true path and were lost in the land for many years

while the gate of wisdom was closed before them.... This is the day for which we had hoped, when the shackles of imprisonment were removed and Israel gained hope in its time of tribulation.

Echoing the prophetic idiom of Isaiah as well as the sonorous rhythm of Handel's "Messiah" chorus, Jeiteles translated the language of Christian annunciation into a Jewish register. In a sly gloss on Christian salvation history, Jeiteles implied that reason had actually saved the world from religious barbarism and redeemed the Jews of Europe from their "imprisonment" in Christian darkness. To commemorate the occasion, he called upon Jewish schools to erect stone monuments dedicated to Mendelssohn, engraved with the dates of his birth and death followed by a quotation, from Alexander Pope's well-known couplet, which conflated the advent of Mendelssohn with Isaac Newton: "Nature and nature's laws lay hid in night/God said, let Moses be! And all was light!" Jeiteles modeled the exegesis of this verse on the recitation of the "four questions" in the Passover liturgy:

> And it shall come to pass that your children shall ask you: "What is this stone to you?" And you shall tell them: "It is a monument [Heb. *even zikaron*] to the man who opened our eyes, Moses son of Menahem whom God filled with wisdom so that he could instruct us. And had Moses not opened the path of learning before us, we would have remained in ignorance and darkness like the generations that came before, untouched by enlightenment and knowledge.... He is the man who established our name [Heb. *yadvashem*] among the nations, speaking on our behalf in order to clear us from imputations of wickedness ... and so we have erected this monument to his memory for generations to come.[11]

Jeiteles envisioned the use of Jewish ritual to mark the historic merger between Jewish redemption and Europe's liberation from its medieval Christian past. He did not, in the process, dispense with the Jewish obligation to keep the commandments. On the contrary, he endowed Mosaic legislation with the force of "nature's law" and all of the symbolic significance of the new age. Jeiteles insisted that there was no contradiction between his responsibilities as a Jew and his "perfect faith" [Heb. *emunah shlemah*] in the triumph of "wisdom." His own sense of duty to God was strengthened by the power of reason rather than weakened by the liberation of conscience. Taking his cue from Saul Berlin's radical deconstruction of the punitive conception of Exile (see above, chapter 5), Jeiteles rewrote the course of Jewish history in a major key. To him, the convergence between Jewish and universal time presented a source of wonderment, strengthening his belief in the benevolence of providence, evident in the prophetic promise to the Jewish people. Historical progress served to justify rather than diminish Jewish pride and elevate the commemoration of Mendelssohn above the contested, mutually exclusive memories of Christians and Jews.

Jeiteles was not alone. Other maskilim similarly entwined the regeneration of Jewish conscience with the moral and intellectual awakening of modern Europe. Addressing his "fellow maskilim and countrymen," Jacob Samuel Bick, an accomplished writer and translator from a prominent family of Jewish merchants in Brody, wrote:

> When God took pity upon the world and removed the obstinacy from the hearts of the people of Europe and the clouds of folly scattered and the lights of wisdom began to glimmer in Germany, France, and Spain and the other countries where people had reached a higher level of general education and earned the right to call themselves civilized, men of knowledge came together and began to cultivate all of the arts and sciences that are needful for human society.... At this time, virtue [Heb. *hatovah*] spread over the House of Jacob as well; for it is in the nature of wisdom to provide universal benefit. And so religious animosity ceased and love of humanity came in its stead and the nations began to embrace the people of Israel in their shared humanity.[12]

Still, such rhetoric rang false in the face of the confessional "conquest" of Hasidism. That Mendelssohn was a contemporary of the Baal Shem Tov (the founder of Hasidism) unsettled the providential course of history. A heightened sense of expectation left behind a feeling of decidedly contemporary unease. Even as Jewish intellectuals proclaimed that theirs was a time of light, they admitted to each other that they were stuck in the "darkest depths of the world." In 1857, Solomon Rubin, a well-traveled maskil with a capacious mind, who originally trained for the rabbinate but who subsequently became a serious scholar of Jewish mysticism and philosophy as well as one of the first Hebrew translators of Spinoza, lamented: "Our land Galicia remains appalling and horrible, mired in darkness and evil stench ... its paths strewn with thorns and barbs."[13] Depictions of progress focused on universal time; but Hasidic resistance to reason was typically reduced to a problem of space. "We imagined ourselves," wrote Samson Bloch, a maskil with a precocious interest in what we would call cultural anthropology, "purifying our hearts, cleansing our minds, and then turning darkness into light and the shadow of death into coherence, for we would be the bearers of the torches of justice and reason in a land of darkness, a candle illuminating the way for people walking in obscurity and a light onto their path."[14] Casting Hasidism in the role of its own uncanny, diabolical double, maskilic polemics depicted the contest over the soul of Jewish Galicia as a cosmic battle. "I was despised by my own brothers, the children of Israel," declared Zelig Mondshein, a popular teacher and one of the founders of the modern Jewish school in the Western Ukrainian town of Bolechow. Despite the fact that Mondshein was actually a prominent local figure, he lamented his own destiny to be "persecuted by the wretched flock of hypocrites [Heb. *ha-hasidah ha'evyonah*—this is an untranslatable pun on the word "hasidah," which refers both to Hasidism and to the word for "stork," an emblem of hypocrisy] which has spread its wings over our entire land of Galicia. . . . They blocked out the shining rays of wisdom, for they are rebels against the light. They strove to bolt the doors against it and to cover the earth with their folly. And they reserved their most implacable hatred for me and my friends. They fought against us because of our desire to expand understanding."[15]

The discrepancy between Mondshein's defensiveness and the actual course that his career took shows that the social history of relations between maskilim and Hasidim is more complicated than such rhetorical militancy suggests. That, however, was just the problem. Lowering the temperature of the literary assault on Hasidism invited the possibility of reading the Hasidic revolution from a secular perspective. Isaac Markus Jost, a German Jewish historian and educator who had "never mustered much faith in the future of Judaism" and who was a vocal advocate of political emancipation, had done precisely that.[16] Jost subjected Hasidism to more dispassionate scrutiny. Contrary to the persistent claim in the writings of maskilim that Hasidism was a pathological deviation from the rational path of Jewish historical development, Jost placed Hasidism within the context of the modern Jewish revolt against the rule of the rabbis. According to Jost, Hasidic emphasis on personal "spiritual satisfaction," although "exaggerated" in the relationship between the *tzaddik* and his followers, had helped to weaken the authority of Jewish law over the individual. Hasidism, Jost implied, ultimately served the cause of Jewish emancipation.[17] In this long view of human progress, Jost, heir to the Enlightenment, displayed his detachment from the "future of Judaism," a commitment that Eastern European Jewish Romantics refused to abandon.

Driven by the same doubts that informed contemporary hysteria about Hasidism, Nahman Krochmal, a philosopher whose work provided a touchstone for several generations of Eastern European Jewish thinkers, projected the collective anxieties of his peers onto a powerful new vision of Jewish historical development. Krochmal invigorated maskilic faith by translating the heightened awareness of the difference between outer darkness and inner light into a guiding principle of modern Jewish metaphysics. His unfinished *Guide for the Perplexed of Our Time* (Heb. *Moreh nevukhei ha-zman*, 1851), a polemical rereading of Maimonides' classic of medieval Jewish philosophy, *Guide for the Perplexed*, sought to alleviate the "perplexity" of living in a pathological present when imminent expectations of renewal seemed to have collapsed into the black hole of "fanaticism, superstition, and sanctimony." These three, in turn, bred the corresponding "sickness" of "materialism" and the "abandonment of religious practice altogether."[18] Like Perl, Krochmal invoked the language of modern dis/ease—what Heine called *"Zerrissenheit"*—to refer to the impossibility of faith and the pain of unbelief. Krochmal treated secularization not as an aberration but as a symptomatic response on the part of "perceptive people whose eyes are open to the contemporary degeneration [Heb. *anashim mifkahim 'ayin 'al ha-ma'avot ha-na'aseh*]" of Judaism to the latest manifestation of a "deep-rooted, ancient pathology." The modern cure, Krochmal said, was at least as bad as the old disease. The real danger of Hasidism and the persistence of false piety more generally was the way in which it discredited the Jewish tradition not so much for the "average man [Heb. *adam ha-prati*] and for the great mass of people [Heb. *kibbutz ha-rabim*]," who were "by nature" unlikely to relinquish their faith entirely but for those finer spirits who were scandalized by the discrepancy between their philosophical ideals and the contemporary degradation of Jewish life. In response to potential apostasy from the faith of Jewish intellectuals, Krochmal sought to produce a philosophically compelling defense of the modern age and to inspire "perceptive people" with moral purpose and a sense of Jewish self-consciousness.

Krochmal set out to show that to be modern and to live as a Jew did not constitute a historical contradiction in terms, an "act of self-negation," as Hegel had called it. Krochmal argued that the legal "content" of "faith in Scripture" (Heb. *ha-emunah ha-torayit*) was consistent with categories of rational reflection and spiritual experience characteristic of a mature and original "philosophy of religion" (Heb. *hokhmat ha-emunah*).[19] Moving beyond Wessely's claim that the "teaching of man" was fully compatible with the "teaching of God," Krochmal now insisted that Jewish law, properly understood and observed, was identical to the law of humanity, because it *was* the law of humanity. This idea did not originate with Krochmal; it goes all the way back to Philo, who considered Moses mankind's first legislator. Gentiles, Philo said, had appropriated the idea of moral and spiritual self-regulation from the Torah.[20] Paul had made much the same point in Romans; moral law was the special privilege of Jewish election inaccessible to gentiles without the direct intervention of God. But of course Krochmal did not have to go that far back. Krochmal had read Wessely.

Like Wessely, Krochmal defined the universal in terms of the Jewish particular. In his dialectical conception of the relationship between universal history and the eternity of Israel, the progressive development of "philosophy of religion" actually served the unfolding of the "spiritual essence" of Judaism, always already implicit in its "scriptural faith."[21] Other nations, Krochmal said, were subject to a "natural order" of generation and decline, but "our people, even though they are under the same law of nature with respect of material and sensible faculties, ever remain, as the rabbis said, 'with God in Babylon, with God in Elam' [alt. eternity]."

> For the universal [alt. absolute] spirit [Heb. *ha-ruhani ha-klali*] within us protects us and redeems us from the law that governs all things that are made to pass away.... All that has befallen us from the time that our nation first flowered to this day shows clearly how the three eras [of spiritual birth, flowering, and death] have come and gone, not twice but three times over, and how with every period of exhaustion, atrophy and loss, we have been renewed and always a new and vital spirit arose within us. If we fell, so too we rose, strengthened, and did not abandon God.[22]

Only through an "awareness of themselves as the bearers of "universal spirit" would Jewish intellectuals—the "perplexed of the modern age"—ensure that "Jewish culture remain[ed] vital and alive."[23] Where many of his contemporaries saw insoluble conflict between light and darkness, Krochmal saw an opportunity for moral growth and spiritual self-realization. One of the strengths of his argument lay in his transposition of wavering maskilic faith in the renewal of Jewish society into the realm of psychology. Krochmal transfigured the intellectual hope for Jewish renewal into an urgent ethical quest and channeled maskilic feelings of prostration before the forces of history into a heightened sense of personal responsibility.

The crisis of modernity revealed the imperative of discovering a "middle path" between two extremes of contemporary "idolatry," neither of which was authentically Jewish but a "symptom" of the general crisis of meaning that led to false piety and unbelief.[24]

> For, in the fullness of time [Krochmal wrote] and in our present vexation, with the multiplication of needs and the struggle for power over one another, it has become difficult to resolve the contradictions that now beset the heart on every side. The [philosophical] breach will only get wider and each of the two tendencies [false piety and unbelief] will become more extreme. Or there shall arise and flower from those tendencies, upon the first steps toward perception [of the truth], roots that bear gall and wormwood, beliefs, ideas, and mores as do uproot the

foundation of faith and sink its ramparts, and that will surely lead to death and destruction—and it is to this that the aforesaid quotation speaks, in fear and trembling for the fate of the believer who ascends God's mountain to ask: "What shall I do?"[25]

Referring here to a quotation from the Jerusalem Talmud, cited in the epigraph to chapter 2 of the *Guide*, Krochmal redefined the maskil as an observant Jew who made a conscious and deliberate choice to "walk in the middle."[26] According to Krochmal, the narrow path of Jewish renewal lay in avoiding two extremes, both based in "distorted interpretations of the Torah," and therefore complicit in the corruption of "modern times." Esotericism led to "fanaticism," signified by the path of the sun, and empirical science produced "unbelief," signified by the path of snow and ice.

Krochmal did not invoke Hasidism directly, since he saw it as part of the generic pathology of the times. He did not anticipate a resolution to the problem of "backwardness" that obsessed his readers and disciples in Galicia. He made no promises about the future eradication of Hasidism and the imminent return of the masses to a purified form of Judaism. Instead, he provided the "perplexed" with a non-messianic form of messianism. The conclusion of the long punitive period between the destruction of the Temple and the modern age was signified not by miraculous restoration of Jewish sovereignty but by the morally sovereign act of psychological resistance to evolutionary processes that turned some Jews into fanatics and others into atheists. The centerpiece of this apotheosis of Jewish moral autonomy was Krochmal's defense of the commandments based, I think, on a left-Hegelian reading of the second part of Mendelssohn's *Jerusalem*.

Krochmal's *Guide* presents the commandments as the practical—in Hegelian terms, historical—bridge between the "universal essence" of the Jewish people and the inner life of the modern individual. For Krochmal, the commandments constitute an "essential part not only of the individual's attachment to God but of the national attachment to God. It is through the commandments that a Jew and Jews as a people realize the knowledge of the absolute that is the goal of modern philosophical thought."[27] Krochmal insisted that the commandments have lost none of their relevance in the modern age. With communal discipline on the wane, they have actually gained in psychological and spiritual significance as an instrument of Jewish renovation. The commandments are at the core of Jewish self-liberation from the pressure of materialism—the force of things—and from blind obedience to the temporal authority of the state. Moral autonomy, the source of Reason in history, involves the willed transcendence of political necessity to which Jews, like everyone else, had to submit. The possibility for transcendence is the providential gift of the commandments, duties that Jews owe to God alone. Inscribed in the original Jewish language of freedom, the commandments explicitly contest the ideology of "civil union" that threatens the Jewish "nation" with dissolution and political enslavement by another name.

The discourse of moral renewal underpinning Krochmal's intellectual defense of Jewish modernity was not, as we have seen, directed chiefly against Hasidism but against liberalism. Although many Eastern European Jewish intellectuals connected the spread of Hasidism and the general atmosphere of social dissipation that also produced religious apathy, only Krochmal systematically linked both "fanaticism" and "atheism" to the ineluctable secularization of history in the modern age (a concern that informed his interest in Hegel). Produced in the 1830s and published ten years after Krochmal's death, the attempt at a genuinely Jewish philosophy of history stands out against the contemporary work of Jost, whose history provided liberal readers with an etiology of Jewish emancipation. It is not impossible that Krochmal's struggle to imbue the Jewish experience of modernity with religious significance was a direct response to Jost.

Devoid of any form of Jewish metaphysics, Jost's version of a Jewish usable past was a strictly political account of the "Israelites" that anticipated the dissolution of the Jewish collective and the political liberation of the Jewish individual from rabbinic authority, constituted and maintained by an oppressive medieval Christian state. As we have seen, Jost had discerned in Hasidism that beginning of a modern revolt against the authority of the medieval Jewish "church," and, implicitly, a progressive step toward the removal of internal obstacles to citizenship. Indifferent to the prospect of Jewish renewal, Jost granted no philosophical quarter to the Jewish modernism of Galician Romantics. For him, political emancipation meant that the individual was free to choose any form of worship, even one that was as manifestly "irrational" as Hasidism. A thoroughgoing rationalist himself, Jost anticipated that the course of history would in and of itself ensure the eventual disappearance of religion in any case. In the meantime, he was prepared to tolerate it; for liberals, the fight for Jewish political equality represented the real battlefront.

In contrast, Jewish Romantics in Galicia and elsewhere were inclined to read the contemporary German struggle for emancipation as a self-serving defense of religious laxity and social ambition. Maskilim were pained by the tension between personal freedom and moral autonomy. The first was, at best, a mixed blessing as well as an enormous risk because, as history had shown, people would not necessarily use it in order to embrace a rigorous program of intellectual and spiritual self-discipline that Krochmal prescribed as the ethos of the modern age. Maskilim deplored Jost's political "disinterestedness" as disloyal and delusional and rejected "citizenship" as a brittle juridical construct that could not compete with the bonds of ancestral faith that tied Jews together. "And when, you wise men of Germany [lit. 'Ashkenaz']," thundered Samuel David Luzzatto, a scholar, poet, and historian from Habsburg Trieste in a letter to Jost (1840), "will the Almighty open your eyes?"

> How long will you fail to see that in following the mob, you are causing national pride [Ger. *Nationalstolz*] to be laid low, and the language of our forefathers to be forgotten by our children, and for "Latinism" [Heb. *latitsizmus*] to grow in our midst every day? For as long as you give leave to our brothers to imagine that perfection resides in nothing other than resembling their neighbors and becoming important in their eyes, your hearts cannot be inclined, in the spirit of zeal for God, for the truth and for the love of your brothers, to teach them that virtue does not reside in what is visible to the eyes but reposes in the recesses of the heart and that the success of our people does not depend on emancipation but on the love of each for his brother, for we are bound together in fraternity like members of a single family. This is our great fortune.[28]

Luzzatto juxtaposed "emancipation" with "love"; the first represents the manifest truth of political rationality, the second the higher spiritual truth of the heart. Adopting a posture of aggrieved, Eastern European Jewish marginality, Luzzatto tars Jost, the German Jew, with the insidious pagan influence of "Latinism," the symbolic victory of imperial "Rome" over the national purity of colonial "Jerusalem." His romantic ideal of an affective "fraternity" between all Jews "reposes in the recesses of the heart" and erases the legacy of mutual recrimination, social hostility, and polemical rancor that characterized the "visible" differences between maskilim and their Hasidic opponents. In fact, Luzzatto's imaginative embrace of his "brothers" illustrates the proposition that the opposite of hate—in this case, the hatred of Hasidism on the part of Jewish Romantics—was not love, but Jost's political indifference and rational detachment.

This dialectical connection between "love" and "hate" had surfaced in maskilic debates about emancipation back in the 1820s. Jacob Samuel Bick, a writer, translator, and repentant Jewish Romantic from a prominent merchant family in Brody, enjoined his fellow maskilim to adopt a spirit of tolerance and fraternity in their treatment of the faith of the great masses of Jewish people. The well-connected Solomon Judah Rapoport, a leading figure in nineteenth-century Jewish scholarship as well as a notable talmudist who descended from a long line of Lemberg rabbis, was moved to respond to Bick's provocative defense of Hasidism. Rapoport retorted by invoking the link between faith and critical reason, anterior to "brotherhood," which was presumably blind. "For the Almighty has enlightened our minds only so that we could give light to the masses who remain in darkness. This does not mean that we ought to go mad ourselves. Nor should we start to caper wildly like goats just because all around us people have taken leave of their senses. Obviously, our position does not imply intolerance."[29]

Rapoport was responding directly to Bick's comparison of Galician intellectuals with the authors of the Terror during the final stage of the French Revolution. His clever rejoinder merged a stock image of Hasidic revelry with the revolutionary image of the wild dance of French sans-culottes who were thirsty for blood. In other words, he was calling Bick a Jacobin, mindlessly in thrall to the intemperance and folly of the Jewish crowd. Rapoport took care to remind Bick that the catastrophic violence of the French Revolution was not the result of too much reason, but too little: "The first cause of the revolt of the French in 1789 . . . was, as is well known to every scholar, only the excessive poverty of the people and their claims against the caprice and greed of the nobility, which, as far as the people were concerned, was the reason for every one of their troubles. The rebels did not scream for knowledge, only for bread."

Evidently, Bick and Rapoport were not really arguing about the merits of Hasidism. At stake was the relationship between Jewish intellectuals and the Jewish masses. Such debates became particularly significant against the background of political changes that made it impossible to take for granted the social authority of those who shared Rapoport's familial background and scholarly credentials and to rely on government support in the creation of a model Jewish society. The debate over Hasidism tapped into a much deeper crisis of conscience that ultimately moved many Jewish Romantics to declare themselves "lovers of Zion." Rapoport's letter to Bick (which had circulated only among friends) was first published in 1873, by Peretz Smolenskin, a maskil who had abandoned the Kantian moral imperative for the "wild dance" of "national pride."[30]

8 Paradise

In 1860, Sh. J. Fuenn published the first-ever history of Jewish Vilna. Entitled *City of Faith* (Heb. *Kiryah ne'emanah*), the book located Vilna at the center of rabbinic learning. But its author was hardly a traditional rabbi. Throughout his long life, Fuenn continued to play a leading role in the various projects and social initiatives that consumed the attention of maskilim in the "Jerusalem of Lithuania." An eminent talmudist, Fuenn also had a distinguished career in the Russian civil service. In 1844, he was appointed to teach Jewish history and the Hebrew language at the Vilna Rabbinical Seminary. In 1856, the liberal governor-general of the Vilna district promoted him to the office of inspector for all the government-funded Jewish schools in the province, a position Fuenn held until the government curtailed its support for Jewish education in the late 1870s. While employed by the state to promote the "official enlightenment" of Russian Jewry, Fuenn produced numerous original works of Jewish scholarship, translated German Jewish historical fiction, and founded a Hebrew literary and critical journal called *The Vineyard* (Heb. *Hakarmel*), which endured for twenty years.

City of Faith was a reflection of Fuenn's personal experience of Vilna as a place where Jewish intellectuals traced their own collective identity back to the rabbinic ideal of scholarly rigor and independence of mind, exemplified chiefly by R. Elijah ben Solomon. Known as the Gaon (Heb. "genius") of Vilna and venerated for his erudition, his dedication to Torah study, and the broad range of his interests that extended from mysticism to mathematics, Elijah ben Solomon held no communal office and had no school of his own. In the 1770s, the Gaon emerged from the seclusion of the study house to take a public stand against Hasidism. His principled resistance to the spirit of popular folly provided a model of progressive leadership for Vilna maskilim who likewise adopted a lofty, disinterested perspective even when they descended into the fray of communal politics. While *City of Faith* located the Gaon firmly within the precincts of traditional Jewish learning, Fuenn described the personality of the great sage in a way that anticipated his own Romantic intellectual ideal. He took pains to stress the Gaon's stalwart moral heroism and characterized his deep understanding of the relationship between Torah and "philosophy" as rooted in a perfect synthesis of "reason and feeling, the mind and the heart."[1] But *City of Faith* also made another important point about the Haskalah. Fuenn's Vilna, the northern paradise where the ambience of the study house suffused the culture of modern Jewish renewal, was providentially marked by imperial favor.[2]

Fuenn devoted the introductory part of *City of Faith* to a brief history of legal privileges granted to Vilna's Jewish community. The last and longest section focused on the Russian period between the end of the partitions in the 1790s and the reign of Alexander I (r. 1801–1825). In Fuenn's narrative, the modern age of the pax Romanov began between the Russian defeat of Kościuszko's Polish army in 1794, which ended more than a century of intermittent war and violence along the Polish frontier, and Alexander's victory over Napoleon in 1812. Thus, the "medieval" age of Polish discord and communal conflict culminated in the intellectual triumph of the Gaon over Hasidism and closed with his death in 1797, almost simultaneously with the beginning of Russian rule. The Russian era of "peace" opened the way for the Gaon's disciples, with whom Fuenn implicitly placed his own generation, although the book never actually reaches this point—and with good reason. By 1860, the benefits of imperial rule in Vilna had become an increasingly sensitive subject, as rumors of another Polish rebellion against the autocracy began to flow back to St. Petersburg, not only from Warsaw but from the northwestern periphery. Local tensions between Polish patriots and the Russian government had gotten so heated that, in 1861, martial law had been imposed on the Vilna, Kovno, and Grodno districts. Throughout the late 1850s and early 1860s, the question of Jewish loyalty was continuously discussed both among Jewish and Polish writers. Fuenn was not an antiquarian: the connection between empire and Vilna's identity as a Jewish city was, for him, an immediately urgent concern. Drawing a straight line between the dawn of "enlightenment" under Alexander I and the era of intellectual renewal, vouchsafed by the wise policies of Alexander II, Fuenn made this point clear:

> One is apt to harden one's heart against the generation [of Alexander I], for they did not have the intellectual capacity to understand his royal will. They did not take advantage afforded by his good and wise [policies] in order to be of use to themselves and so to benefit their descendants. But heaven forbid that we should blame them, for they did not act maliciously in rejecting the good that was put before them, but rather from ignorance, from failure to appreciate their political position, and from a short-sighted view of what history expected of them: learning Russian and acquiring other forms of knowledge that prepares a person [to be self-sufficient] instead of waiting for handouts at the doors of the rich.

For the Polish government had kept them at a distance from the world and did not offer them any opportunity to get near institutions of higher learning. And now that the sun of our own Alexander has risen, who is to light their path? Who is to point out the significance of this moment . . . so that people may open up their ears to hear the voice of time and to do that which is incumbent upon us all.[3]

Fuenn's language becomes increasingly elliptical as he moves toward the present; he needs to acknowledge the decisive nature of the choice between "Poland" and "Russia" without explicitly conceding that the issue is still very much alive. Jewish Vilna, Fuenn argued, despite ready evidence to the contrary, had always been a peace-loving, reasonable "loyal city," not a hotbed of religious and political fanaticism (here, the relevance of the Gaon's struggle against Hasidism becomes immediately obvious). His title attests both to the moral integrity of Vilna's modern Jewish elite—the faithful "disciples" of the Vilna Gaon—and to their unimpeachable loyalty to the emperor.

To Jewish intellectuals who might have felt persuaded by the justice of Poland's cause, Fuenn's polemical point was plain: Judaism was always already enabled and supported by imperial patronage. Polish nationalism was a false idol, akin to other popular delusions, such as Hasidism. In 1860, such a position was no longer a given in Jewish educated circles, which is why Fuenn felt compelled to write *City of Faith*. During the reign of Nicholas I, Russian authorities could take the loyalty of northern maskilim for granted. Vilna's "official enlightenment" was a brainchild of Nicholas's minister of education, S. S. Uvarov. Moreover, the first Polish uprising in November of 1830 had hardly touched Jewish Vilna at all (in Warsaw, it was a different story). But by 1860, the civic identity of "Jewish Vilna" had become much more complex. For one thing, the noble conspiracies of the late 1820s were spilling into the streets. In 1830, the struggle against Russia could still be treated as a war over the question of political legitimacy. Thirty years later, the rhetoric of the January uprising explicitly stressed the promise of popular liberation and involved the contested and confessionally diverse territories of the northwest. Nurtured by the local memory of Polish Romanticism and attached to the figure of its own native bard, Adam Mickiewicz, Vilna's Polishness was no longer the preserve of a small aristocratic circle. Mickiewicz had translated the exclusive ethos of noble republicanism into an accessible lyric idiom that stressed the pathos and universality of Polish suffering under foreign rule. "After Mickiewicz," writes Czeslaw Milosz, "Lithuania . . . became a seat of the Muses."[4] Indeed, by mid-century, modern Polish poetry, Polish historical writing, and Polish drama had made Polish culture available to

Vilna's educated middle-class readers, many of them Jewish. At the same time, Polish intellectuals were beginning to recall the memory of the eighteenth-century alliance between the Polish nobility and the Jews as the literary ground of a modern Polish-Jewish symbiosis. In the overheated climate of the late 1850s, Fuenn was thus aware that the past of the "loyal city" was open to multiple interpretations.

After 1863, the imperial identity of the northern paradise became a still more pressing source of anxiety. Set against the background of the revolt that had just taken place, a Russian novel called *In the Heat of Time* (Rus. *Goriachee vremia,* 1871) invoked the imperial genealogy of Jewish modernity as a form of ideological prophylaxis against the appeal of Polish nationalism. The author, a Vilna maskil named Lev Levanda, drew a direct line between Vilna and St. Petersburg in opposition to the line linking Vilna and Warsaw, the capital of a past and future Poland. During the late 1860s, when Levanda was writing his book, Vilna's civic identity continued to generate heated debate, inspired by a shift in government policy. Responding to the threat of peasant participation in the January uprising, Russian authorities had undertaken an ambitious Russification campaign in the northwest borderlands. This educational initiative, tainted by corruption as well as recourse to physical and administrative coercion, failed to counteract the appeal of Catholic patriotism and Romantic nationalism, succeeding only fitfully in producing reluctant converts to Russian Orthodoxy.[5] In the dimmed light of a second and much less successful pass at "official enlightenment," Vilna's Jewish intellectuals confronted the legacy of their own imperial loyalties.

> We must never forget [cautioned the male Jewish protagonist of Levanda's novel] that it was *barbarous* Russia and not *civilized* Poland which first began to concern itself with our education and development. The awakening of our self-consciousness we owe to Russia and not to Poland. In a certain sense, Emperor Nicholas I was for us, the Jews, what Peter I had been for the Russians. What, on the other hand, did Prince Czartoryski ever do for our education? We did not exist, as far as he was concerned. But exist we did for Count Uvarov. He invented us [Jewish intellectuals] for the sake of Russia's education.[6]

The author of this little speech is Arkadii Sarin, a modern Jewish intellectual and a character with whose point of view Levanda obviously sympathized. But the novel also offers a Romantic counter-text to its own explicitly stated identification with empire. In contrast to Sarin, Levanda presents the reader with a trio of Jewish women, Polina, Sofia, and Meri. He juxtaposes the evolution of their erotic aspirations and their romance with Poland against the political education of Sarin. Levanda was not a pioneer here; Fuenn's image of Jewish loyalty was also heavily gendered. His biblical conceit of the "city of faith" is drawn from Isaiah 1:21, where the prophet chronicles the dereliction of "Jerusalem" in sexual terms. Fuenn's "city of faith" is a potentially errant woman, a "harlot," poised for a fall. Levanda, inspired by the dramatic tension inherent in the feminization of Zion, devised *In the Heat of the Times* as a dialogue between masculine reason and feminine sensibility.[7] The ambiguous resolution in favor of the former is considerably attenuated by the appeal of the transparently named Polina Krantz, the most unconventional and "liberated" figure in the novel who is also most closely identified with love for Poland, which, tragically, remains unrequited.

The author's own empathy for these passionate girls defeats his attempt to discipline the plot so that it conforms neatly to the ineluctable logic of historical progress, which rests with the Russians and with Sarin. The "heat" in the title alludes both to uncontrollable female desire and to the intensity of the moment of Polish independence that throws the orderly history of the Russian state and the modernization of the Jews off course. In fact, the novel ends in an ideological and temporal impasse. Levanda could not resolve the conflicting claims of progress and peace, associated with empire, and the moral claims of Polish freedom, which the Russian autocracy continued to suppress. Neither could Levanda get away from the fact that the condition of the Jews in the northern paradise of the Haskalah and throughout the Pale of Settlement was much like that of the Poles. The ideological "crisis" of the plot, says ChaeRan Freeze in her astute reading of Levanda's "politics of love," moved the author toward "some sort of Jewish populism."[8] Indeed, by the late 1870s, both Levanda and Fuenn had become enthusiastic "Palestinophiles." Their turn to Zionism may be read as an attempt to cut the Gordian knot between contending and contradictory loyalties and, instead, to create an autochthonous cultural space where the mind of Arkadii ("the Russian bear") Sarin and the loving heart of Polina Krantz could at last be reconciled.

By the time Levanda wrote *In the Heat of Time*, the association of women with social anarchy and sexual disorder was a well-established theme in the literature of the Haskalah. Projected onto images of ungovernable femininity, the problem of desire was also bound up with the politics of empire. In Levanda's work, the impossible Polish-Jewish romance elevates love above reason and impinges on the author's attempt to represent the historical triumph of Sarin, the Russian Jewish *raisonneur*. While the novel itself "speaks" in the same formal Russian as its hero, its rebellious, cosmopolitan heroines shuttle easily between polite French, street-wise Polish, and poetic English (the language of

Byron, who was both a Romantic revolutionary and a rebel against sexual convention). Charged with the taint of cultural promiscuity, female polyglotism drowns out the author's insistence on linguistic discipline and political containment. At the same time, the multiplicity of voices is what makes Levanda's novel a novel, rather than a transparent defense of Jewish assimilation into Russian society. Levanda's imaginative complicity with his irrepressible female characters, compared to whom poor Sarin is rather a stick, undermines the political point that he was trying to make; but the multiplicity of female voices also enabled him to put words to thoughts that he could not bring himself to articulate in his own name.

The affinity between imaginative freedom and sexual desire wreaked havoc with the poetics of Jewish transcendence, the language of which was Hebrew and the inspiration for which was God's own timeless words. The difficulties of adopting the unstable register of the novel, an idiom explicitly identified with the vagaries of female taste, to the divine language of reason and truth became especially acute when Jewish intellectuals lost the support of the state and began to depend more on the love of their readers. The ambiguities attendant on the "emancipation" of Hebrew literature during the era of the Great Reforms are evident in the contrast between the treatment of female desire in Abraham Mapu's historical novel *Love of Zion*, written during the Nicholaevan era of "official enlightenment" and published in 1853, and Judah Leib Gordon's "The Tip of the Yud," a novel in verse, first published in 1875, just after the government of Alexander II closed the rabbinical seminaries in Vilna and Zhitomir and withdrew all administrative funds from Jewish schools.

Against their own best intentions to reproduce a utopia of "perfected Jewish manhood," the writers of the Lithuanian Jerusalem set forth a modern Jewish discourse that consistently eluded their attempts at policing desire. In Mapu's *Love of Zion*, the most popular Jewish novel of the nineteenth century and possibly the century's most popular nontraditional Hebrew book, the divine language of paradise became a tantalizing idiom of feminine persuasion. In his penetrating critique of the novel, H. N. Shapira noted that despite his own best intentions Mapu wrote "not for love of the maidens of Jerusalem, but just for the love of girls."⁹ Like Levanda, Mapu adopted the subject position of his male protagonist but identified his own imagination with the fantasy life of the young girl whose erotic dreams control the movement of the plot. In *Love of Zion*, authorship itself reflected the unaccountable and unreasonable contrivance of female wishes to thwart divinely appointed plans. Conventionally read as a naive biblical pastoral "for children," *Love of Zion* is actually the first Jewish novel of development (Ger. *Bildungsroman*) concerned with the moral education of a desiring woman.

As Shapira intimated, the "love" in the plot of Mapu's novel supplanted the prophetic language of "Zion." In his correspondence, Mapu described his own work as a form of imaginative "ingathering." He saw himself as an original Romantic "visionary" engaged in the redemption of the "holy tongue" from its betrayal by contemporary translators from French and German.[10] The person that Mapu held chiefly responsible for this literary apostasy and for the corruption of Jewish taste was actually Kalman Shulman, a fellow maskil from Vilna. Shulman's very popular Hebrew translation of Eugène Sue's scandalous novel *Secrets of Paris* (Fr. *Mystères de Paris*, 1842) gave Mapu no rest.[11] Hebrew was supposed to elevate a bad "foreign" habit (reading novels) to the status of "Jewish matters," pursued for the sake of heaven. However, Mapu's treatment of his material actually blurred the difference between the modern language of sensibility and the divine language of Hebrew prophecy. The "love" in *Love of Zion* lowered the state of scripturally induced attentiveness to the ground of erotic self-absorption. Male readers of Mapu—and most of his Hebrew readers were male as well as young, although certainly not children—probably read this highly provocative book with one hand. The libidinal appeal of the plot unbuttoned the mind of even the most abstemious reader, so that it became difficult to tell whether one was being inspired or seduced. To M. L. Lilienblum, a Lithuanian maskil whose own struggle against the refractory life of the body became the subject of an overheated confessional autobiography called *Sins of Youth*, Mapu's biblical novels (after *Love of Zion*, he wrote another, *The Guilt of Samaria*) seemed to hover ambiguously between the sacred and the profane. Precisely for this reason, Lilienblum admitted, they had the power to arouse "the most prodigious excitement" (Heb. *hitlahavut 'atsumah*); the language here evokes an image of male sexual arousal. Lilienblum apparently did his illicit reading in the study house while standing erect at a lectern designed to hold rabbinic texts. This setting was bound to make the thrill of infraction still more delicious. In the ultimate act of religious displacement, Lilienblum juxtaposed his miraculous discovery of Mapu's work with his repudiation of the messianic "mysteries" of Kabbalah, a subject highly charged with erotic secrecy.[12]

Named Amnon and Tamar, the lovers in *Love of Zion* originated in the story of Amnon and Tamar in II Samuel, chapter 13. Besotted by her beauty, Amnon, the son of King David, rapes his half-sister Tamar. The violation triggers a chain of events that the biblical narrator connects to the eventual fall of the royal house of Israel. The challenges to David's rule ensuing from the rape of Tamar constitute the condign punishment for David's own "taking" of Bathsheba in chapter 12. After the rape, Amnon abandons Tamar. To avenge her, Tamar's brother Absalom, who also happens to be the king's favorite and the presumptive heir to the throne, kills Amnon. In the aftermath, Absalom rebels against his father. With David's armies in pursuit, Absalom is accidentally killed. The final act in the domestic tragedy of Amnon and Tamar, Absalom's senseless death, leaves David humiliated and inconsolable. Now, the future of the dynasty rests in the hands of Solomon, David's son from his near-adulterous and morally suspect union with Bathsheba. Solomon, associated by name with "peace," ironically ends up fulfilling Nathan's prophecy that the "sword will never depart from the house of David" (II Sam. 12:10) because David is responsible for getting Bathsheba's husband killed. Thus David's own extravagant appetites, both sexual and political, undermine support for the dynasty and eventually lead to the split of the Davidic empire under his grandson, Rehoboam.

Tamar's role as sexual catalyst in II Samuel recapitulates the seductive but essentially passive part of Bathsheba; the biblical historian never examines the extent of Bathsheba's willingness to cooperate with the plans of the king. In the case of Tamar, the question of female desire is rendered still more ambiguous because the figure of Tamar in II Samuel recalls the story of her namesake and ancestor in Genesis 38. This Tamar is a twice-widowed daughter-in-law of Judah, the ancestral progenitor of the Davidic dynasty. Fearing that his third son will also die if he weds her, Judah refuses to accede to the rule of levirate marriage. But Tamar will not be put off. Setting out to seduce Judah so that the family line may continue, she disguises herself as a prostitute. Her ruse is successful and she becomes pregnant; however, as an unmarried woman, she is charged with prostitution. Bringing forth the "signs" (the cord and the staff) that she had demanded from Judah when they were together, Tamar proves her "righteousness" and bears twins, a sign of divinely appointed plenitude.

The biblical intertext between Genesis 38 and II Samuel 13 juxtaposes a comedy of female sexual initiative with the tragedy of female sexual denial. The narrator in II Samuel suggests that Tamar's "virginity" is both a source of temptation and the only available means of female resistance to male power. In the first instance (Genesis), erotic activism promotes life. In the second (II Samuel), the refusal of sex leads to death and the near-destruction of the royal family. But the parallel between the two stories assumes that the moral and social threat attendant on the expression of female sexuality cannot be resolved, only contained. Whether she does or she doesn't, the biblical Tamar is equally damned, because in both instances she flouts male authority over her body. Whether she will or no, it is the exercise of sexual agency that ultimately leads to the loss of sexual value and ultimately puts an end to desire altogether. Neither in

Genesis nor in II Samuel does Tamar ever reenter the marriage market or have sex again.

The biblical texts about Tamar position female desire at the center of a power struggle between men; for the biblical historian, gender politics *is* politics. The same is true for Mapu, so much so, in fact, that he is prepared to send the reader back to II Samuel. *Love of Zion* picks up where the biblical intertext leaves off, in order to make Tamar fall in love with Amnon and thus repair the "house" that the original leaves in ruins. The act of marriage between Amnon and Tamar symbolically reconstitutes the Davidic dynasty and makes good on the messianic promise, broken in the biblical original as the result of the insoluble conflict between Amnon's desire and Tamar's resistance. Mapu capitalizes on the ambiguity—should she or shouldn't she?—in order to reconcile the tension that the biblical doubling of the enterprising widow and the violated virgin poses in such dramatic fashion. Unlike the biblical Tamar (Amnon's half-sister and victim), her modern namesake, the object of Amnon's love, must choose the object of her desire, but she must choose wisely and well. Insofar as she herself must settle on the proper suitor, she is also required to play the part of the other Tamar, Judah's daughter-in-law, who solicits her conquest by the side of the road.

Whereas the Bible creates a primal scene of sexual struggle in which there are only two opposing terms (Amnon/Tamar and Judah/Tamar), Mapu constructs a scenario in which female desire is first formed and developed (Ger. *gebildet*) and then rewarded. In the biblical story, the woman loses even when she wins; in Mapu's story, her submission is the ultimate sign of her victory. Disarmed rather than suppressed, the power of sex must be disciplined in the name of "love" and in the name of "Zion." Neither comedy nor tragedy, Mapu's novel of marriage conciliates individual wants with social and political goods, a philosophical compromise that the biblical historian cannot conceive. In *Love of Zion*, the education of desire becomes the true story of a "Jewish enlightenment."

Marriage between Amnon and Tamar represents the righting of a biblical wrong. Their union is affirmed by faith in the idea that history can reconcile freedom and necessity. In the Bible, desire presents a particular problem because the design of the divine creator remains obscure to human actors. Commandments are necessary because the traditional reader of God's words has no other way of knowing what God wants people to do. Just like Judah, he must be confronted with "signs" in order to reassure himself that Tamar has not truly "sinned" even though she acted in every way like a prostitute. In the absence of metaphysical certainty, only the results of their actions can distinguish Tamar the prostitute in Genesis from Tamar the virgin in II Samuel. Giving them the same name, the biblical narrator takes pains to underscore the possibility that the prostitute and the virgin may actually be the *same woman*. This is the reason that the expression of desire is always a dangerous mystery. In order for Judah and the reader to recognize whose side God is on, Tamar the prostitute must bear children; their appearance is the equivalent of the "signs" that she displays to Judah (maybe that's why there have to be two of them). Meanwhile, the conspicuous childlessness of Tamar, the eternally grieving, disgraced sister of Absalom, reflects the withdrawal of divine favor. In either case, the will of God cannot be anticipated, only followed.

In Mapu's work, the convergence between personal desire (sex) and the social order (marriage) constitutes a frontal assault on the biblical argument that the plain meaning of history, determined and revealed by God in any manner He chooses, is inaccessible to human reason. What is good, says the biblical author, is what God wills. Even His prophets cannot always understand what He is up to and try fruitlessly to evade His mysterious injunctions; Jonah's unwillingness to go to Nineveh and Moses' to return to Egypt are lessons in divine transcendence. But in *Love of Zion*, the "visionary" novelist understands God's purpose better than the reluctant prophet because, unlike the prophet who is only an instrument of revelation, the novelist identifies his own work of creation with God's. The marriage of Amnon and Tamar represents the essential affinity—the marriage—of human will and historical reason. The radical implications of the difference between Mapu's point of view and that of the biblical historian for the normative reading of Exile are clear, even though Mapu never actually suggests that he is rewriting the terms of the covenant. He doesn't have to; the omniscience of the creator-author shatters the impregnable darkness of biblical secrecy.

Mapu's attempt to domesticate the metaphysics of Jewish modernity demonstrates his faith in human perfectibility, a faith that was, perhaps, singularly at home in the Jerusalem of Lithuania. Still, in order for his trial to succeed, the heroine must be a worthy object. Unlike Amnon, who is always already the model of moral perfection with an obedient, impregnable body (even if that body is socially displaced), Tamar must be a woman poised to fall. The efficacy of the power of reason is measured against the distance that she is prepared to travel in order to defy it. There is no greater triumph for the Kantian ideal of personal autonomy than the conscience of a seductive, desiring woman—for Mapu, the very place where humanity proves most vulnerable to biological necessity. This is why, in the depiction of Tamar, Mapu must stack the deck against his heroine.

First, Tamar is the product of a union, initiated by her mother Tirzah, a renowned beauty, between her own idolatrous northern tribe of Ephraim and their pious southern neighbors. Tamar's father is Yedidiah, a "philanthropist, a descendant from the King of Judah, Minister of Finance, and worshipper of [the] one true God."[13] Pursued by all the young nobles of her own kin, Tirzah "despises [the men of Ephraim] with all their riches" and wants a man of "Judah and a resident of Jerusalem." A foil for her daughter, Tirzah wishes to have "him whom she may choose."[14] Under the wise rule of her husband's patriarchal order, peace between the two rival states is temporarily secured. The marriage of Tirzah and Yedidiah represents an initial act of female subversion of male authority in the name of their social conciliation. The moral education of Tamar recapitulates this generative scenario. When she becomes Amnon's wife, Tamar is reborn into her destiny as the daughter of desire.

However, the name Tirzah is double-edged: "tirtsah" can be read as either "she will desire" (Heb. *tirtseh*) or as "she will appease" (Heb. *tiratseh*). And, indeed, Tirzah's "choice" complements the wishes of her father entirely. An instrument of exchange between her father and her husband, Tirzah does not even consent in her own name. "Be you the messenger to my father for me," she tells Yedidiah, "and what he will tell you shall reveal my heart's best wish." In the courtship scene, Tirzah plays the part of the passive recipient. The amiable Yedidiah represents the corruption of "wisdom" by appearances. For all his good intentions, he is consistently deceived by the false suitor Azrikam because his capacity for judgment between truth and falsehood is rooted in the sensible world. Thus, despite the ironic nod to "God's blessing," the union of Tirzah and Yedidiah is only a secular joining of parts, an empirical exchange of beauty for honor. Significantly, in the list of his virtues, Yedidiah's "faith"—the purity of his reason—comes third, only after his more visible assets. In this scheme of things, Tirzah's practical marriage of convenience stands for "pseudo-enlightenment," Tamar's for freedom and truth.

Second, Mapu stresses Tamar's ambivalent sexual identity. On the one hand, she is sweet and gentle and has an innate sense of right and wrong. Associated with the pastoral qualities of the Judean landscape, she lives in harmony with the countryside. She is loving, gentle, and kind. On the other hand, Mapu repeatedly associates Tamar with the changeable, seductive power of the moon.[15] She is herself double-natured, like the figure of Tamar in the Bible, both a sexual risk-taker and a militantly chaste virgin. Like the "bisexual" date palm (Heb. *tamar*) in the Zohar, she possesses both masculine and feminine traits.[16] The fact that she has a twin brother, Teman, who is almost identical (in Hebrew, only a single consonant separates his name from hers), highlights her androgyny.

Aggressive and argumentative, Tamar can be the very image of "wrath." She will not hesitate to kill those who cross her. The detestable false bridegroom Azrikam compares her tongue to a "sharp sword."[17] When she herself suspects Amnon of infidelity, Tamar says that her "jealousy is deeper than the grave. I will crush the stranger [the other woman] and . . . with the storm of my vengeance I will destroy her."[18]

Like the widow Tamar in Genesis who tempts fate by the side of the road, Mapu's Tamar is inclined to wander off by herself. She challenges the feminine precincts of the home that the novel otherwise maintains. Her venturesome temperament suggests sexual risk. To highlight this point, Mapu sequesters Tamar's female double, her future sister-in-law. Named Peninah, this hidden "pearl" remains "concealed behind a rampart of rocks, and screened by trees and brushwood."[19] When her suitor, Teman, attempts to approach her, she tells him to talk to her mother and refuses even to tell him her name. At their second meeting, he asks for a formal introduction. Peninah again intones: "Ask my mother. I can do nothing. Let her do as she pleases with me."[20] The courtship of Teman and Peninah takes place in full view of Peninah's mother and offers a striking contrast to Tamar's highly charged first encounter with Amnon.

Unlike Peninah, Tamar meets Amnon outside and alone. She also makes the initial contact, by tossing a wreath across a stream. Naturally, as if to punish this immodest, come-hither behavior, the author unleashes a lion upon his wayward heroine. But here Mapu's provocative prose defeats his well-intentioned moralizing. To appreciate the dramatic point of Tamar's sexual escapade, the passage needs to be quoted in full.

> Tamar lifted her eyes, gripped by deadly fear, for out of the bushes came a vicious lion. His aspect was dreadful, his mane stood out like bristles, his tail was thick like an oak, his eyes darted with fire, his maw was like an open grave, and his tongue like a red flame, dry and thirsting for the blood of helpless victims. And here he was, sneaking up quietly and surely, his gaze fixed on the flock that grazed across the stream. He crouched, ready to pounce on the prey that suddenly crossed his field of vision. And Amnon made ready his bow, as quick as lightning, another second, and the lion, with one awful roar, was no more. For Amnon's arrow had pierced his guts [Heb. *klayot*, lit. "kidneys"] and he fell dead not ten paces from Tamar, who lay in a faint, languishing from fear. But Amnon's heart, which had been strong enough to defeat a lion, melted when he saw the beautiful swooning maiden Tamar. He left his herd, waded into the stream up to his neck, and he was like a man perplexed [leaning] before Tamar who was lying unconscious before his very eyes. And he called out to her in his strong voice, and his tears flowed like

living waters [Heb. *mayim hayyim*] down her cheeks; and he tried and tried to rouse her, until finally Tamar awoke. And her eyes opened and saw the lion fallen dead and her ears heard the words of the young man whispering to her: "Be still my lady, have no fear. The danger has gone, the peril has passed, for God strengthened the hand of your servant and my arrow has pierced the guts of the predator, here he is rolling in his blood before you, look at him and rejoice."

But Tamar's heart still beat fast from fear and happiness, and her eyes, filled with tears, moved up to the heavens and down to her beloved, her savior. Her heart whispered a million thanks, but her words failed her, and Amnon tried to still the storm raging in her heart until she was becalmed.[21]

There is no need for an elaborate Freudian intervention to appreciate the richly erotic affect of Mapu's best prose. Lest we miss the point, however, Mapu continually underscores the scopic quality of the scene. This one short passage contains fifteen separate references to eyes, sight, and seeing. Tamar exposes herself to Amnon and to the reader, so that the latter becomes complicit in Amnon's conquest. The wreath is a sexual invitation to her own deflowering, signified by the killing of the lion. Amnon pierces the "beast" through its kidneys, a word that may also be loosely translated as "loins." At any rate, all the action takes place below the waist.

The bloodletting yields to Amnon's release of "living waters." Like all the water imagery in this passage, this is an overdetermined sexual reference, both to ejaculation and to the ritual immersion of the bride that precedes traditional Jewish nuptials and subsequently follows consummation. The lion, of course, is not just a cigar. The animal is a transparent reference to Tamar's aggressive, phallic sexuality, dramatically penetrated by Amnon's own arrow. To underscore the symbolic proximity of the ravening animal, Mapu positions the swooning girl "not ten paces" from the very spot where the beast lies unconscious. In what can only be called a post-coital flutter of "fear and happiness," Tamar opens her eyes to see the "face of her beloved." Amnon, in turn, directs her gaze to the lion "rolling in his blood." Mapu's allusion to Ezekiel 16:6–7 evokes the image of a young girl in the moment of her sexual awakening; Amnon tells Tamar (and us) how to read this scene. This well-known verse is also used in the circumcision ceremony, where it refers to the impending "marriage" between God and Israel. Here, too, it marks the consummation of a divinely appointed union. With the "help of God" Amnon has killed the girl in order to make the woman live, like the lion, "in her blood." By this point in the story it is not difficult to imagine why the book scored such a hit with yeshivah boys.

Mapu presents Tamar as an object of male delectation. Although this association goes back to the biblical stories in which she was cast as the object of desire, quite possibly Mapu relied on more contemporary literary sources for his project. Tamar had appeared in the "erotic fantasies of Amnon" in the biblical verse drama *Amnon and Tamar* (Breslau, 1832) by Eleazar Raschkow, an Austrian physician, whose work in Jewish history and Hebrew poetry was deeply appreciated by Jewish intellectuals in the northwest provinces of the Pale.[22] The Hebrew poet Shalom Hakohen likewise included similar scenes from the story of Amnon and Tamar in his biblical saga about the royal house of David, *Nir david* (Vienna, 1834).

However, Mapu had hit on a crucial aspect of a familiar seduction scenario that had eluded his predecessors. The gendered logic of the novel presents a delectable Jewish princess not as a dangerous temptation to masculine powers of self-restraint but as a coveted sexual prize of male entitlement. Amnon does not actually have to undergo any kind of a trial to win the girl, because he is always already a prince and cannot help but conduct himself in a princely manner. The novel does not allow him much to do, except throw his weight around. For all of her natural discernment, it is beautiful, brilliant, seductive Tamar who must be convinced of his essential merits. In order to be worthy of him, she must fall in love with him before she finds out that he is rich and well-born. Unlike Yedidiah, whose "honor" is displayed before Tirzah, Amnon remains hidden from Tamar and must be continually sought out.

While Mapu continues to test his heroine's constancy until the very end of the novel, even when it no longer serves the plot, Amnon's nobility is never in doubt. In contrast to the purity of Amnon, the deliberate deferral of the anticipated happy ending demonstrates how unsure a thing female desire is. The moral of the story works according to the double standard of the fairytale, in which a princess's willingness to kiss a frog while he is still a frog brings her the potential reward of marriage to a prince. But the frog always knows that he is really a prince. For the frogs who may be reading this story, the message goes something like this. You too may be a prince waiting to be kissed by a princess. If you turn out to be only a frog in the end, it is not your fault. You just have not met a princess who is prepared to see past the fact that you appear to be a frog and discover your true inner prince. Any woman who sees you only as a frog cannot be a true princess and must not be worthy of you.

For princesses, the message is rather different. If the frog you've kissed turned out to be a frog and not the prince you were expecting, it is your own fault. Obviously, you should have known better. Whether it is your ability to tell the difference between a frog and a frog who is really a prince, or just the quality of your kissing, the problem still lies with you. Mapu wrote his novel for both frogs and princesses—there is evidence that *Love of Zion* found an audience among women, which would help to account for its unprecedented success—but he adopts the point of view of the frogs waiting desperately to be recognized as the princes they (and perhaps their mothers) thought they were.[23]

Thus, whatever suspense the novel generates does not come from the conflict between good and evil, which is summarily dispatched by the mechanical plot.[24] The reader knows that goodness will triumph because he is meant to identify with Amnon, whose victory is a matter of narrative certainty from the start. From Amnon's point of view, the pleasure of the text lies rather in watching the education—the taming—of Tamar. However, for the historian of Jewish culture, the main question raised by *Love of Zion* is this: why does Mapu have to work so hard to get Tamar properly married off? Why does female desire have to be so carefully stage-managed by the author? From their relative weight within the story, one might think that Tamar's potentially unstable and uncontrollable sexuality presents a greater obstacle to the triumph of enlightenment than all the material forces that Mapu arraigns on the other side. And one would be right, because desire leaves a crack in the foundation of modern Jewish metaphysics that cannot be healed.

For despite Mapu's strenuous efforts to reassure the reader that she can be redeemed, the persuasion of Tamar remains a fantasy. What starts out as a love match, driven by her sexual desire, ends up as a conventional social contract, a marriage rooted in the political realities of the relationship between two noble houses. That is the way it has to be, because once the fly of desire has been released into the ointment of history, there is nothing to ensure that Tamar will, in fact, stay tamed. At the end, in order to keep Tamar bound to Amnon, Mapu must rely on the same institutions of authority—the family, the community, and the state—that he was initially prepared to let her flout in the name of love. This is why he is so careful not to shift the ground beneath his own feet. He never questions the rightful rule of Yoram ("his highness"), the warrior-judge, whose fortuitous absence at the beginning leaves the principals free to act in accordance with their desires and therefore allows the story to take place. Yoram returns, as he must, to bring the "hearts of the parents to the children and unite the hearts of the lovers."[25] In the moral economy of the novel, the former is ultimately more significant than the latter because continuity must be assured. And, of course, some of Mapu's original readers must have seen, as his readers now see, this ending as a failure of nerve on the part of an author who was unwilling to face the implications of his own work. Indeed, the novel itself defeats Mapu's attempt at cultural prophylaxis against the charms of the desiring woman.

Love of Zion celebrates the very thing that makes Mapu most uncomfortable. In the act of disclosing the autonomy of desire, Mapu reopens the gap between self and society that the marriage between Amnon and Tamar was supposed to close. The last-minute return of Yoram, who embodies not only justice but also force, is a last-ditch effort to ensure history against the risk presented by Tamar. After all, what would happen if all the princesses suddenly realized that all the frogs they were supposed to kiss were really just frogs with a nice bedside manner? Or if the princesses decided that they no longer wished to take the risk involved in kissing anyone? Or, heaven forbid, that they preferred to start kissing each other and left the frogs to fend for themselves? After all, even the prospective marriage to a prince may not be all it's cracked up to be. Apparently no one is telling, since all fairytales, including Mapu's, seem to end with the tantalizing promise of happily ever after.

Like the taming of Tamar, the restoration of order under Yoram is a fantasy. Mapu's novel associates the union of reason and imagination with wise imperial administration that transcends local disputes, tribal rivalries, and provincial conflicts. Underpinning the marriage of Amnon and Tamar is a romantic vision of social conciliation that anticipates Fuenn's political ideal in *The City of Faith*. Indeed, both Mapu's novel and Fuenn's history were conceived in the long shadow cast by Nicholas's "official enlightenment." During the 1840s, administrative support for modern Jewish education created unprecedented employment opportunities for maskilim and enabled the pursuit of Hebrew literature and Jewish scholarship. For the first time since the 1780s, the project of Jewish renewal, buffeted by Hasidic opposition and the impact of secularization, seemed to gain ground. In Vilna, where traditional learning often served rather than inhibited the development of a "perfected Jewish manhood," state patronage of Jewish intellectuals generated near-messianic hopes. In his praise of Nicholas I, Fuenn reached back to Wessely's post-partition image of Joseph II. "Now our master the emperor," wrote Fuenn in a private letter to Betsalel Stern, the founder of Odessa's first modern Jewish school, "has taken it upon himself to be the tiller of our soil, to extirpate from among us every root that bears gall and wormwood, to purify the hearts of Israel of every evil design and to shower the dew of blessing upon this thirsty, yearning soil."[26]

Social conflict and political discontent in the era of the Great Reforms severely tested the political faith of Jewish Romantics in Russia—just as the withdrawal of the reforming state had done in Galicia. A historicist commitment to the redemptive ideal of imperial conciliation became increasingly difficult to sustain. During the last decade of his life (he died in 1867), Mapu's plots were getting more forced and his images of desiring women more abrasive. With the closing of the Vilna seminary in 1873, Jewish intellectuals lost their institutional connection with the reforming autocracy. At the same time, the state began to seem less and less like an effective instrument of ensuring progress and peace. Russian liberals and Russian conservatives both held the government responsible for failing to manage the disruptive consequences of "unserfment." Dispirited by the results of Russia's unfinished revolution from above, Russian educated society came to view the state as a "self-perpetuating apparatus responsible for the ignorance and misery of the population."[27]

Political disillusionment forced modern Jewish writers into direct confrontation with a refractory and unpredictable Jewish reading public. As the promise of imperial patronage faded, maskilim found themselves in the inglorious position of suppliants for the attention of middle-class Jewish consumers, uninformed and untrained readers of literature who had more interest in profits than prophets. By this point, too, Jewish orthodoxy had become more sophisticated in its efforts to counteract the incursions of Jewish intellectuals into Jewish education. Religious polarization and a conspicuous diminution of social power produced a revolution in the literature of the modern Jewish revival. In place of Mapu's marriage plot, Judah Leib Gordon, the last lion of Vilna's Jewish renaissance, installed "The Tip of the Yud," his story of the "chained wife," a dark fantasy of the poet's romantic despair.

Rich in interpretive possibilities, "The Tip of the Yud" is, among other things, an attack on the rabbinic monopoly on Jewish knowledge. At the core of the plot lies the problem of talmudic mediation of Scripture. Gordon skewers the language of rabbinic argument as the corrupt "speech" of Exile, in place of which he seeks to install the biblical language of the visionary poet, the vehicle of redemption and transcendence. The tipping point, as it were, is the figure of the Jewish woman, a representation of the desiring reader and the "creation" of the poet himself. If Mapu stacks the deck against Tamar in order to make her domestication that much more a triumph, Gordon does just the opposite. The text prepares the heroine for love, but ends with her refusal.

In *Love of Zion*, the author achieves a moral victory over his readers and rewards their expectations with Tamar's marriage. In "The Tip of the Yud," the poet concedes his defeat and then dooms his heroine to perpetual widowhood. *Love of Zion* enlists faith in the possibility of reconciling desire and responsibility through the process of sentimental education that the novel both represents and advocates. "The Tip of the Yud" taps into the impotent rage of Jewish intellectuals, deprived of authority over the future of Jewish culture. Abandoned by a new generation of modern Jews, the Hebrew poet transforms Mapu's biblical fantasy of literary seduction into a fantasy of punishment and revenge on the desiring reader, again projected onto the body of a woman. Her desolation represents his failure, her rejection of him, a sign of his unbearable guilt for his complicity in her seduction. The final desertion of the poet culminates in the renunciation of poetry for the prosy language of "train schedules" and the exhaustion of the Romantic impulse.

"The Tip of the Yud" tells a story of a beautiful woman named Bat-shua who enters into a conventional Jewish marriage to a talmudic prodigy named Hillel. Completely unprepared for the tasks of supporting a family, Hillel departs for America to make something of himself. Bat-shua, left with two children to support, opens a little store. In the meantime, the scene shifts to the era of the Great Reforms. Modernity comes to Bat-shua's pre-emancipation shtetl in the person of Fabi, a young widower with great prospects. Fabi arrives in town to oversee the building of the local railroad line. Unlike Hillel in every possible way, Fabi is enterprising, well spoken, charming, and rich. He falls in love with Bat-shua and offers to take her and her children away from her misery. Naturally, she falls for him as well. The only obstacle to their marriage is Hillel, now far away in Liverpool. Fabi dispatches a messenger to extract a divorce decree from the errant husband. For a sum of money, Hillel complies. Soon after, he boards a ship to America, only to disappear at sea as the victim of a wreck that leaves no survivors to testify to his death. The divorce decree is submitted to rabbinic judgment, but the local rabbi, a rigorist named Vofsi, declares it null and void because the name Hillel is incorrectly spelled; it's missing the letter "yud," the smallest jot in the Hebrew alphabet. The "tip" or "end" (Heb. *kotzo*) of the yud in the title is a play on the word *ketz* (end), alluding to the terrible consequences or end result of the missing letter out of all proportion to a cause of minute significance. Thanks to the corrupt document, Bat-shua remains forever "chained" (Heb. *'agunah*) to her dead husband. Fabi tries to persuade her to accept financial help from him but she refuses because the pair is now officially "estranged" from one another. In disgust, Fabi abandons Bat-shua to her fate. Left in poverty and squalor, she becomes a figure of pity and scorn for the local gossips. Eventually, she is forgotten by everyone. Even the yeshivah boys are more interested in railroad timetables than in the laws of the "deserted wife." By the end, Bat-shua presents a picture of utter desolation, "undone" by the tiny point of Jewish law represented by the letter yud.

At the heart of Bat-shua's story lies a struggle over language. Arrayed on one side is the traditional rabbinic "Aramaic," the male-marked vernacular of Jewish knowledge. The grammar of talmudic exegesis presumes to set boundaries on reading biblical texts but, in fact, enables a kind of interpretive abandon that gives rabbis virtually unlimited power to represent their own pronouncements as the word of God. Thus, Vofsi has a reputation for being a "strict" constructionist of the law (which means he is "never lacking for proof texts for his decisions"), but he wields his "formidable" dialectical skill like a cudgel. Vofsi is a "gaon"—a genius of talmudic interpretation—with the fist of a "Tatar."[28]

On the other side of the divide, Gordon positions the language of biblical metaphor in which "The Tip of the Yud" is composed. The imaginative work of the poet renews the inspired idiom of God's own creation and represents the "way of peace" (Heb. *derekh shalom*) between human will and divine goodness. Unlike the rabbi who requires the social and religious mediation of Aramaic, the poet writes in a language stamped straight upon the heart. The love between Bat-shua and her creator mirrors the love of Fabi, likewise expressed in the divinely inspired "voice of doves" that issues directly from the "depths of [his] soul."[29] Both languages are inscribed onto the body of Bat-shua, the locus of Jewish corporeality. Bat-shua constitutes the body of Israel, both profane and holy. Thematized in the parallel structure of the introductory material, Bat-shua's double-nature is the problem that anticipates the novel's plot.

In the first introduction, Gordon indulges in a vivid depiction of the Jewish female body as the source of sin and physical abjection. She is a thing, an instrument of reproduction, an animal, born in blood and destined so to die, after passing from one masculine "domain" to another. The poet can barely contain his sadistic pleasure and his self-induced disgust at the spectacle of female degradation that he has managed to conjure up. Stunned by the dramatic effect of Gordon's imagery, we are likely to miss the rhetorical point that the poet's generic "Jewish woman" is entirely made up of talmudic quotations. Thus, the poet's denigration of women to the status of animals and their exclusion from the temple of learning becomes an effect of rabbinic language. The perfected Jewish body has been reduced by deliberate rabbinic misprision of divine creation.

Viewed in this light, the first part of the introduction becomes a highly self-conscious grotesque, a very funny parody of talmudic mediation, implicated in Gordon's own poetic quest for a biblical poetics of transcendence. It is not, in other words, an indictment of the social conditions under which nineteenth-century Jewish women actually lived.[30] This investment in the significance of language becomes even clearer as we move to the second installment of the proem, in which we are introduced to the beautiful Bat-shua, who is both like and unlike all of the other "daughters of Israel."[31] In contrast to the female "object" of rabbinic textuality elaborated in the first part of the introduction, Bat-shua is an integral (Kantian?) subject, an autonomous being fashioned by the poet-creator-God. Composed of biblical metaphors, transmuted through the prism of the poetic imagination, Bat-shua—Gordon tells us—is "made up of whole stones."[32] Born of God's kiss, she is unlike all other human beings. Motherless, she passes directly from spirit to flesh. She is a queen, both virgin and temptress, who moves not only the most dedicated ascetic but the divine presence itself. Bat-shua is the product of art and of a language that is linked expressly to imaginative creativity. She is the Jewish body "in exile" redeemed by the poet's gift. Sculpted rather than born, Bat-shua is Galatea to the Hebrew poet's Pygmalion.

The ambiguity of Bat-shua's parentage is signified by her odd name, which is actually not her own name at all. She is called only the "daughter [Heb. *bat*] of Shua"; in Genesis 38:2, she first appears as the daughter of a Canaanite "named Shua" and the common-law wife of Judah. Her brief mention here anticipates the story of David and Bathsheba, whose name is also linked to this anonymous predecessor. In both instances, she catches the eye of her would-be seducer and husband and then becomes the matriarch of a royal line remarkable both for its proclivity to promiscuity and for its divinely appointed messianic destiny. It is possible to take this reading one step further; obviously, the name Judah also refers to Gordon in his self-appointed role as Bat-shua's lover, seduced, as it were, by his own creation. Indeed, the poem itself leaves the identity of Bat-shua's "maker" deliciously open: "Who is the craftsman," Gordon invites the reader to guess, "of such deft virtuosity / Who has hammered these [the various aspects of Bat-shua's beauty] at his forge?"[33] Indeed, Gordon himself is not only reflexively tied to the biblical *Judah* as well as to his descendant, King David, the first Hebrew poet—that is, to the two lovers of Bat-shua / Bathsheba. He also has a paternal tie to the "daughter" of Shua; in I Chronicles 7:32, a woman named "Shua" is the granddaughter of Asher, the eighth son of the patriarch Jacob. Asher was also the name of Gordon's father. What we have here, then, is a series of intricate textual references that connect the symbolically overdetermined figure of Bat-shua to Gordon's own identity as a "maker" of poetic effects and the author of a new language.

The story of Bat-shua's miraculous creation, related in the second part of the introduction, is undone by her imprisonment both in her father's house and in her married life. The shtetl where Bat-shua lives is a place governed by the corrupt semblance of Jewish language; as long as she is prepared to be governed by its arbitrary and despotic rules, she remains in a state of exile, estranged from herself. Subject to the authority of her father, himself a creature of talmudic dialectic, Bat-shua is "given" to Hillel, a talmudic genius whose words are dry and fruitless.

Appropriately, he displays his alleged exegetic command on a passage of text the subject of which is death inside the womb, one that, even by its own terms, represents an interpretive dead end about which there is nothing to say.[34] Hillel effectively kills the text before Vofsi, a much more distinguished talmudic expert, kills Bat-shua.

The only chance for Bat-shua to be restored to her true nature, to be redeemed from textual exile, arrives in the person of Fabi. Like Bat-shua herself, her lover is transparently named. Fabi is the diminutive of Faivush, the Yiddish version of Phoebus Apollo, the god of the sun and of poetry. The name echoes the Russian "Feb," the conventional designation for poet in Russian literature. Fabi is yet another self-reflexive reference that puts Gordon inside the text of the poem and defines his relationship to his own creation. But the most immediate and perhaps most complex source for Gordon's identification with Fabi comes from Heine's "The God Apollo," which appeared in Book I of *Romancero* (1848–1851). In this poem, a young nun nearly seduced by the divine music of the god of poetry goes in search of Apollo. Her fruitless quest gives way to a story about the "leading cantor ... in the German synagogue" known as "Rabbi Faibisch/Which means Phoebus in High German."[35] This Rabbi Faibisch is not exactly divine. Although he can strum the lyre "with feeling," he is more inclined to cards and other secular diversions. A free-thinker and a traveling actor, he can play at being "King David" or a fool or the devil with equal ease and to the same enthusiastic applause. While he can "sing the psalms of David" in their original Hebrew "mother-tongue," his only "muses" are the whores of Amsterdam. This is the problematic lineage that Gordon bestows on his hero, and, by extension, on his own "laurels" as the crowned king and "idol" of modern Hebrew poets. The intertextual link between Fabi/Gordon and Heine's "Rabbi Faibisch" will emerge with singular clarity in the consideration of Bat-shua as a signifier of Gordon's female reader, figured here in the collapse of the difference between the chaste, worshipful nun and the prostitute, always open for business.

In the poem, Fabi, the railroad "engineer" is both a romantic and an intellectual—"*maskil bkhol drakhav, libo lev matanah*." His persona is a manifestation of the Pygmalion effect that suffuses the plot of "The Tip of the Yud."[36] Like King David and the patriarch Judah, Fabi is initially seduced by the sight of Bat-shua. He is the modern version of the biblical original, a voyeur with a "telescope."[37] Like Apollo in Heine's poem, Fabi nearly seduces Bat-shua with "the voice of doves" and pries her out of her sexual prison with the elusive promise of freedom. In a reprise of her divine creation by a kiss, she kisses Fabi and is reborn.[38] And then—disaster!

What exactly happens at this point? To anyone even remotely familiar with the rabbinic system of deliberation and decision making, the so-called "legal" plot of "The Tip of the Yud" must seem absurd. If Gordon's intention was to indict rabbinic stringency in the face of human needs, he could not have picked a less credible scenario, so apt to be trivialized as polemical exaggeration. Gordon himself surely knew that the rabbinic emphasis on legal innovation (Heb. *hiddush*) works precisely against the kind of legal inflexibility that Vofsi the "Tatar" is allowed to exercise in the poem. In the real world, Bat-shua and Fabi would have gone to another rabbi; in fact, even within the poem, there are two other judges who are prepared to sign off on the divorce decree and to provide textual justification for their opinions. The whole point of talmudic dialectic is creative negotiation, based on the infinite play of rival precedents, not the establishment of absolute statutory edicts. As an attack on the so-called legal power of rabbis, the story fails. Gordon's modern biographer is perfectly right to insist that the poet had written a "satire, not a legal brief."[39]

But he is just as wrong to identify the "cause" of Gordon's satire as the "emancipation of women." At stake in "The Tip of the Yud" is a struggle over the heart of the Jewish reader, the issue that mattered to Gordon most *as a poet*. The object of satire here is the Jewish internalization of rabbinic language and the colonization of the Jewish body by the regime of the study house. In the crucial scene of confrontation between Bat-shua and Vofsi, the rabbi does not win by means of a superior ability to manipulate texts. His victory is not interpretive but "formal," based on the *Set Table* (Heb. *Shulhan 'arukh*), the early modern manual of Jewish law that by the nineteenth century had become a standard reference book for rabbis and for the educated laity. In other words, Vofsi's "decree" displays none of the extraordinary talmudic virtuosity for which he is supposedly famous. This is because Vofsi speaks in the collective idiom of the Jewish tradition; he articulates what everybody already knows. Tellingly, he pronounces his unimpeachable verdict in a "loud voice in Yiddish" (Heb. *bekol gadol yehudit*).[40] The phrasing and the syntax are ambiguous and, without stretching the text too much, could be rendered as a "loud Jewish voice." In other words, Vofsi speaks in the name of Judaism. At any rate, he speaks in the same language as Bat-shua and all other Jewish women. His authority cannot be gainsaid not because it has anything to do with interpreting the biblical text, but precisely because it has nothing to do with it.

The source of the problem, we recall, is a missing letter, a yud. Into that tiny space, the great collective voice of the oral tradition inserts itself and renders the meaning of Scripture beside the point. Vofsi speaks in the language of religious power, while Fabi only has the language of the heart, a language that tempts Bat-shua to freedom and extracts no further commitment. As in *Love of Zion*, the language of female sexual autonomy potentially disables masculine privilege. But the institution of talmudic culture—*not* the work of interpretation the poem itself performs—is infinitely potent and brooks no resistance. It has overtaken the Jewish body so completely that its effects on Bat-shua are instantaneous and palpable:

> The way a lead ball shoots forth from a cannon
> Wherever it touches down, there be murder, despair and death
> Just so the word-blast [Heb. *dibbur mefotsets*] from the rabbi's mouth
> Did touch the heart of the wretched one sitting there.
> How her hope became her disaster in one instance!
> Suddenly seized by a tremor, she fainted
> With a sound, like that of soul leaving body
> Fell to the ground, as though dead or senseless.
> And then the rabbi motioned to both his attendants
> And they picked her up and removed her.[41]

It is difficult to capture the "explosive" effect of Gordon's imagery here. Nevertheless, the quotation repays close scrutiny. Vofsi's "pronouncement"—the Hebrew turns the rabbi's "word" into a "thing" (Heb. *davar*)—is both punishing and phallic. Here, Vofsi reveals the hidden power of the letter yud, which "classical midrashic sources ... conceived as the letter or mark of circumcision," an "imprint" of the divine potency, the "sign of the Holy One himself ... inscribed onto the flesh."[42] The missile hits its target immediately, insofar as the absent-present yud goes straight to the heart of Bat-shua, to reverse the effects of the dangerous kiss that Bat-shua bestows on Fabi, thereby awakening her desire and bringing her to life. Here, the language of Bat-shua's instantaneous demise that undoes her temporary liberation is patently ambiguous, a parody of the covenantal consummation scene between Amnon and Tamar. Bat-shua has succumbed but she has also been penetrated unto death.

Insofar as the scene undoes Bat-shua's sexual submission to Fabi, Vofsi takes the place of the spectral Hillel, the absent husband who now reclaims his wife from her would-be seducer even from beyond the grave (Gordon has rewritten the David-Bathsheba-Uriah plot, where the prophet Nathan similarly invokes the presence of the dead husband in order to recall the lover to his sin). We have been mistaken in writing off the dead husband; Vofsi knows better. Behind Hillel—who only *seems* impotent—lurks the collective masculine power of the study house. Vofsi will restore to Hillel that which is rightfully his. By contrast, despite all his wealth and connections, Fabi has only his own words. In tempting Bat-shua, they also threaten to turn her into a "woman of pleasure," whose will may be beyond the control of any words that Fabi has to offer. Once she goes with Fabi, she can go with anyone else; once she goes searching for her Apollo, the nun in Heine's poem runs the risk of becoming one of Rabbi Feibisch's whores. In this impossible choice between the talmudic language of Jewish textual discipline and the fugitive biblical language of desire lies the real tragedy of the Jewish poet. He cannot command where he wishes gently to persuade. Jewish tradition does not speak with the voice of a dove.

The rabbinic "no!" silences Fabi. He knows now that there is no salvation. His words reach Bat-shua from an impassable distance. Leaving town, he writes her a letter in which he offers to support her in secret; but her "eternal answer" (Heb. *teshuvah nitsahat*) is "No, Fabi, I shall not."[43] The everlasting nay puts Bat-shua in the company of Vofsi. As happens so often throughout Gordon's work, rabbis and women speak the same language. Like the rabbi's, Bat-shua's is the adamantine "voice" of collective discipline that reduces a woman to her "husband's wife." There is an untranslatable pun here that beautifully makes the point implicit in Bat-shua's refusal. Bat-shua refers to herself as "ishah beit ishah." In the first instance, "ishah" means woman; in the second instance, "ishah" is a noun with a resumptive suffix, a construction that renders it as "of her husband." Only the most subtle phonetic difference separates the two words; a *mapik* (a dot inside the final letter *heh*) and an extra yud, both of which are literally points. Contracted to her husband forever, the woman (Heb. *ishah*) named Bat-shua nearly disappears. She has become Beit-ishah, "chained" forever to the empty house that belongs to a man who no longer exists. What brings about the tragic impasse at the end of the poem is not what the rabbi does; it is what Bat-shua does that matters. By the end, she is fully at one with the language that reduces her to someone else's body. Paradoxically, in this act of self-diminishment, Bat-shua reaches a kind of celestial, bodiless integrity that raises her above mere desire and personal feeling. Bat-shua does her duty and in that there is a passion all its own. The poet denies this dignity to Fabi, who stoops to make her an offer that one extends to a prostitute, a kept object that Bat-shua can never be. It is the offer one makes to a woman who is presumed to have fallen already; it is also an offer that makes us think Fabi is the one who has missed the point of the yud. While Bat-shua stands firm, it is her creator who falls. In that one irreversible gesture, Fabi the lover-poet becomes Rabbi Faibisch the procurer.

Against Bat-shua's own intractable will, Fabi can do nothing. Like Samuel Richardson's Clarissa and Pushkin's Tatiana (the heroine of

Eugene Onegin), Bat-shua transcends the instrumental moral code by which her society lives and against which her lover can offer only physical and economic relief, substituting one kind of chain for another. Loyal unto death, she is the only kind of woman worthy not only of the poet's desire but of his love. She is his steadfast, serious reader, who has narrowly avoided becoming a "woman of pleasure." But she is impossible, because serious readers—both Pushkin and Richardson knew this too—are not made by novels. They are made by stronger words than any that the modern author can offer. This, Gordon also knew full well, for the "explosive speech" of his own verse can only reach someone who is prepared to be destroyed by it.

The poet must make his own bid for textual authority from within the same language that he rejects. He must have Jewish readers who are "chained" to the tradition, the hold of which he is desperately trying to break. This is a paradoxical, Romantic ideal of culture, both integral and free, that Gordon here depicts as unsustainable. Either yeshivah boys will remain like Hillel or they will study railroad schedules and leave the study house for good. In either case, the story of the "chained wife" will be "effaced" as if she and her creator had never existed.[44]

Although the story is about the victimization of Bat-shua, her dejection mirrors Fabi's. Doomed to eternal "widowhood," like Mordechai Gold in *Revealer of Secrets*, he leaves town without even the consolation of a borrowed child. In the end, it remains unclear who leaves whom. Fabi's prostration in the face of Bat-shua's intransigence is a reflection of Gordon's own sense of helpless dependence on his reader. The poet imagines himself bereft of an audience, speaking in the voice of a dove but reaching no one. But, in fact, Gordon was a well-known supporter of women's education; women were among his most devoted readers.

In some sense, then, Fabi represents not the reality of Gordon's public position on the woman question, but the poet's ambivalent relationship to the modern Jewish lay reader—gendered female—whom he had expressly courted from the beginning of his career and whose heart he eventually won. Scholarly literature celebrates Gordon as an enlightened feminist, a pioneer in the relatively new sphere of Jewish women's education. Actually, his involvement with women's schooling was, for him, a sign of his own marginality. Despite his literary ambitions and his enormous erudition, the only job of public influence that he could get was as a teacher of girls, while his intellectual inferiors (provincial rabbis) commanded exclusively masculine attention. The love of his female readers was, for much the same reason, a mixed blessing. As Mapu already knew, the affections of the desiring reader were, by definition, unreliable. A poet and a Romantic, Gordon aspired to futurity. Like Bat-shua, he was "chained" to the tradition that threatened to "efface" his work, which could never inspire the extraordinary loyalty of Bat-shua. That is exactly the paradox that Gordon could not resolve. Indeed, if Bat-shua had given in and gone off with Fabi, how could Fabi have prevented her from falling for someone else with even nicer words? Once freed from Hillel and the all-powerful collective voice that he represents, what would have kept her tied to Fabi? Once liberated from the Text, readerly desire becomes unaccountable, unpredictable, uncontrollable.

The tragic elevation of Bat-shua and Gordon's identification with Rabbi Faibisch, the singing jester and whoremonger, is a measure of the poet's guilt about his own role in liberating the female reader. "Sir!" asserted Sheyna Wolf, a devoted admirer of Gordon's work, "had you written nothing but 'Tip of the Yud,' you would have made yourself a great name and earned eternal love." Nevertheless, "I do not know," Wolf allowed herself to wonder, "if the words of [that poem], depicting the power of defiance and the enchantment of love, had moved the hearts of its male readers as they had moved the women who had read them."[45] Gordon responded to the feminization of his audience with bemusement; but after "The Tip of the Yud," his work grew increasingly darker, "obsessed with the idea of destruction and a meaningless and desecrated history."[46] The prospect of being better understood by women than by men reduced the language of transcendence to the impermanent and ambiguous status of mere literature in which the poet was powerless to convey anything but the irremediable "moral chaos of human existence."[47] The love of women that Wolf promised to him was cold comfort when the assurance of popularity testified to the erosion of the sacred; once the nun flees from the convent besotted by the "lilting air" of an idol she will never return to her God.[48] Wolf's sincere adulation may have appealed to the poet's vanity; but her interpretive initiative also forced Gordon to acknowledge that the "birth of the reader must be at the cost of the death of the author."[49] Removed from the study house, Hebrew would soon be displaced either by Russian, or worse, by the language of women—the *mame-loshn*, the *vaybertaytsh*, the language that, as if in defiance of the holy tongue, dared to call itself Jewish.

9 Fall

If the northern paradise of "perfected Jewish manhood" had a bad conscience, then it spoke Yiddish and presided over the infamously "lawless world" of the southern provinces of the Pale of Settlement. Of course, the use of Eastern Europe's Jewish vernacular was not confined to Volhynia and Podolia. The Lithuanian Jerusalem nourished not only traditional Jewish learning and the beginnings of a modern Jewish literature in Hebrew. It also produced Ayzik Meyer Dik, the most successful Yiddish writer among Russia's Jewish Romantics. But in the imaginary geography of the Haskalah, the semantic and grammatical "chaos" of the Jewish vernacular was bound up with the moral and political disorder of the south, conquered by rapacious Hasidic confidence men and far away from the northern centers of civilization, Vilna and St. Petersburg.

In Volhynia, wrote Baer Levinsohn, "folly triumphs." But Lithuania "knows nothing of rebbes and diviners." There, "sages and learned men are most important."[1] Himself a lifelong southerner from the border town of Kremenetz, Levinsohn was one of the most prolific and well-informed writers of the Haskalah. His own career bore proof against his constant grousing about being stuck in a "benighted and obscure" place, a region impervious to the influence of "new people" where no one ever read newspapers or books.[2] For Levinsohn, the southern Jewish "argot" represented the psychological distance between the colonial hinterland and the metropolitan center where "great scholars, sages, and faithful Jews with the fear of God in them" knew "how to address the authorities" in languages that had an army and a navy. More problematically, the "dialect" without a classical Jewish past suggested the troubling possibility of Jewish life without a future.

The idiom of an unredeemed Jewish present, Yiddish reified the pathological condition of "these profane times" when philosophy was finding it impossible to "speak even afar off of the unspeakable."[3] Associated with a fallen world, Yiddish was a supremely unholy tongue, a language in which it was good to lie. Following Perl's *Revealer of Secrets,* a Hebrew novel "built upon a Yiddish foundation" that both affirmed the heroic struggle for truth and exposed the limits of all human knowledge, maskilim deployed Yiddish in the same spirit of romantic irony.[4] In its macaronic profusion of sources—midrash, proverbs, folktales, Hasidic stories, Central European vernacular literature—its rootedness in ordinary life, and its characteristic self-consciousness, maskilic Yiddish exemplified the "truly transcendental buffoonery" of all modern literature.[5]

Despite the avowal of Hebrew purism, the appeal of Yiddish proved irresistible to the Romantic Jewish imagination. What the twentieth-century linguist Zelig Kalmanovich said of Perl's "secret" affair with Yiddish was true of his successors as well. While deploring Yiddish as hopelessly unliterary, trivial, and ugly, Perl evidently approached his own Yiddish manuscripts (which he refused to publish) with a "true writer's loving attentiveness," lavished upon a language in which it was possible to express every "subtlety of thought and feeling."[6]

The first maskil to produce a programmatic rationale for writing in Yiddish was neither Perl nor Levinsohn, but Israel Aksenfeld, another native Jewish southerner and a renegade from the Podolian court of the *tzaddik* and mystical virtuoso, R. Nahman of Bratslav. Aksenfeld abandoned the Hasidic fold during the Napoleonic Wars when he was twenty-five years old. Employed as a military contractor, he traveled in Central Europe and eventually settled in Odessa. Aksenfeld turned to writing in Yiddish sometime in the 1830s when he was already financially independent. He saw an opportunity to publish some ten years later, during the era of "official enlightenment." In the 1840s, the government was most receptive to the reforming projects of the maskilim. Without state support, Aksenfeld had almost no hope of getting his work into print: Jewish publishers operated on a slim margin and thus tended to stick to traditional material. Censorship restrictions likewise stood in the way of experimentation. Aksenfeld took matters into his own hands and petitioned Uvarov (the minister of education who was also, we recall, the inventor of "official enlightenment") to incorporate Yiddish literature into the modern Jewish curriculum:

> Many Jewish writers have made attempts to help liberate their brethren from the errors which they nourish and to point out to them the primitive character of their superstitions. They have been striving in particular to save them from the injurious influence of the *hasidim*. . . . Moved by genuine patriotism and pure morality, Jewish writers have directed their works against these *hasidim* but without success. One could hardly expect them to be successful with the means which they applied to eradicate an evil which had become so deeply rooted. They wrote their works in Hebrew and German. Could these works ever have had any influence when the simple people for whom they were intended do not understand either of these languages?
>
> It is, therefore, necessary to apply different means, i.e., to write in such a language which the simple Jewish masses understand, to seek out the

comic as well as the educational events of real life, to attract the reader with a story so that the truth is always apparent but in the fine form of an interesting story. This difficult task I have undertaken.[7]

In *The Wimple* (1842), his only surviving novel, Aksenfeld again invoked the importance of producing a credible and convincing performance of the "educational events of real life" in order to unmask Hasidic depravity and popular folly. The theater, intones Oxman, a character who provides a kind of running commentary on the intrigue that drives the plot, "is more useful than a preacher's sermonizing. Here, in the theater, you enjoy a bit of 'make-believe' . . . but in the process moral lessons are smuggled into the hearts of the people who are watching and listening."[8] Yiddish, the only language in which it was possible to fool the masses, would also inoculate them against taking reality for "make-believe."

That, of course, was just the trouble: the merely tactical recourse to Yiddish in order to strip Hasidic "magic" of its aura reduced all speech to a pack of lies. The protagonist of *The Wimple*, an aspiring Jewish intellectual called Mikhl the Gravestone, revolts against Oxman's sophistic logic. The hasidim, he says, are consummate performers too. The "rebbes, with their [own] make-believe," turn everyone into "liars, windbags, and cripples."[9] If Jewish intellectuals begin to dissimulate in order to outwit their opponents, how shall the "people who are watching and listening" tell what is true and what is false? What is to keep the writers from catching the same "theater fever" that makes Hasidism so popular? Maskilim themselves are not immune to the temptations of play.

Mikhl's reflexive deconstruction of Oxman's philosophical innocence (a form of narcissism, really) potentially extends the metaphor of theatricalization to the gates of the northern paradise itself. Southern Jewish literature often depicted the "enlightened" *litvak*, a clever stranger from the Lithuanian Jerusalem, as a maker of mischief, a weaver of plots, a shape-shifter and a trickster.[10] But Mikhl, a radical skeptic, a self-appointed scourge of Jewish society, and the most successful deceiver in Aksenfeld's novel, is the first maskil to join the devil's party.

Aksenfeld's ambivalence about the signifying potential of Yiddish possibly reflected the lingering influence of the Bratslav court, where R. Nahman, the mystical storyteller, endeavored to turn the vernacular into a powerful medium of Hasidic magic. Originally recited in Yiddish, Nahman's tales brought the listener directly into contact with the divine. "Embarrassingly frank and concrete . . . too much like the life of ordinary human beings . . . the Bratslav tale illuminated the entire scheme of creation, the government of the universe and—most important—of redemption."[11] A disillusioned listener, Aksenfeld may have wished to demystify Jewish speech altogether.

Unlike Levinsohn, Aksenfeld did not fetishize Vilna as the paradise of order and "lawfulness." The first Jewish author to write exclusively in Yiddish and to write nothing but fiction, Aksenfeld produced an original Jewish novel based on a clever confidence game that was a mirror image of the Hasidic swindle. Perl, his only predecessor, could not bring himself to implicate his virtuous hero, Mordechai Gold, in the movement of the plot and kept him entombed in the prison house of his own metaphysics, the fictional equivalent of the drawer where Perl consigned his treasured Yiddish manuscripts. Aksenfeld accepted the fool's license granted to Yiddish and transformed the educational potentialities of realism into the most impressive conjuring trick of all. The apocalyptic conclusion of *Revealer of Secrets* foreclosed the possibility of modern Jewish literature; the removal of the hasidim portends the end of all plots. *The Wimple*, by contrast, interpreted the confrontation between maskilim and hasidim as a rhetorical play of surfaces or, better yet, a battle of wits that might go on interminably to fill the pages of a hundred novels, which Aksenfeld himself proceeded to write. Unfortunately, his prodigious output of manuscripts did not survive a disastrous fire that broke out at his publishers.

Jewish intellectuals vested their hopes for Jewish renewal in the providential completion of Mendelssohn's modern Jewish Bible. Aksenfeld transposed these messianic expectations into an ironic register by associating them with the proliferation of secular fiction. Anticipating the adoption of Russian "by decree," Yiddish becomes the language of infinite jests that emancipates the reader from the authority of sacred Jewish text. Stripped of a divine assurance of truth, Yiddish exposes the connection between the power of rhetorical persuasion and brute force. "You have to fight fire with fire," exhorts Oxman, the modern Jewish philistine.

> You have to use the weapons [of the *tzaddikim*] against them, their pointless, inane biblical nonsense, their smirking, their twisted grimaces. You have to ridicule them so that simple people will laugh at them in the streets. That's the only way to destroy their prestige. Furthermore, we have to ask the tsar to issue an order, compelling all the Jews to learn how to read and write. If Jews read the excellent works by modern Russian authors, our whole life would change. Jews would cast out the hasidim with stick and brick. God willing, I hope that happens within fifty years throughout the lands of the partitions [lit. Russian Poland], and herald the redemption and salvation of the shtetl.[12]

Until one gets to the last sentence of Oxman's assault, it is easy to miss that Aksenfeld is actually mocking him. The "Ox" represents himself as a civilized man of the world but ends up sounding like a petty thug who wishes to destroy the shtetl in order to save it. Oxman, the man who accuses Hasidic wonder-workers of exploiting human credulity, is actually a cynic and a materialist. His defense of culture boils down to "stick and brick," weapons liberally borrowed from the arsenal of the Russian military. This is the master that Oxman, the contractor, ultimately serves. Mikhl, initially enamored of Oxman's sophistication, barely escapes his mentor's moral blindness. The influence of Oxman nearly ensnares him in a dangerous confusion between a wish for freedom and a will to power. Oxman is, in his own way, Mikhl's rebbe. To gain a sense of moral autonomy, Mikhl must free himself from his pernicious tutelage. In the end, Aksenfeld's romantic comedy of "enlightenment" leads not to the apocalyptic "salvation of the shtetl" but to the Kantian "redemption" of the hero's self-critical faculty from political abjection and personal greed.

Despite the potential mass appeal of the vernacular, Aksenfeld's work had little to say to the masses. *The Wimple* aimed much more explicitly at middle-class Jewish readers who identified their own rising fortunes with the Russian state. Such people were all around Aksenfeld; indeed, he was one of them. The uneasy relationship between Mikhl and Oxman represented the secular double-consciousness of their creator. Both government "contractor" and Jewish intellectual, Aksenfeld could not resolve the tension between the objective historical "necessity" of enlightening the Jews, to which he was himself beholden, and the subjective aesthetic experience of freedom and play that he inscribed into his fiction. Writing in the 1830s and 1840s, Aksenfeld anticipated the emancipation anxieties of Jewish Romantics in the reign of the tsar-liberator.

In the era of the Great Reforms, Jews began to enter Russian universities and joined the ranks of the diplomaed intelligentsia. Alexander II introduced a policy of "selective integration," also known as "partial emancipation," that permitted certain categories of individuals—primarily university graduates, wealthy merchants, artisans, and a small number of professionals—to detach from their home communities and leave the Pale. "Selective integration" contributed to the growth of a Russian Jewish middle class, not only in Odessa but in St. Petersburg, Moscow, Warsaw, and other large cities. Educational opportunities and the development of commerce magnified social differences and promoted secularization. The relaxation of censorship restrictions helped to expand the literary marketplace and opened doors to careers in journalism and publishing. Family life was changing, too; divorce rates ran higher than in any other period in Russian Jewish history, and women appeared with increasing frequency as independent petitioners to state courts. A new generation of Jewish children, both sons and daughters, flocked to universities, to professional courses, and into the ranks of a restive Russian student movement.

To be sure, in the Nicholaevan period, Russian history had not stood still. Many of the dramatic changes that people experienced under the impact of the Great Reforms during the 1860s and 1870s originated in the policies of the previous reign. The abolition of serfdom had been much discussed within the Nicholaevan bureaucracy, and the establishment of a Western-style judiciary, which included the professionalization of the bar and the institution of open jury trials, was carried out by ministers who had trained in Nicholaevan law schools. But the post-reform climate of "openness"—the first era of *glasnost*—raised the palpable effects of Russia's social revolution to public consciousness. The impact of the abolition of serfdom was immediate and far-reaching and the general implications of emancipation became an urgent topic of discussion.

The "peasant question" went hand in hand with no less contentious public questions about women, young people (the so-called *studenchestvo*), and Jews. Their uncertain status in post-reform Russia touched off a common set of anxieties: how much freedom was enough to transform docile subjects into loyal and productive citizens? Would anarchy ensue once wives, children, laborers, and non-Christians got out from under the patriarchal tutelage of the state and the protection of their betters? Could they be trusted to maintain the peace, defend the frontiers, speak their minds, and dispense justice? Once freed from direct supervision, how could they be influenced, taught, and governed? As newspapers began to report on social disorders, revolutionary unrest, and the high incidence of urban criminal activity, topics that had been taboo under Nicholas I, it began to seem as if emancipation created more problems than it solved. Russian thinkers who had just recently decried the scandal of serfdom as the root of all evil were deeply disappointed with the state's apparent incapacity to manage the consequences of "unserfment." Gradually, progressive educated professionals began to insist on playing a more active role in the reconstruction of post-reform Russia. More and more, the talk among doctors, psychologists, lawyers, philanthropists, and teachers focused on devising benevolent and efficient means of social control in order to keep the empire together.

Against the background of partial emancipation, the future of Jewish renewal looked increasingly uncertain. Beginning in the 1860s, bourgeois Jews began to dominate the project of creating modern Russian Jewry. Organized and endowed, a new "Society for the Education of the Jews in Russia" (OPE), founded in St. Petersburg in 1863, symbolized the entry of educated professionals—doctors, lawyers, professors, accountants—and commercial elites into the business of enlightening the Jews. To the leadership of the OPE, "enlightenment" did not mean what it meant to Jewish Romantics. Socially conservative and deeply divided on the question of culture, the membership of the OPE was most invested in promoting Jewish entry into Russian institutions of higher learning. The OPE spent the lion's share of its liquid funds on student stipends and occupational training; its support of literature and scholarship was tentative and bore meager results. Aimed at making more Jews fit into the categories of the "emancipated" according to Russia law, the OPE fell in perfectly with a policy that rewarded "productivity" with civic integration. It was an agency dedicated to restructuring, rather than transfiguring, Jewish society. Although the OPE coopted the promise of "promoting enlightenment," its relentlessly practical ethos actually pushed the philosophical idealism of the Haskalah to the sidelines.[13]

Nevertheless, the patronage of Russian Jewish educated society remained the best hope for the creation of modern Jewish culture. Upwardly mobile, middle-class Jews were its only reliable consumers. In the 1860s and 1870s, their desire for self-improvement and their income sustained the slow growth of a Jewish periodical press, initially in Russian and then in Hebrew and Yiddish. For the first time, there were readers of a "fine" (Rus. *khudozehstvennaia*) literature dealing with Jewish themes. Many of these readers were women, accustomed to a broad range of reading matter in European languages and in the Jewish vernacular. With this new audience in mind, a small number of Jewish intellectuals began to consider a professional career in fiction writing. They started to experiment with a new style of middle-brow Jewish literature, written in Russian, and aimed at urban Jewish professionals and businessmen with only the rudiments of a traditional Jewish education but with a strong sense of Jewish attachment.

Together with Lev Levanda (see chapter 8), Osip Rabinovich and Grigorii Bogrov founded a literature for the modern Russian Jewish reader. Although traces of Jewish Romanticism could still be found in their work, Bogrov and Rabinovich were southern liberals, drawn to the secular virtues of self-help and faith in material progress. Levanda, whose connections to Jewish Romanticism were stronger, stood out as the only northerner among the three. Confining Judaism to the intimate sphere of family life, Levanda, Rabinovich, and Bogrov did not entirely abjure modern Jewish metaphysics. The maskilic ideal of transcendence instead found expression in the celebration of romantic love and domestic "bliss" (Rus. *shchastie*), the ineffable blessings of which justified the pursuit of wealth and legitimated the more earthly appetites for sex, comfort, and status. But even to them, the middle-class myth of a *good* fortune, although seductive, was not entirely satisfying, especially when viewed against the background of steep divorce rates, intergenerational, marital, and religious conflict, legal and residential restrictions, and endemic poverty.

In the work of Levanda, Rabinovich, and Bogrov, the language of great expectations was, naturally, Russian. For Sh. J. Abramovich, Yiddish became the language of middle-class Jewish frustration, disappointment, and unresolved guilt. Levanda, Rabinovich, and Bogrov represented the high hopes of progressive, educated Jews; Abramovich tapped into their worst fears—downward mobility, moral emptiness, alienation, the dissolution of family ties. Abramovich entered Jewish literature not as a vernacular writer for the masses, but as a participant in the heated debate among maskilim about the impact of secularization and the meaning of the emancipation experience. His provocative recourse to Yiddish was deeply implicated in the mid-century development of secular Jewish culture in Russian, which Abramovich saw as a symptom of moral capitulation on the part of Jewish intellectuals rather than as a sign of social success and cultural progress.

Adopting the language of Jewish lost causes, Abramovich translated Mendelssohn's pessimism about the "education of mankind" into a dystopian idiom of regression and decline. His most famous creation was the figure of Mendele the bookpeddler, a folksy alter ego who served as the narrator in most of his stories. Through Mendele, Abramovich spoke to a Jewish revival that had gone astray and was in danger of losing its original philosophical and ethical moorings. Mendele, the homegrown Jewish intellectual, whose stock and trade consisted primarily of ideas rather than goods, recalled the Haskalah to resistance against the material blandishments of a shallow and one-sided "civil union" with the gentiles, originally dismissed by Mendelssohn as a bad trade for an exclusive covenant with God. Mendele, whose name deliberately sent the reader back to Mendelssohn, recapitulated the philosopher's original doubts about the possibility of reconciling the unbreakable laws of Jewish life with temporal plans for universal "improvement." Abramovich, a "northerner" by origin but a "southerner" by vocation, contracted Mendelssohn's heavenly "Jerusalem" to the size of a Ukrainian shtetl, a tiny provincial hole on the edge of the Jewish world, in order to expose with devastating clarity the corruption of "Rome," relocated to the "northern" imperial capital of St. Petersburg, where the lure of a university diploma now beckoned to Jewish talent.

Abramovich's skepticism about the "utility" of secular education was ultimately traceable to Mendelssohn's wariness toward the politics of Jewish "improvement." His critique of Jewish materialism went much deeper than a distaste for middle-class ambition that the discourse of Jewish enlightenment increasingly seemed to serve (especially in the hands of the people who ran the OPE). In the 1860s, enlightenment had become virtually synonymous with positivism, a philosophical doctrine based on the premise that all rational judgments are subject to experimental verification and mathematical proof. Positivist morality was secular, and utilitarian, positivist aesthetics was a tool of social analysis. Representation, argued a new generation of radical Russian and Jewish intellectuals, had to be grounded in accurate description and methodical classification of all phenomena according to a set of common biological and economic norms.

Although positivism found its most vocal adherents within the Russian student movement and among revolutionaries, its influence was also discernible in the philanthropic ethos of the OPE, which supported individual efforts at self-help but for all intents and purposes abjured Jewish communal life and encouraged the abdication of social ties by making it possible for people to flee the Pale. Worse yet, positivism, in its stress on objective laws of social development, absolved the individual from moral responsibility for the persistence of poverty and squalor and justified self-seeking, egotistical behavior by reference to the survival instinct. From the perspective of Russian and Jewish Romantics, positivism bred a form of rational cynicism that spared no one and held nothing sacred; the most famous positivist of nineteenth-century Russian literature was the repentant murderer Rodion Romanovich Raskol'nikov, the hero of F. M. Dostoevsky's terribly current *Crime and Punishment* (1866). Echoing Dostoevsky, maskilim saw in positivism not a source of scientific progress but a pernicious form of "dreadful nihilism." "Enlightenment without faith and the fear of God," warned Vilna's David Gordon, the editor of a Hebrew weekly called *The Preacher* (Heb. *Hamagid*), "bears the seeds of death."[14]

In this cultural context, the attainment of secular education, the goal upon which Jewish society was supposed to stake its future, appeared not only vulgar but ethically suspect. If the Kantian imperative dignified the autonomy of each thinking individual as an end in itself, the acquisition of "useful" scientific information threatened to reduce every human being to the level of a laboratory specimen. At the end of the positivist dream of absolute knowledge, Abramovich glimpsed the onset of an obsession with "facts," which led to moral stupefaction followed by descent into mental paralysis. This was the dark Faustian plot of a fantastic novella called *The Nag* (Yid. *Di kliatche*, 1873), one of Abramovich's best-loved and most frequently reprinted works. The result of being driven into madness by a desperate accumulation of data for an exam, the breakdown of the protagonist—an aspiring Jewish university student whose efforts at self-improvement are underwritten by his association with a "benevolent" philanthropic "Society for the Prevention of Cruelty to Animals," obviously modeled on the

OPE—represented positivism not as a fulfillment but as a parody of enlightenment.

By the end of the novella, the diminutively named Yisroelik virtually crawls back into his mother's womb. His regression replays in a psychological key the most salient characteristic of the Mendele universe—its unredeemable backwardness. The collapse of Yisroelik signals the slippage between personal and collective interest that the new diplomaed intelligentsia refused to acknowledge despite hard evidence of a growing gap between rich and poor. Unlike deluded Yisroelik, Abramovich's Jewish grotesque, drawn on the margins of the empire, exhibits an impressive indifference to the political encroachments of reform, regulation, and order. Furthermore, Mendele's world threatens to throw the meaning of "emancipation" completely off-kilter. The southern *shtetl* accommodates a wide range of human eccentricity and redefines the northern ideal of a "perfected Jewish manhood" as a blissful state of freedom from the political responsibilities of good citizenship, the demanding habits of thrift, and the hygienic imperatives of bourgeois housekeeping. With Abramovich, Jewish literature leaves the study house for the bathhouse.

Born in 1836, Abramovich was a latecomer to the Haskalah. He came of age during the age of emancipation and was too old to reap the rewards of "official enlightenment." His initial years of professional floundering were symptomatic of the difficulties faced by Jewish intellectuals during the transition from the Nicholaevan period to the reign of Alexander II. Although he was known in Jewish intellectual circles as the author of an impressive range of works both in Hebrew and in Yiddish, Abramovich had difficulty finding a permanent place of employment. Despite his reputation for talmudic genius and his attempt to gain accreditation from the Zhitomir Rabbinical Seminary, Abramovich could not find steady work. Until the age of forty-five, his economic prospects were dim and his social position uncertain. At the mercy of the expanding Jewish private sector, Abramovich finally got a permanent paying job in 1881, as the director of the largest Jewish charity school (Talmud Torah) in Odessa. The appointment was engineered by his friends and admirers, most of whom were professionally educated, Russian-speaking, and middle-class.

By the time Abramovich arrived in Odessa, it was already better known for its cafés than for its yeshivahs. God-fearers claimed that seven fires of hell burned around the city, and learned "northerners," like Lilienblum, deplored the ignorance and greed of its leading citizens. Abramovich might have easily despaired of his place among the parvenus whose donations to the Talmud Torah now paid his salary. Instead, he came to see his arrival as the inception of a new literary vocation on

Jewish native ground. The writer's imaginative "return" to the shtetl in the breakthrough book *The Abridged Travels of Benjamin III* (Yid. *Kitser masoes binyomin hashlishi*, 1878) marked his permanent relocation and his attainment of status and security. After years of wandering through the small towns of the Volhynian backwoods, trying, like Mendele, to hock his literary wares, Abramovich finally settled in a city that was nothing at all like a shtetl. The construction of an autobiographical myth of return depended on the permanence of departure, as if the Jewish people could be loved only from a safe distance.

In the early years of his work as a writer, Abramovich actually lived far closer to the reality of the Jewish small town that subsequently became his trademark. The stories he had written back then read like modern chapbooks, in which the exercise of critical reason was linked with the possibility of transcending necessity and achieving a state of moral autonomy. The highly compressed, diverting plots of the early versions of *The Wishing Ring* (Yid. *Dos vintshfingerl*, 1865), *The Little Man* (Yid. *Dos kleyne mentshele*, 1864), and *Fishke the Lame* (Yid. *Fishke der krumer*, 1869) all turned on the effective resolution of ethical crises through self-conscious acts of contrition and reparation. In these stories, the *shtetl* served as a laboratory of personal redemption from the secular temptations of greed, ambition, and lust.[15] After *Benjamin III*, Abramovich went back and revised these early works as if he were actually revisiting the original site of his own enlightenment. Only at this point did his shtetl become stuck in time, permanently disfigured not so much by the "ugliness" of human misconduct—in the early works, such "ugliness" had always been open to the possibility of redemption—but by ineluctable material forces. Rooted in biological and economic competition, these forces were systemic and irremediable. While they could be manipulated or evaded with a varying degree of success, they could not be "improved" out of existence. Abramovich's imaginative return to Glupsk (Yid. "town of fools") and Kabtsansk (Yid. "town of beggars") represented the impossibility of overcoming contingency—the impossibility of ever leaving the Pale.

Beginning with *Benjamin III*, Abramovich set out deliberately to disfigure the shtetl. One of his most characteristic devices involved creating an illusion of proximity that was actually a form of deliberate distortion. The dynamic effect of a too-close reading is itself a form of estrangement from normal perception that strives toward the enlargement of the contextual field. It is the opposite of objectivity—and thus a parody of the positivist demand for more information—and it is crucial for an understanding of the disturbing impression that Abramovich's reductive readings often produce.

Abramovich adopted a form of "distended discourse" as a deliberate "assault" on the perception of the reader.[16] His myopia has the power to shift an indifferent account of physical realia (literally a list) into an eccentric register of an obsession. In the process, chaos breaks in on the attempt to impose meaning on an ungovernable material reality. Here, for instance, is Benjamin's microscopy of Glupsk's perilous ditches that threaten to engulf the armchair tourist of the shtetl in a flood of filth. Space is at war with the regulative, rational function of time, and space appears to be winning:

> When you arrive in Glupsk, by way of Teterev Street, you should, if you will excuse me, hop over one ditch, then another, and a little farther ahead, over a third, the biggest one, into which flow, if you will pardon my saying, all of the sewers and all of the town's chamber pots. This stream carries all kinds of goodies [Yid. *kol-tuv*] along, each day of a different color and smell, so that without much difficulty, one can determine the day of the week by the appearance of the puddle. If, for instance, the puddle contains rivulets yellowed by the sand that's used to clean floors, and they happen to carry fish scales, chicken bones and heads, shreds of wool, and shards of burnt hoof—then you know, today is Friday! Take your besom and your ladle and go on, if you will excuse me, to the bathhouse! If the rivulets are carrying egg shells, onion and radish peelings, liver tendons, herring tails and chewed up marrow bones—congratulations, children of Israel! It is Sabbath day. Celebrate and rejoice! Eat up your pudding in good health! If the rivulets are barely moving, and dragging along burnt clods of kasha, dried up bits of dough, torn rags, a mildewed sponge—this means today is Sunday.[17]

The ceaseless circulation of garbage mocks the orderly passage of time, the signifier of Jewish transcendence in a world full of random debris. The transition from holy to profane, from Friday to Sabbath and back again, is marked by the detritus of digestion continuously vomited up the sewer, where Benjamin, both the narrator and the hero of the novel, appears to be entirely at home. The proximity of "chamber pots" evokes, "if you will excuse me," the inevitable appearance of shit to which the Jewish presence in Glupsk is ultimately reduced. Animal parts stand for the distinct possibility of human "dismemberment." In fact, just a little further down the page, Benjamin considerately warns the reader of the possibility of "breaking a leg" on the jagged cobblestones, lying "upturned" in the middle of the street. The treacherous space of the shtetl takes its revenge on the reader and brings him to his knees.

In his ironic introduction to the late (1888) version of *Fishke the Lame*, Abramovich makes explicit the point of the debilitating encounter with the shtetl solicited by Benjamin's travelogue. The introduction addresses Abramovich's intended audience, represented in the person of Menashe Morgulis, his friend from the Zhitomir Seminary. Unlike Abramovich, who never graduated, Morgulis got his diploma and eventually rose to become a successful Odessa lawyer and a respected Jewish scholar and journalist. Addressing Morgulis directly, Abramovich subverts the comforting teleology of Romantic historicism: "Yes," he acknowledges to Morgulis, "you and I started our literary work at one and the same time."

> But my fate was different from yours. You have climbed very far up, to deal with the diamonds, both polished and rough, of Jewish history. You have exhibited the most beautiful jewels of the past of our people, the best and most precious things in its life . . . But I was destined to lower myself to the lowest rung of Jewish life, to the very cellars. My heritage consists of rags and rot. I am constantly preoccupied with beggars, with the poor with the indigent, with useless small-timers, clowns and other creatures, squalid and vile. I dream only of scroungers. The Jewish beggar's pack, that enormous, everlasting Jewish burden ceaselessly hovers before my eyes. Everywhere I turn, it flickers in front of me. Every story I try to tell, the beggar's pack comes immediately to mind.[18]

The shtetl presents Morgulis, a beneficiary of "universal" progress and a believer in the redemptive myth of Jewish time, with a treacherous Jewish present-continuous. Exile, signified by the "everlasting beggar's pack," is an interminable, incurable condition of human neediness, the enormity of which can only be conveyed through the power of fantasy born not in the head, but in the "cellar" of the body. The "beggar's pack" that everyone is dragging around is the human body itself, a bottomless pit of desire, a begging, "scrounging" thing, "squalid and vile," the real counterpoint to the illusion of intellectual self-sufficiency and moral restraint that "R. Hillel, R. Meir, R. Akiva, and other men of renown" represent to Morgulis. Abramovich ironically casts his own "stories" in contrast to the idealized Jewish "history" that Morgulis was even then attempting to write. The names "R. Hillel, R. Meir, and R. Akiva" refer to an actual piece of scholarship that Morgulis was working on during the late 1880s and finally published as a series of historical "Sketches from the Talmudic Era" (Odessa, 1900).

Abramovich contrasted the reasonableness of such a usable past with the compulsive power of fiction-making to which he had willfully and abjectly succumbed. Like all fantasies, Abramovich's "low" stories are ones that he could not help telling. Unbidden, noisy squatters, they set up camp in his imagination and then refused to leave. In *Fishke*, Abramovich figured his literary "return" to the shtetl as a form of corporeal imprisonment (signified by Fishke's physical debility), but in *Benjamin III*, the Jewish mind, tempted by the promise of transcendence, found freedom within, not beyond, the body. Reproduction had replaced new creation as the proper object of modern Jewish writing.

Benjamin III is the youngest, best-beloved son of Israel (the patriarch Jacob) as well as the proverbial "third" son of Russian fairytales, generally named Ivan and depicted as an innocent dreamer, a charmer who lives in a world of his own. Like Ivan, Benjamin spends most of his time warming his backside, although he does so at the study house rather than at home by the hearth. Unlike Yisroelik, the ambitious modern protagonist of *The Nag*, driven mad by a positivist quest for useful information, Benjamin is a romantic Jewish reader, a Quixote whose imagination is transported by messianic fantasies. Inspired by a bit of dried carob brought by an emissary from the Holy Land, Benjamin decides to leave his hometown, Tuneyadevke ("village of deadbeats"), for Jerusalem. Along with his sidekick and loyal Sancho, here named Senderl, Benjamin wanders through the Ukrainian hinterland and gets as far as the district capital of Dneprovitz (probably Kiev). But the journey is summarily interrupted when Benjamin and Senderl are impressed into the army by a couple of Jewish thugs. After spending some time in the garrison, Benjamin decides that he has had enough soldiering; there is delicious irony here, derived from the fact that the biblical tribe of Benjamin epitomizes strength and ferocity. In a surreal court-martial, Benjamin acquits himself of all future military service and is allowed, along with Senderl, to depart, after being declared mentally unfit. At the end, the two return to Tuneyadevke and to their spousal responsibilities. A Yiddish romance, *Benjamin III* upstages the historicist conventions of the European novel and, unlike the real Quixote, culminates in a refusal to be reconciled to reality.

One of the most conspicuous narrative incongruities of *Benjamin III* has to do with Abramovich's representation of military service. On the one hand, Benjamin's court-martial before a mixed military-civilian tribunal is distinctly post-reform. In 1874, the government had replaced the impressment system with universal conscription by lottery and began to issue formal deferments. Under Nicholaevan military regulations, Benjamin would have been entered under the Jewish quota of recruits. If he had been released, he would have been required to supply a substitute for himself. On the other hand, the Jewish thugs (Yid. *khappers*) who nab Benjamin and Senderl are drawn from the repertoire of Nicholaevan horrors. Abramovich explicitly informs the reader that the story is set in the previous reign, but he confuses the issue by introducing transparently sarcastic allusions to the imperial ambitions of "Alexander the Great," references that pertain unmistakably to the Russo-Turkish War (1876–1877). This incongruity is another example of the way in which the space of the shtetl consistently defeats the orderly passage of time.

But there is more to it: the difference between the Nicholaevan draft and conscription by lottery is crucial to Abramovich's supple critique of Russian Jewish liberalism. Under Nicholas, the state had relied on existing "corporations" of estate and confession to gather recruits. The army did not draft individuals. Rather, the Ministry of War issued its quotas to communities to which each individual legally belonged. These included the peasant *mir,* the Jewish *kahal,* and the urban municipality. Each community was responsible for filling the quotas with able-bodied men. If a recruit was subsequently "remitted" by the army, if he fled, or if he refused to serve, the leaders of the community had to find a replacement. In the last two years of the Nicholaevan period, the state was fighting a ruinous war in the Crimea. As a result, recruitment quotas were significantly stepped up. By this time, people had become more experienced and more resourceful at avoiding the draft. Under increasing pressure, the *kahal* hired muscle—the infamous *khappers.* Any man who was found without paperwork attesting to his exemption from the draft by the community in which he lived would be swept by the *khappers* into the jurisdiction of the community that paid them for their services.

Following the abolition of serfdom, peasants acquired the legal right to leave the *mir* in exchange for redemption payments. More generally, emancipation loosened the hold of established communities, including Jewish ones, over its members. It became more difficult to administer conscription through the estate system. The state turned, instead, to a district lottery, which rendered every man within a particular age group eligible for the draft. Whether he actually ended up serving depended on the number he drew. Draft boards, staffed not only by military personnel but also physicians and sometimes other kinds of experts, took over the function of local communities, both in deciding which draftees were fit to serve and in making sure that registered, that is, enlisted, men appeared for the call-up. There was no further need for *khappers;* but, of course, the state had far greater resources at its disposal to enforce its policies than any community could command. It is highly likely that the effectiveness of the *khappers* in snaring recruits was vastly exaggerated in Jewish conscription literature.

The new policy proved both more efficient and more ruthless in collecting and sorting potential soldiers. Most significantly, however, it was universal. This means that military regulations now defined human beings exclusively as bodies rather than as members of different estates, ethnic groups, and confessions, reducing personhood entirely to a man's capacity to perform certain routine tasks on cue, with the ultimate aim of efficiently disposing of other bodies who were similarly reduced. Let me be clear: the Nicholaevan system was neither better nor worse than the post-reform army, not least in terms of achieving its ultimate purpose that, in both cases, was organized murder. But it operated under a different set of assumptions about what constituted a human being.

For the Nicholaevan "confessional" state, a person remained, even if he wore a uniform and wielded a weapon, a member of some concrete, definable, visible community. The conscription system depended on the preservation of established social and religious hierarchies in order to function. When these failed—as when potential recruits resisted the authority of their elders—the system stalled and broke down. Life in the Nicholaevan military "estate" likewise replicated the conservative patriarchal patterns of Russian peasant life. For this reason, extending the draft to non-Russian and especially non-Orthodox minorities remained controversial, the conscription of Jews and Polish Catholics especially so. Universal conscription, by contrast, stripped men of their social identity and therefore rendered ethnic and confessional distinctions theoretically moot.

Under the circumstances, the stubborn persistence of such differences threatened to become disruptive; imperial diversity now undermined morale and vitiated military discipline. Nervous about the absence of a common national ideology to bind enlisted men together, military elites began to invoke the xenophobic and vaguely racialist doctrine of "Pan-Slavism." The idea of the Slavic nations united by faith and ruled from Moscow began to resound in the Russian press during the Russo-Turkish War, the first war fought by the recently integrated citizen-army, reformed by statute in 1874. The irony, for those who chose to see it, was plain; equality before the law did nothing but compel greater numbers of men to die in the dubious cause of Russian chauvinism and Orthodox intolerance. The government of the "tsar-liberator" was more reactionary than that of his father. His reforms served his own political ambitions rather than the people for whose welfare he was responsible.

The reforming state under Alexander is thus at the center of the confrontation between Benjamin and the military authorities. Meanwhile, the *khappers* are holdovers from a Jewish communal regime that plays no other part in the plot; what are they doing in Benjamin's story? To understand their role, we need to set Abramovich's shtetl-world in its proper "Nicholaevan" perspective. As I have said, Benjamin's messianic journey takes place not only in space but also in time. The shtetl is backward, stuck in the unregenerate pre-reform period. No matter what time it is outside, the Jewish town, like Benjamin, who will never be first or even second, but perpetually a distant third, is always already behind.

When he leaves Tuneyadevke, Benjamin is also moving toward the future. However, almost at once, his historic journey is "abridged," foreshortened by the *khappers*. In the world of *Benjamin III*, the *khappers* act as the agents of imperial power rather than as representatives of the community that employs them. Their dealings with Benjamin, despite the fact that they too are Jews, mirror the way in which the state treats him. Entirely indifferent to him as a person, they see him only as a body, an object to be manipulated. Moreover, like Oxman, they are enthusiastic proponents of self-help, of "Jews getting organized" in order to "put an end to their sorry situation." Eminently practical, they judge progress by material signs such as the "railroad and the telegraph," which are "Jewish" inventions anyhow. Yet they detest the "heretics . . . those weird modern intellectuals [Yid. *di modne hayntike gelernete*]" who are running the schools and, with their heads uncovered, teach the children all sorts of abominations.[19]

What's going on here? Who are these familiar strangers, these Jewish goons, these philistines who profit by ushering Jews into the waiting arms of state officials? The answer is, I think, potentially devastating, more so even than the satiric attack on the OPE in *The Nag*. Abramovich's post-reform *"khappers"* are modern Jewish philanthropists whose self-appointed role, in this dark reading of internal Jewish politics in the era of "selective integration," is to initiate Jews into modernity by making them good citizens, which means helping them to end up as cannon fodder. The *khappers* trade their own younger brother Benjamin for money. In the process, they sell out their place within Jewish society; unlike real *khappers* they are free agents. Associated with no community, they represent the direct intrusion of state power into the inner life of the Jews. Throughout their interaction with Benjamin and Senderl, they remain doubly marginal, alienated from him but also foreign to their political masters. Military authorities are only too happy to use their particular skills but also leave them in the no-man's land of the "anteroom" (Yid. *fartsimmer*) to their own "grand apartments."[20] They are stuck, not only in place but also in time, between their provincial "Nicholaevan" past and a future that will discard them because the army can get its own recruits. Their liminal condition, to which they themselves are blind, encapsulates Abramovich's view of the sorry position of St. Petersburg's Jewish notables, most of whom aspired to forget their Nicholaevan origins as soon as they fled the Pale.

In the new reformed military, the body is an abstraction. Benjamin's body is, in political terms, identical to the body of any other recruit. That is why the *khappers* can dispose of it like a commodity; according to the logic that informed the creation of the OPE, enough money could turn any Jewish boychik into a doctor. But in the Nicholaevan universe, as we have seen, the recruit is socially situated. So too is the pre-reform Jewish body; it is not interchangeable and, no matter what improvements it undergoes during the Alexandrine reign, it seems to revert to its original, unkempt "Nicholaevan" state. It remains, like Benjamin, stubbornly itself. Insofar as it is true only to its own essence, it is always already integral and complete (Heb. *shalem*). In contrast to the *khappers* and the "enlightened" secular people whom they are meant to represent, Benjamin's unregenerate Jewish body is, in fact, a model of "perfected Jewish manhood."

Bred in the study house amidst Jewish books, longing for Jerusalem, Benjamin is a Romantic Jewish intellectual, who is, not coincidentally, the best tour guide to the world of the shtetl. *Benjamin III* is the story of his spiritual rebirth, recorded by Mendele, and interspersed with Benjamin's own travel notes. Benjamin's relationship with the potholes and ditches of Glupsk is both intimate and ironic. Completely at home within this eminently Jewish landscape, he has not, as a result, lost his capacity for thinking critically. By the end of his "adventures," Benjamin has come to understand the categorical distinction between a moral community and a political regime. In abandoning the latter for the former, he opts out of universal history. But in losing the world, Benjamin gains the eternity of Israel. What such a choice means to Abramovich and what it says about the future of the Haskalah, we shall shortly see.

What kind of moral community does Abramovich locate in the shtetl? What is it that Benjamin is choosing when he chooses to go back home to his own "village of deadbeats"? Why should Tuneyadevke remain so far and so foreign to the political organization that is represented by the modern state? The distinction between "secular" and "religious" does not help all that much. Whatever Abramovich may have thought about the shtetl, he certainly did not see it as heir to the Jewish ideal of a holy congregation. Ritual behavior in Tuneyadevke and Glupsk is an extension of the human body. These places, as we have seen, are teeming with the material effluvia of the Jewish lifecycle. One of the criticisms most often leveled at Jewish literature is that it is blind to the beauties of nature; but Abramovich's towns are so completely embedded in human biology that one can almost feel the physical presence of sweating, belching, jostling, shouting bodies. And it is not meant to be a pleasant experience. The point here is that Abramovich does not represent "nature" as a still object of equable contemplation, a construct in every way false to the way nature, red in tooth and claw (Tennyson), actually operates in nineteenth- rather than eighteenth-century literature. Abramovich's Jewish materialism is another version of Darwin's Romantic biology. For him, nature is excess and power and movement, the consummate example of which is human rather than vegetable or mineral.

Furthermore, Abramovich's bodies are always particular. They belong to the residents of Kabtsansk, Glupsk, and Tuneyadevke. He is not interested in a generic human body, because this body cannot be imagined, only abstractly posited. Abramovich's bodies are always physically present and constantly involved with other bodies. They exist by means of contact, which is often too close. No one is ever alone in a town like Glupsk. Intimate relationships define who people are and what they must do. The shtetl is, effectively, an extended biological family. It epitomizes with striking literacy, the familiar, and familial, talmudic principle of mutual responsibility, according to which "all of Israel are entangled with one another" (BT Shavuot 39a). Personal responsibility (rather than religious, much less social or political, duty) defines morality in Abramovich's shtetl. It is a visceral morality born of proximity and it is not incompatible with feelings of disgust, resentment, or even hatred.

Only psychological distance places a person absolutely beyond the pale; Abramovich insisted to Morgulis that while both of them actually resided in Odessa, Abramovich still lived in the shtetl because the shtetl lived inside him. Indeed, "Mendele" is himself never objective or dispassionate about the state of his surroundings; his occasional horror is a measure of his involvement. He finds himself unreasonably touched by people who are every bit as disgusting as Abramovich allows them to be. If they were any less disgusting, it would imply that they were capable of rising above the insistent demands of their bodies. And Abramovich, himself engrossed in "rags and rot," sees this ideal as a delusion, a shiny piece of glass, "polished" by the likes of Morgulis desperately trying to convince himself that Jewish history is about "R. Hillel and R. Akiva," rather than the "poor and the useless" whom Morgulis is as little able to face as his own needy body. Figuratively breaking with Morgulis, Abramovich breaks with the meaning of transcendence in the discourse of the Haskalah. For him, the moment of new creation does not begin with the aesthetic sublimation of desire but with the self-conscious overcoming of narcissism. This is why shame plays such a crucial role in Abramovich's aesthetic. Like the letter to Morgulis, Abramovich's "low" stories seek to provoke the reader to shame, which way lies the end of detachment and the beginning of responsibility.

Abramovich attaches his ethos to the most primal and the most unstable of all biological ties—paternity. The stories he tells focus frequently on awakening the conscience of errant fathers to the fate of the children they have sired and then selfishly abandoned. Fatherhood represents the wages of desire that must one day be paid. The recovery of a lost paternal connection involves a transition from the morally undifferentiated egotism of the child to an adult's awareness that the ego constantly impinges on other people. Unlike motherhood (a relationship that Abramovich never questions), fatherhood requires a willed act of recognition of the claims of another upon the self. In *Benjamin III*, it represents the surrender of civilization to the inescapable reality of the human body; but it also liberates Abramovich from the uncritical embrace of secular political ties, a universal fiction on which the liberal idea of citizenship rests.

Benjamin's initial attempt to leave the Jewish "village of deadbeats" is immediately undercut by the intrusion of his family, signified by the wife from whom he "has no idea how to part."[21] The mother of Benjamin's children represents the limit case of all arguments for progress. But when he does leave, the poor match between biological and political manhood becomes immediately apparent. As soon as Benjamin and Senderl are clad in the uniform, masculine garments of empire, they lose themselves. In other words, they become like women: "Everything was totally strange—the soldiers, the barracks, the language, each and every order they were given [more irony—Senderl and Benjamin certainly know how to take orders from their wives!]. The greatcoats hung on them like sacks, their tunics bulged like bodices, their caps fell over their ears like bonnets."[22]

The light soon dawns, however. Benjamin realizes that in his search for a post-Christian "Jerusalem" he has fallen into the hell of the new secular "Rome." Benjamin's masters appear to have freed themselves from the dogma of estate and confession; there is a certain kind of political logic in the expectation that their colonial subjects ought now to shed their own "corporate" (lit. bodily) bonds, defined as backward, degenerate, and irrational. Benjamin experiences just such a conversion when he is "baptized" by the delousing waters and reborn as a soldier. But Benjamin is a maskil, a Kantian "critic" (Heb. *hoker*) who has come to understand that the difference between "Jerusalem" and "Rome" is a fantasy. He wakes up to the reality of his situation as soon as he realizes that the mind is its own place. Benjamin see his political "transformation" for what it is; an elaborate projection of the human desire for power that reduces him to the position of a child or an automaton, "an appearance that arises when one fixes and kills life by making it into a thing."[23]

Senderl, apparently seduced by this political fiction, must likewise be awakened to his own abjection: "I swear, Senderl," Benjamin says to him, "what a baby you are, playing soldier like a school boy! What are you trying to accomplish? How can a married man, and a Jew to boot, spend all of his time making right-faces and left-faces? What difference does it make?"[24] It is one thing to say such things to Senderl; it is quite another to say them to the military authorities. Here, Benjamin, in his capacity as a ranked Jewish subaltern, tells truth to power: "We wish to make an official statement," Benjamin announces to the "general" and the "colonel" who are presiding over his court-martial. "We hereby declare that the two of us, that we know nothing of military matters; neither do we wish to know anything about them. We are, thank God, married men with other things on our minds and your affairs don't even enter into our minds; as we cannot possibly be of any use to you, you really ought to discharge us."[25]

Benjamin's decisive "departure" ought not be taken for political advocacy; Abramovich was not advising Jewish soldiers to desert. Neither was he claiming that Jews were in any way unfit to serve in the military. Benjamin's fantastic confrontation with the army represents Abramovich's very real refusal to accept the political/medical verdict of the state on his own person as final. Benjamin's "material wit" is an assertion of his creator's aesthetic freedom, at the source of which lies the power of the imagination to make the body act "deliberately without reason or contrary to reasons." Faced with Benjamin's stubborn unwillingness to drink the Kool-Aid—to be deceived into compliance with "regulations" that threaten his life—the "law magnanimously forgoes its rights" because Benjamin's antics break into the system with the all-consuming force of Dionysian chaos.[26] Benjamin's comic exertions reduce *even the officers* to stitches. He must be quarantined because Romantic irony is contagious. The army cannot afford to have a sense of humor.

Benjamin's parting from the military assumes the form of a divorce. The climactic scene takes place in a chapter entitled "A Bride No More, Once More a Maid," in which he asks to be "exempt" from military service in order to return to his estranged wife and marry her for good. His declaration echoes the terms of a talmudic "testament [lit. 'book'] of separation" (Heb. *sefer kritut*), which declares a woman "free" to remarry. Marriage and divorce is the organizing trope of *Benjamin III*. Abramovich's text is itself a *sefer kritut* that releases the maskil from the possibility of a bad political marriage so that he can become a proper Jewish husband to the one who awaits him at home. His return to responsibility is, paradoxically, a "higher" form of freedom, like the spiritual freedom from the demands of liberal citizenship that Kant assigned to the *Gelehrter*. To be sure, Benjamin's wife is not altogether agreeable. She is aggressive and intemperate, not to mention provincial, ignorant, and coarse. She babbles constantly and often without sense. She smells of the kitchen and she is up to her elbows in garbage. But to Benjamin she is irresistibly real, an extension of his own body—flesh of his flesh, bone of his bone, mother of his children.

In *Benjamin III*, the organizing motif of marriage (I hesitate to call it a metaphor because such a term implies a level of abstraction foreign to Abramovich's style) extends beyond the household. It pertains to every relationship in the shtetl, including the friendship of Benjamin and Senderl, who are explicitly described as husband and wife. Like their actual marriages, it is an "uncivil union," in this case a parody of the social contract between men. If anything, it is a decidedly unequal sexual contract, in which Senderl performs the humble tasks of a "housewife," leaving Benjamin free to live the life of the mind.

The Benjamin-Senderl partnership parodies the gender norms of modern middle-class marriage, which sets up strict boundaries between the feminine sphere of private affective relationships and the masculine network of public and institutional ties, governed by a formal code of manly behavior. The perfect separation between private and public sustains the liberal theory of emancipation. From this perspective, what Benjamin and Senderl have between them is both sexually and politically perverse; their Jewish relationship queers the social contract. And that's exactly Abramovich's point, although he would never have said so in precisely those words. For Benjamin, the Jewish Romantic is not a university man; he comes out of the traditional "study house." This is a place where knowledge is produced to no useful purpose, where learning for its own sake is the same as learning for the sake of the divine Name (the Hebrew expression *torah lishmah* means both the former and the latter), where study, like the Romantic pursuit of art, is the only form of transcendence. The study house is a privileged homosocial public space where knowledge circulates without end. But it is also an intimate and exclusive home of the Jewish imagination, where the fantasy of adolescent intimacy between men is sustained and indulged. It is the place where the shtetl touches the heavens. It is the only place where the "parasites" of Tuneyadevke are free. And, of course, the women aren't there.

The motif of marriage that structures every relationship in *Benjamin III* brings the Haskalah back to its beginnings. In *Jerusalem*, Mendelssohn had affirmed without equivocation that Jews would be prepared to renounce "civil union" with the gentiles if it required them to renounce the "laws that we considered binding upon us." In fact, Mendelssohn's genetic definition of a distinctly Jewish "law" bears a striking resemblance to Mendele's principle of familial responsibility. Insisting on the binding experience of "corporate" revelation at Sinai to the entire body of Israel, Mendelssohn said that the biological members of the House of Jacob "and all of their descendants" inherited their original obligation in perpetuity. This familial legacy included all the "laws, precepts, commandments, and rules of life which were to be peculiar to this nation." Israel, Mendelssohn argued, will remain Israel as long as it follows the "rules of [its own] life." The issue here is not the content of revelation. Mendelssohn was deliberately fuzzy on this point, because revelation was, for him, not a source of knowledge about God. Rather, the original moment of revelation, reenacted regularly through collective ritual, informs the identity of Israel. The more important point is that the peculiar nature of the House of Jacob is borne in its "laws, precepts, commandments, and"—note the shift from a normative to an organic register—"rules of life." What makes God's "prescriptions" incumbent upon Jews is that it makes them Jewish; quite literally, it constitutes them as a people. Moreover, these "prescriptions" are to be accepted entirely "on faith" because, like the biological ties of paternity, their origins are invisible: "For no words or written signs preserve their meaning unchanged throughout a generation." Beyond the power of empirical certainty, they must be "propagated through oral, living instructions," sustained by the alliance between the imagination and the body.[27]

Right here, we can see the impetus for Krochmal's Hegelian defense of the commandments. But it is Abramovich who comes closest to Mendelssohn's Jewish determinism. Krochmal's "middle position" equivocates on the question of whether the commandments, by their very nature as God's law, partake of the "Absolute Spirit" or whether they are an expression of Israel's own historical character. For Abramovich, the matter is clear. Following Mendelssohn more precisely than Krochmal, Abramovich does not even attempt to prove that Jewish "law" transcends the "peculiarity" of the Jewish condition. The Hegelian possibility of historical transcendence does not arise. Instead, "Mendele" presents Jewish peoplehood as a corporation of bodies, grounded in the ineluctable material conditions that compose its own "rules of life." The "life" of this extended Jewish family has no history, properly speaking, since its perpetuation is organically bound up with the only universal law there is: the law of evolutionary continuity, governed by the interminable desire to reproduce one's own kind:

> Say what you want about the Jews of Kaptsansk, they're *not* such big self-starters, they *don't* pull any major coups in their humdrum little lives or set the outside reeling with anything at all. Go ahead and say they live from hand to mouth. Say all this and plenty more. But when it comes to increasing and multiplying, don't, God forbid, say a word against them; they are as punctilious as all the other Jews. Not even their enemies can deny that every Jew in Kaptsansk is weighed down, touch wood, with a parcel of children.[28]

This principle of eternal multiplication, which Abramovich nicely mirrors in his own long lists and serial repetitions, undermines all historical teleologies that move toward some sort of resolution between the particular and the universal. In the Mendele world, no such resolution is possible because the universal consists entirely of particulars. The only general rule that complies with the teeming variety of nature is that which attaches to belonging; every being is responsible for its own kind. In this scheme of things, the family that sticks together has the best chances of survival, and the first and last "commandment" is to multiply. Jews, Mendele says, are the "roosters among the peoples of the earth, forever perched by the domestic hearth, close to their wives and children. A Jew's family is his whole life, as much a part of him as his heart." The ultimate good father in *The Wishing Ring* is a "Jew's Jew."[29] And the most reprehensible people are the child-abandoners like Alter, in *Fishke*, and Takif in *The Little Man*.

Abramovich's radical poetics of disenchantment leaves modern Jewish metaphysics rather in shambles. What remains is not very pretty and not very nice. At certain moments, Mendele descends from his usual wry humor into unadulterated disgust with Jewish "fraternity." Here, he begins to sound suspiciously like Abramovich himself, a cranky intellectual raging against the squalor, the whining, the constant demands, the pushing and shoving, the sheer physical indignity of it all. The householders of Kabstansk, Mendele says,

> all like to push their way into someone else's business, step on someone else's toes in the approved Jewish fashion; if there's two, I'll be three; if three, I'll be four, and so on and so forth until things get to the point of ve-KAPTSEYNU yakhad, gather us together, O Lord, KAPTSEYNU, impoverish us, that we might all be KAPTSONIM [beggars] together, and cleave to each other, embrace each other, choke each other in brotherhood, until we all suffocate and drop dead together at one and the same moment.[30]

Abramovich never makes excuses for the shtetl; that would be like complaining about rain being wet. His shtetl is a form of living life, relentlessly and inevitably driven unto eternity by the demands of its own inexhaustible and exhausting reproductive cycle. On the other hand, he does not make the mistake of underestimating or misunderstanding the Romantic imperative to reconcile "all opposition between actuality and the ideal" and thus achieve a blessed state of peace. The "mind must be satisfied," Schiller warned, but "not so that aspiration ceases on that account."[31] No Jewish intellectual could fully abdicate the quest for transcendence. After Wessely, every generation anxiously awaited the hour of redemption. Hurry up please, each kept telling the other, *it's time*. But after Abramovich, it would always be too late. Mendele was forever restarting the clock.

10 The End of Enlightenment

In 1792, a Prussian scholar and litterateur named Karl Philipp Moritz introduced to the German reading public a book of "particular worth," notable for its "nonpartisan and unprejudiced depiction of Judaism." The "story," Moritz promised, would "transport" the reader "into the area among the people where chance let the writer be born and reason let his spirit ripen to a level of education that found no nourishment on this soil, and therefore obliged him to seek under foreign skies what had now become a necessity."[1] Moritz confidently asserted that the "facts" presented in the author's unvarnished account of his own terrible struggle against the "consequences of general ignorance" served the much-discussed cause of the "education and enlightenment of the Jewish nation" much better than "any lengthy treatise on the subject." With that aim in view, Moritz himself had shepherded the volume through the press on behalf of its author, who was his close friend and occasional collaborator. *The Life History of Solomon Maimon* (Ger. *Salomon Maimons Lebensgeschichte*) rewarded Moritz's strenuous labors, having entered modern Jewish history as the paradigmatic account of Jewish Enlightenment and a record of the triumph of Western European culture over the vestiges of Eastern European barbarism.

Moritz represented Maimon's determined quest for the truth as a struggle *against* his Polish Jewish origins. And, for more than two hundred years, even Maimon's Jewish admirers were content to interpret his "life history" in much the same way: as an authentic record of Maimon's struggle after "pure philosophical knowledge" against the seemingly immovable forces of religious superstition and social backwardness, enveloped in the "thickest cloud of Polish ignorance."[2] Like Moritz, Jewish readers have come to know the book as an "autobiography" that relates the transformation of an obscure talmudic prodigy named "Shlomo ben Yehoshua" (Solomon son of Joshua) into "Solomon Maimon," a German savant and public intellectual who made his name as a contentious and subtle critic of Kant. "Maimon," asserts Shmuel Feiner without the slightest trace of self-consciousness, "underwent an extreme, remarkable metamorphosis. He began as a Jewish Polish *melamed*, teaching small children in smoky, filthy huts in a Polish village, where only the faintest murmur from the European Enlightenment reached his ears, and later became a brilliant philosopher, writing in German in end-of-the-century Prussia."[3] Following Moritz's prescription almost exactly, Feiner reads the "unique [and] surprising intellectual development" of the Polish prodigy as a milestone in the "education and enlightenment of the Jewish nation." For the contemporary historian of "Jewish secularization," Maimon's successful liberation from "religious supervision" happily portends a "revitalization in Jewish life."[4]

Only recently has scholarship begun to challenge the normative view of the "life of Solomon Maimon" as an "example of more or less complete progress from pre-modern Judaism . . . to Enlightenment philosophy." Abe Socher, author of a critical study of Maimon's intellectual evolution, locates in his self-presentation a "site of uneasy heretical hybridity."[5] Maimon's self-portrait, Socher says, is "crucially ambivalent," an "expression of . . . a divided psyche of a minority thinker," estranged both from "the culture in which he was raised and the one to which he aspired." In this reading, the "life history" testifies to Maimon's ambiguous position as a radical Jewish thinker misprised and misplaced among both tolerant Christians and traditional Jews. "Maimon's narrative stance," Socher points out, "continues to oscillate between confession and that of a kind of bemused participant-observer" who seems to be detached from the enlightened ideal that was the endpoint of his ambitions.[6] For Socher, Maimon's literary "life" sounds like a "profoundly broken" record that represents the "spectacular failure" of Shlomo ben Yehoshua to become a "*gebildet* (educated) modern Jew."[7]

Although Socher is sensitive to the distance between Solomon Maimon the author and "Solomon Maimon" the narrator, his interpretation still assumes that the book known as *The Life History of Solomon Maimon* is a candid autobiography: an imaginative but sincere attempt to present an accurate picture of its author's personal history. This means that the sense of failure that the "life" conveys at the level of its "literary deep structure" must also "replicate the intellectual and cultural conflicts in which Maimon's [real] life was formed."[8] Socher does not say what these "conflicts" are, but we can guess. Either they are rooted in Maimon's own bad conscience about his betrayal of the tradition, or in the bad faith of enlightened society that was only prepared to endure a Polish Jew but could never really accept him. In both instances, Maimon's apparent inability to fashion a coherent story of development is a symptom of what went wrong with the Enlightenment of the Jews. Whether we define his problem in psychological or political terms, the unresolved tensions that make up Maimon's "life history" epitomize a failure of integration.

But what if Maimon's ostensible incoherence is a deliberate strategy, a set of elaborate rhetorical effects? What if we take more seriously the imaginative status of "Solomon Maimon" as a character in the "life story" that Moritz commissioned from his Jewish friend? What if the narrator named "Solomon Maimon" is not a mirror image of the person who actually went under the name of Solomon Maimon but a fiction, deliberately offered to Moritz in place of a real autobiography that Moritz was hoping for? What if the literary creation of "Solomon Maimon" is a way of concealing rather than revealing the Jewish identity of its author? What if the *Life of Solomon Maimon* was not written by "Solomon Maimon," the German philosopher who emerged from obscurity in 1780, but by the maverick Jewish intellectual from the Polish town of Nieśwież, who was born in 1754 under the name of Shlomo ben Yehoshua? This supposition is not as far-fetched as it sounds: Maimon's earlier experiments in "life-writing," also initiated by Moritz and published in his *Journal of Practical Psychology* in 1792, were written under the name of "Ben Josua," a Germanized form of "ben Yehoshua."

Based on the introduction that Moritz subsequently wrote for *The Life of Solomon Maimon*, one can imagine the kind of story that he was trying to get his protégé to tell. Deeply sympathetic to Maimon's tribulations, Moritz saw in his ostensible "conversion" from Judaism to philosophy an argument for Jewish integration into German society and a model of what a modern education in science could accomplish. Moritz effectively wanted a book in which Maimon would represent himself to the German reading public as Moritz saw him. Moritz, who had grown up in a strictly pious Christian home, had described his own liberation from religion in a psychological novel called *Anton Reiser*, the last part of which was published in 1790. In some sense, *The Life of Solomon Maimon* was meant to pick up where Moritz's own autobiographical project had just left off. The problem, however, was that the life of Shlomo ben Yehoshua did not conform to the pattern that Moritz established in *Anton Reiser*; unlike Moritz's alter ego, Shlomo ben Yehoshua did not have to "convert" from his ancestral faith in order to achieve enlightenment. Just the opposite; as Abe Socher points out, the Jewish tradition within which Maimon was raised and in which he continued to work throughout his life was "not as alien to either the technical philosophical concerns or the radical anticlerical spirit of the Enlightenment as its exponents often liked to think."[9]

Even though Moritz did not know him as well as he came to know the man who called himself Solomon Maimon, Shlomo ben Yehoshua did not disappear just because he had changed his name to something German-speakers could pronounce. In fact, his new name was not exactly neutral, alluding to the Jewish origins of his modern persona. It was Maimonides, the exemplary Jewish thinker of the Middle Ages, who became the "basis of [Maimon's] self-invention" as a philosopher.[10] Tellingly, Maimon never invoked this new name in his Hebrew writings, where his Jewish connections were obvious and noncontroversial. The person who had styled himself after Maimonides manifestly had no need to "convert" to philosophy, because he was always already a philosopher. As Socher argues, the "radical enlightenment" of Shlomo ben Yehoshua was, essentially, a Jewish heresy. In this light, *The Life of Solomon Maimon* may be read not as the quintessential tragedy of a modern Jew, but as a comedy of mistaken identity that deliberately subverted Moritz's expectations. Under the confessional cover of autobiography, an unrepentantly Jewish Shlomo ben Yehoshua of Nieśwież recounts the disintegration of "Solomon Maimon," a show-off and a nudnik, whose existence might have been a convenient fiction from the start.

The story of becoming "Solomon Maimon" moves westward, from squalor and ignorance to culture and knowledge. But the person we come to know as Solomon Maimon does not start out ignorant. Nor is he quite as poor and provincial as his Polish origins suggest. His grandfather, Heimann Joseph, was a "farmer of some villages in the neighborhood of the town of Mir, in the territory of Prince Radzivil."[11] Heimann Joseph left the business to Maimon's father, who expanded the family trade in agricultural products with merchants in Königsberg and "introduced into the house a more refined mode of life."[12] Following unexpected reverses (which Maimon attributed to the machinations of "Herr Schachna," Radziwiłł's unscrupulously competitive Jewish steward), the family relocated to the small town of Mohylna, about forty miles west of Minsk. Maimon was six when "everything went backward." According to the revealing evidence of the text (written, we remember, by Shlomo ben Yehoshua), Maimon never fully got past this initial injury to his sense of social entitlement.[13] Throughout his "life" Maimon, the aspiring modern Jew, appears to be not so much poor as déclassé; Shlomo ben Yehoshua unmasks Maimon's pursuit of "enlightenment" as an attempt to recover his status.

Writing about his departure from his hometown, Maimon invokes God's call to Abraham, in Genesis: "It was only in search of the truth that I left my people, my homeland, and my family."[14] But the passage, which insists that there was nothing personal about the desire to depart, tells only half the story. The biblical text reads: "Now the LORD said unto Abram: 'Get thee out of thy country, and from thy kindred, and from thy father's house, unto the land that I will show thee. And I will make of thee a great nation, and I will bless thee, and make thy name great; and be thou a blessing.'"[15] Thus, what remains implicit in the allusion, meant to be decoded by the wise Jewish reader, is Shlomo ben Yehoshua's suggestion that Maimon's abandonment of his "father's house" was also a journey of return undertaken in order to repair the family fortune and "make [his] name great." Maimon's decision to go to Berlin retraces his father's travels to Königsberg, journeys that were made with the same aim in view. In leaving provincial Poland for bustling Prussia, the errant son retraces the footsteps of his father.

The theme of return everywhere subverts the implacable movement forward that propels the creation of "Solomon Maimon" and his removal beyond the pale of his own culture. It would seem that the "truth" he is meant to acquire "under foreign skies" is already there, in his own Jewish Lithuania. In the course of writing the *Life History,* Shlomo ben Yehoshua delights in showing the reader how Maimon comes upon it again and again. The "autobiography of Solomon Maimon" is supposed to illustrate the ways in which traditional Judaism ill serves his desire for "enlightenment and education." But Maimon is already an experienced scholar and an accomplished philosopher by the time he arrives in Berlin. It is his early exposure to Jewish books that expands his mental universe and determines his future greatness. His own father, a "good rabbi," had "felt a secret pleasure that his young son, without a guide or previous training," had "transgressed his command to meddle with nothing but the Talmud" and "mastered an entire work of science" written by the sixteenth-century chief rabbi of Prague, which Maimon snagged from (where else?) the family bookcase.[16] Maimon insists over and over again that he picked up whatever bits of philosophy and culture he could solely at his own initiative, without guidance, systematic training or help from anyone.[17] But the text, written by Shlomo ben Yehoshua, who knows better, tells us something else. It is not only his father who tacitly encourages his mental development but every other "good rabbi" with whom Maimon comes into contact. Jewish learned society knows a genius when it sees one.

When, for instance, Maimon begins to "dispute" with his elementary schoolteacher, no less respectable a person than the chief rabbi of Iwieniec (a small town on the outskirts of Wołożyn, which was a center of talmudic learning, where Maimon began his formal education) steps in to "set [his] mind in activity."[18] After his marriage, another "chief rabbi," who was not only personally "acquainted with the sciences" but "had a fair library of German books," enables and supports Maimon's efforts to learn German.[19] Through the generous assistance of his new friend, Maimon's "eyes are opened" to physics and biology as well. When subsequently ejected from Berlin and forced to become a "vagrant in a strange land," Maimon ends up in Posen/Poznan, Prussia's recently acquired Polish province. Here, among fellow Eastern European Jews, Maimon finds relief and still more appreciation. Unlike the "orthodox"

Jewish leadership in Berlin which had Maimon expelled from the Prussian capital, the "chief rabbi" of Posen "who was himself a scholar" welcomes him with honor. One of the "most prominent people of the town," who also happens to be the rabbi's brother-in-law, hires "Herr Solomon" to tutor his only son; so much for Feiner's "smoky, filthy huts."

Most important, however, the Eastern European rabbi appreciates and values Maimon's "inclination to solitary study."[20] In this crucial respect, Polish Posen proves far more receptive to Maimon's disinterested commitment to philosophical truth than German Berlin. In Posen, the "young scholars of the town" immediately attempt to enlist Maimon to deliver a course of lectures on the *Guide for the Perplexed*. The contrast with what transpires in Berlin could not be more revealing. Upon discovering Maimon's plans to issue a new edition of the *Guide* with his own commentary, Berlin's rabbi, a "zealot in his orthodoxy," denounces Maimon as a heretic to the town elders. What disturbs the peace of the former "polacken" in Berlin is the fact that Maimon intends to "devote [himself] to the sciences in general and to extend [his] knowledge" rather than study medicine, presumably with the aim of acquiring suitable means of earning a living. Unlike provincial Eastern European Jews who understand and value the pursuit of scholarship for its own sake, the social climbers who live in Berlin are enlightened philistines who "look upon [pure study] as something dangerous to religion and good morals."[21]

Although not exactly ripe with opportunities to obtain the kind of practical knowledge that might make one respectable to bourgeois Jewish society, traditional Eastern European Jewish culture provides Maimon with repeated opportunities for extending his natural faculties as a philosopher and to pursue the only kind of knowledge that matters to Shlomo ben Yehoshua. Thus, Maimon's first exposure to metaphysics comes in the form of Kabbalah. His desire for "perfection" is nourished by Jewish speculative philosophy, represented chiefly by the work of Maimonides where Maimon obtains "accurate ideas of God."[22] While Maimon dwells on popular superstition and the persistence of folly among Polish Jews, in order to emphasize his own superior intelligence, Shlomo ben Yehoshua represents rabbinic Judaism as an ideal synthesis of faith and philosophy. For the latter, Judaism is not just *a* religion; it is *the* religion, singularly free of the taint of false belief. Although "in its origin *natural* and *conformable* to reason," rabbinic Judaism has been long "abused" both by force of historical circumstances and through extended contact with the "manners and customs of other nations in whose neighborhood the Jews have lived."[23] If the philosophical essence of rabbinic religion has been adulterated in the course of time, such is the unfortunate result of association with non-Jews. Despite the bad influence of the majority, however, Jews continue to uphold a much higher standard of ethical behavior than everyone else because they adhere to the rabbis' code of personal conduct, which combines "genuine Stoicism" with attention to other "serviceable principles" such as "universal benevolence," charity, and care for the poor.

Indeed, "Polish Jews" exemplify the excellence of "rabbinic morals." Although they have no reason to love their Christian rulers, they "remain loyal to the country in which they live and support themselves in an honorable way." They may appear "rude," but they "adhere faithfully to the religion of their fathers and the laws of their country. They do not come before you with courtesies, but their promise is sacred."[24] Unlike the superficial "young gentlemen" who mistake a man from "Polish Lithuania . . . of a tolerably stiff beard, in tattered dirty clothes, whose language is a mixture . . . for an ignoramus," "Polish Jews" do not judge by appearances.[25] In this description, Shlomo ben Yehoshua foregrounds an Eastern European critique of Berlin's homegrown "Jewish enlightenment" as a pale shadow of the real thing. The implications of the position that Shlomo ben Yehoshua takes here become immediately clear in his account of what happens to Maimon as the result of a disastrous and ill-conceived decision to leave Posen, the place where he had spent "the happiest and most honorable" years of his life.[26]

Maimon explains that his purpose in going back to Berlin was "to . . . destroy by enlightenment the remnant of superstition which still clung to [him]" in Posen.[27] But if we are reading a story written by Shlomo ben Yehoshua, we are not so inclined to take Maimon at his word. The incidents that immediately precede this precipitous move lead us to the conclusion that Maimon had "by this time . . . emancipated [himself] pretty thoroughly from superstitions . . . by diligent study" of the *Guide for the Perplexed*. The superstition that still clings to Maimon is not, of course, his own, but that of the "fanatics" among whom he has found such a welcome reception. Maimon, in other words, wants to go to Berlin not in search of truth, but because he feels socially displaced and personally affronted by his association with the colonials. He wants to leave Posen not because he wants to become enlightened (the whole point is that he is enlightened already), but because the provincial Jews of Posen, although good enough to keep him in food, clothes, and books, are not good enough to satisfy his family pride, his intellectual conceit, and his relentless need for public acclaim. Posen is too small to contain his enormous ego, already irritated by his initial expulsion from the Prussian capital. The text's "ambiguous" treatment of Maimon's motives is not the work "of a divided psyche of a minority thinker"; it is the work of

Shlomo ben Yehoshua unmasking Maimon's "search for the truth" as a self-serving and ultimately self-destructive fantasy. What follows is Shlomo ben Yehoshua's unflinching—and very funny—deconstruction of Maimon's pathetic narcissism, as he attempts to avenge himself on the people who once rejected him by demonstrating his superiority over them. The last third of the book is a case study in denial; nothing that poor Maimon does is ever his own fault.

Once he gets to Berlin, Maimon gives free rein to his snobbery. All the people he meets are "well-to-do," "prominent," and "wealthy." He immediately charms and impresses everyone. Every encounter is an exercise in self-stroking, an act of revenge on Berlin's Jewish society for having rejected him two years before. Maimon constantly shows off his genius and speaks German better than these cultivated upstarts who can only stand back and marvel at his abilities. He becomes a tutor to the son of a wealthy widow (a nice contrast to Posen, where his charge was related to the "chief rabbi"), who challenges him to "explain Adelung's *German Grammar.*" And what do you know? "I, who had never seen Adelung's *Grammar* . . . not only expounded it, but added glosses of my own."[28] Apparently, Maimon can't leave *any* book alone, although he feels especially compelled to rewrite the volumes that testify to gentile learning. Thus, whatever it is that enlightened Berlin has to teach him, he apparently knows already. He begins to read Spinoza only to discover that "his system had already been suggested to [him] by the Cabbalistic writings" he had studied in Poland. In the end, Maimon proves *too* smart for German society: his local "friends and well-wishers" are "unable to follow him in his opinions" because they do not understand him.[29]

Maimon is such a success that "jealousy" inevitably causes his downfall. He makes the acquaintance of some "clever fellows" who have "insinuated themselves into the most prominent and wealthy families of the Jewish nation. . . . Now, they began to observe that my reputation was always on the increase and that the respect for my attainments and talents went so far, that they were being thrown into the shade."[30] The insistence on the contrast between the superficial "accomplishments" of these other "young men" and Maimon's own extraordinary learning is Shlomo ben Yehoshua's ironic swipe at the pretensions of his protagonist, defeated not in the empyrean heights of philosophical controversy but much lower down. Of course, his rivals cannot compete with Maimon when it comes to philosophy (no one can), so they attempt to discredit him in the good opinion of his social superiors by means of a "stratagem." They entice him "into gay society, to taverns, on pleasure excursions, and at last also to [brothels]." His dissolute behavior leads to Maimon being asked to leave Berlin. But of course it is not his fault; just like the grandfather who was ruined by the plots of a jealous competitor, the grandson is a victim, similarly undone by the envy of malicious schemers. Projected onto the iniquitous designs of others, his dissipation has nothing to do with him.

Shlomo ben Yehoshua promptly shows up the specious quality of Maimon's self-justifying reasoning. Mendelssohn himself cautions Maimon about his lack of "prudence." By this point, the expectations of ordinary social propriety are well beyond our young seeker, however. He informs Mendelssohn with the tired sophistication of a seasoned reprobate that "we are all Epicureans."[31] On this note he departs, having, apparently, bested even Mendelssohn in an argument. Now there really is nothing left for him to do in Berlin, although he continues to skate on Mendelssohn's recommendation for several more years.

The second departure from Berlin leads to more wandering, with no purpose and certainly no attempts at "systematic" learning. His efforts to endow the travails he experiences in his "search for the truth" with some measure of dignity and pathos are largely fruitless. Throughout the second volume of the book, Shlomo ben Yehoshua continually exposes Maimon as neurotic and insufferable. For instance, his one attempt to complete a course of study at a secular institution of higher learning (the gymnasium at Altona) ends after less than two years, because Maimon gets bored. Unlike the other students who made "very slow progress," it "was natural . . . that I, who had already made considerable attainments in science, should find the lessons at times somewhat tedious."[32] Once again, Maimon has nothing to learn. Nevertheless, for some inexplicable reason, the director gives him an "honorable certificate." When he leaves, all the "teachers and officers of the gymnasium . . . unanimously paid me the compliment that I had done honor to their institution."[33] Not entirely unanimously: the math teacher grouses that Maimon hardly ever went to class and, when he did, paid no attention. But the director conveniently shuts him up. This slight discrepancy spoils the impressive effect of a "unanimous" recognition of Maimon's irrepressible genius. It is just one small example of the multiple ways in which Shlomo ben Yehoshua undermines the putative sincerity of Maimon's narrative.

The culmination of Maimon's ostensible efforts at "education and enlightenment" are not "education and enlightenment," but fame. Finally, in Kant, Maimon finds sufficient difficulty to present a challenge to his perception of his own genius. When Kant recognizes in him evidence of a "no common talent for the profounder sciences," there is obviously nothing left to say. The master's own testimony enables Maimon to dispose of those other "arrogant Kantians who believe themselves the sole proprietors of the Critical Philosophy."[34] The *Life History* concludes with a "characteristic of [Maimon's] own work," a summary of the scholarly articles that he published in various German periodicals.[35] What we have here is not an account of intellectual triumph over religious parochialism but confirmation of Maimon's unshakeable faith in his own genius, represented in his magisterial contribution to "science" and his "correction" of Kantian idealism. And, despite Socher's misgivings about Maimon's injured psyche, this is not the track record of someone who saw himself as a "spectacular failure."

In fact, Maimon's dubious and incomplete "conversion" from Jewish textual culture to philosophy highlights Shlomo ben Yehoshua's unprecedented success in "converting" Kant to "an alternative [Jewish] idealism that draws, especially, on Maimonides, Narboni, Spinoza . . . and anticipates that of such later figures as Fichte and Hegel."[36] Their work was, as we know, essential in the nineteenth century's continuing struggle to reconcile the self-determining power of subjectivity with the irrevocable structure of things. In the course of writing the *Life History of Solomon Maimon,* the man who had never ceased to be an importunate Jewish skeptic named Shlomo ben Yehoshua of Nieśwież triumphs over the historical "necessity" of a "Jewish Enlightenment" to become the unacknowledged father of European Romanticism, a ferment that may well have begun with the Haskalah.

Notes

CHAPTER 1 — WRONG TIME, WRONG PLACE

1. For these approaches, see Roy Porter and Mikulas Teich, eds., *The Enlightenment in National Context* (Cambridge: Cambridge University Press, 1981), and David Sorkin, *The Religious Enlightenment: Protestants, Jews, and Catholics from London to Vienna* (Princeton, N.J.: Princeton University Press, 2008).

2. On ancient Greece, see Paul Zanker, *The Mask of Socrates: The Image of the Intellectual in Antiquity*, trans. Alan Shapiro (Berkeley: University of California Press, 1995), and on France, see Venita Datta, *Birth of a National Icon: The Literary Avant-Garde and the Origins of the Intellectual in France* (Albany: State University of New York Press, 1999).

3. Cited in Charles W. J. Withers, *Placing the Enlightenment: Thinking Geographically about the Age of Reason* (Chicago: University of Chicago Press, 2007), 109.

4. Graeme Garrard, *Rousseau's Counter-Enlightenment: A Republican Critique of the Philosophes* (Albany: State University of New York Press, 2003), 100.

5. Jean Starobinski, *Jean Jacques Rousseau: Transparency and Obstruction*, trans. Arthur Goldhammer (Chicago: Chicago University Press, 1988), 210.

6. Kant, "Conjectures on the Beginning of Human History (1786)," *Political Writings*, ed. H. S. Reiss (Cambridge: Cambridge University Press, 1991), 228.

7. Starobinski, *Rousseau*, 124.

8. See Béatrice Longuenesse, "Kant's 'I Think,' versus Descartes' 'I Am a Thing That Thinks,'" in *Kant and the Early Moderns*, ed. Béatrice Longuenesse and Daniel Garber (Princeton, N.J.: Princeton University Press, 2008), 9–31.

9. Sebastian Gardner, *Kant and the Critique of Pure Reason* (London: Routledge: 1999), 71.

10. Longuenesse, "Kant's 'I Think,'" 28. Emphasis in the original.

11. Gardner, *Kant and the Critique of Pure Reason*, 258. Emphasis in the original.

12. See James Schmidt, "What Is Enlightenment? A Question, Its Context, and Some Consequences," in *What Is Enlightenment? Eighteenth-Century Answers and Twentieth-Century Questions*, ed. James Schmidt (Berkeley: University of California Press, 1996), 1–44. Kant's essay is reprinted in Schmidt, *What Is Enlightenment?*, 58–64.

13. See Michel Foucault, "What Is Critique?" in Schmidt, *What Is Enlightenment?*, 382–398.

14. Isaiah Berlin, *The Roots of Romanticism*, ed. Henry Hardy (Princeton, N.J.: Princeton University Press, 1999), 70.

15. See Don Garrett, "Spinoza's Ethical Theory," in *The Cambridge Companion to Spinoza*, ed. Don Garrett (Cambridge: Cambridge University Press, 1996), 267–314.

16. Significantly, Spinoza began to exercise Jewish minds at the same time that the philosophical idealism of the Haskalah began to be subjected to political criticism on the part of Jewish secular nationalists. See Gideon Katz, "In the Eye of the Translator: Spinoza in the Mirror of the *Ethics*' Hebrew Translators," *Journal of Jewish Thought and Philosophy* 15 (2007): 39–63, and David Biale, *Not in the Heavens: The Tradition of Jewish Secular Thought* (Princeton, N.J.: Princeton University Press, 2010), 92–134.

17. See Michael A. Meyer and Michael Brenner, eds., *German-Jewish History in Modern Times*, vol. 1 (New York: Columbia University Press, 1996), 352–353.

18. On the maskilic use of the word *hoker*, see Shmuel Feiner, *Jewish Enlightenment*, trans. Chaya Naor (Philadelphia: University of Pennsylvania Press, 2003), 71–72. On the Enlightenment term "men of letters" (Fr. *gens des lettres*), see Roger Chartier, "The Man of Letters," in *Enlightenment Portraits*, ed. Michel Vovelle, trans. Lydia G. Cochrane (Chicago: University of Chicago Press, 1997), 142–189.

19. See Jay M. Harris, *Nachman Krochmal: Guiding the Perplexed of the Modern Age* (New York: New York University Press, 1991).

20. See Marcus Moseley, *Being for Myself Alone: Origins of Jewish Autobiography* (Stanford, Calif.: Stanford University Press, 2006), 1–36, 333–376.

21. On pastoralism in maskilic literature, see Jean-Christophe Attias and Esther Benbassa, *Israel, the Impossible Land*, trans. Susan Emanuel (Stanford, Calif.: Stanford University Press, 2003), 128–130.

22. See Feiner, *Jewish Enlightenment*, 342–364.

23. The quotation is from Berlin, *Roots of Romanticism*, 30.

24. Susan Manning and Francis D. Cogliano, eds., *The Atlantic Enlightenment* (Hampshire: Ashgate, 2008), 1.

25. The classical literature on the Enlightenment is enormous; see, for example, Ernst Cassirer, *The Philosophy of the Enlightenment* (Princeton, N.J.: Princeton University Press, 2009), Peter Gay, *The Enlightenment: An Interpretation*, 2 vols. (New York: Norton, 1977), Norman Hampson, *The Enlightenment* (New York: Penguin, 1991), and Paul Hazard, *The European Mind: The Critical Years, 1680–1715*, trans. J. Lewis May (New York: Fordham University Press, 1990). The most recent version of the master narrative that adopts a North Atlantic perspective is Jonathan Israel's massive three-volume history: see Israel, *Radical Enlightenment: Philosophy and the Making of Modernity, 1650–1750* (Oxford: Oxford University Press, 2001), *Enlightenment Contested: Philosophy, Modernity and the Emancipation of Man, 1670–1752* (Oxford: Oxford University Press, 2006), and *Democratic Enlightenment: Philosophy, Revolution and Human Rights, 1750–1790* (Oxford: Oxford University Press, 2011).

26. Manning and Cogliano, *The Atlantic Enlightenment*, 3.

27. See Wim Klooster, *Revolutions in the Atlantic World: A Comparative History* (New York: New York University Press, 2009).

28. Israel, "General Introduction," in *The Anglo-Dutch Moment: Essays on the Glorious Revolution and Its World Impact*, ed. Jonathan Israel (Cambridge: Cambridge University Press, 1991), 25. See also Steve Pincus, *1688: The First Modern Revolution* (New Haven, Conn.: Yale University Press, 2009).

29. Israel, "Introduction," *The Anglo-Dutch Moment*, 35.

30. For a summary account of these factors, see Israel, *Enlightenment Contested*, 26–38.

31. On these contradictions, see Dorinda Outram, *The Enlightenment* (Cambridge: Cambridge University Press, 1995), 47–76.

32. For a comparative perspective, see Daviken Studnicki-Gizbert, "*La Nación* among the Nations: Portuguese and Other Maritime Trading Diasporas in the Atlantic, Sixteenth to Eighteenth Centuries," in *Atlantic Diasporas: Jews, Conversos, and Crypto-Jews in the Age of Mercantilism, 1500–1800*, ed. Richard L. Kagan and Philip D. Morgan (Baltimore: Johns Hopkins University Press, 2009), 75–98.

33. On the inner life of the Iberian Jewish diaspora, see Miriam Bodian, *Hebrews of the Portuguese Nation: Conversos and Community in Early Modern Amsterdam* (Bloomington: Indiana University Press, 1999), and Daniel M. Swetschinski, *Reluctant Cosmopolitans: The Portuguese Jews of Seventeenth-Century Amsterdam* (Portland, Ore.: Littman Library of Jewish Civilization, 2004).

34. Bodian, *Hebrews of the Portuguese Nation*, 152.

35. On the religion of Iberian "Judaizers," see Yirmiyahu Yovel, *The Other Within: The Marranos, Split Identity, and Emerging Modernity* (Princeton, N.J.: Princeton University Press, 2009), 227–239, and Miriam Bodian, *Dying in the Law of Moses: Crypto-Jewish Martyrdom in the Iberian World* (Bloomington: Indiana University Press, 2007), 23–46.

36. Frances Malino, *The Sephardic Jews of Bordeaux: Assimilation and Emancipation in Revolutionary and Napoleonic France* (Tuscaloosa: University of Alabama Press, 2003), 17.

37. See Steven Nadler's analysis of Spinoza's notorious excommunication in Nadler, *Spinoza's Heresy: Immortality and the Jewish Mind* (Oxford: Oxford University Press, 2004), 157–181.

38. See Israel, "Was There a Pre-1740 Sephardic-Jewish Enlightenment?" *Arquivos do Centro Cultural Calouste Gulbenkian* 48 (2004): 3–20, and his "Philosophy, Deism, and the Early Jewish Enlightenment (1655–1740)," in *The Dutch Intersection: The Jews and the Netherlands in Modern History*, ed. Yosef Kaplan (Leiden: Brill, 2008), 173–201. The idea of a "Sephardic Jewish Enlightenment" was first entertained by Salo Baron. In the early version of his *Social and Religious History of the Jews*, Baron wrote, confusingly, of an early modern "Dutch and Italian Haskalah." See his *Social and Religious History*, 3 vols. (New York: Columbia University Press, 1937), 2:205–212. Because of the persistent and unhelpful equation of "Haskalah" with Enlightenment, Baron's point about Italian

Jewish "humanism" and the "new spirit" of "capitalist and Protestant Holland" was summarily rejected (eventually even by Baron himself). See the wrong-headed but very revealing critique of Baron by Isaac Barzilay, "The Italian and Berlin Haskalah (Parallels and Differences)," *Proceedings of the American Academy for Jewish Research* 29 (1960–1961): 17–54, and its most recent reappraisal by Adam Shear, "'The Italian and Berlin Haskalah'—Isaac Barzilay Revisited," *Simon Dubnow Institute Yearbook* 6 (2007): 49–66. Although Shear's essay perpetuates the same misleading analogy, his point about the "difference" of early modern Jewish rationalism implicitly supports the argument that the Haskalah is not the same thing as Jewish Enlightenment.

39. For an example, see Matt Goldish, "Newtonian, Converso and Deist: The Lives of Jacob (Henrique) de Castro Sarmento," *Science in Context* 10.4 (1997): 651–675.

40. Trivellato, *The Familiarity of Strangers: The Sephardic Diaspora, Livorno, and Cross-Cultural Trade in the Early Modern Period* (New Haven, Conn.: Yale University Press, 2009), 50.

41. Matt Goldish refers to the Sephardic community in Amsterdam a "hotbed of heterodox ideas"; see his *Jewish Questions: Responsa on Sephardic Life in the Early Modern Period* (Princeton, N.J.: Princeton University Press, 2008), xlv.

42. On Spinoza's immersion in contemporary Sephardic culture, see Yosef Hayim Yerushalmi, "Divrei Shpinoza 'al kiyum ha'am hayehudi," *Divrei haakademiah haleumit hayisraelit lemada'im* 6 (1983): 171–213.

43. See David Ruderman, *Jewish Thought and Scientific Discovery in Early Modern Europe* (Detroit: Wayne State University Press, 2001).

44. See Hava Tirosh-Samuelson, "The Ultimate End of Human Life in Post-Expulsion Philosophic Literature," in *Crisis and Creativity in the Sephardic World, 1391–1648*, ed. Benjamin R. Gampel (New York: Columbia University Press, 1997), 223–253.

45. Ruderman, *Jewish Enlightenment in an English Key: Anglo-Jewish Construction of Modern Jewish Thought* (Princeton, N.J.: Princeton University Press, 2000).

46. See Malino on the career of Abraham Furtado, *Sephardic Jews of Bordeaux*, 59–61.

47. On the formation of the state in early modern Russia and the relationship between the nobility and the monarch, see Nancy Shields Kollmann, *By Honor Bound: State and Society in Early Modern Russia* (Ithaca, N.Y.: Cornell University Press, 1999).

48. On state development in Brandenburg Prussia and the Habsburg Empire, see Peter H. Wilson, *Absolutism in Central Europe* (New York: Routledge, 2000).

49. On noble republicanism in early modern Poland, see Antoni Mączak, "The Structure of Power in the Commonwealth of the Sixteenth and Seventeenth Centuries," in *A Republic of Nobles: Studies in Polish History to 1864*, ed. J. K. Fedorowicz (Cambridge: Cambridge University Press, 1982), 109–134.

50. On church-state relations in early modern Russia, see James Cracraft, *The Church Reform of Peter the Great* (Stanford, Calif.: Stanford University Press, 1971), 63–112.

On Prussia, see Mary Fulbrook, *Piety and Politics: Religion and the Rise of Absolutism in England, Württemberg, and Prussia* (Cambridge: Cambridge University Press, 1983), 153–173, and Richard L. Gawthrop, *Pietism and the Making of Eighteenth-Century Prussia* (Cambridge: Cambridge University Press, 1993). On "state piety" in the Habsburg Empire, see Wolfgang Zimmermann, "Die 'siegreiche' Frömmigkeit des Hauses Habsburg," *Rottenburger Jahrbuch für Kirchengeschichte* 19 (2000): 157–175, and Robert Bireley, "Confessional Absolutism in the Habsburg Lands in the Seventeenth Century," in *State and Society in Early Modern Austria*, ed. Charles W. Ingrao (West Lafayette, Ind.: Purdue University Press, 1994), 36–53.

51. On the relative political weakness of the Catholic church in the Polish-Lithuanian Commonwealth, see Magda Teter, *Jews and Heretics in Catholic Poland: A Beleaguered Church in the Post-Reformation Era* (Cambridge: Cambridge University Press, 2006).

52. On social relations and the state in early modern Prussia, see Hanna Schissler, "The Social and Political Power of the Prussian Junkers," in *Landownership and Power in Modern Europe*, ed. Ralph Gibson and Martin Blinkhorn (London: HarperCollins, 1991), 99–110; and William W. Hagen, *Ordinary Prussians: Brandenburg Junkers and Villagers, 1500–1840* (Cambridge: Cambridge University Press, 2002). On the Habsburg empire, see Herman Rebel, *Peasant Classes: The Bureaucratization of Property and Family Relations under Early Habsburg Absolutism, 1511–1636* (Princeton, N.J.: Princeton University Press, 1983), and Roland Axtmann, "'Police' and the Formation of the Modern State: Legal and Ideological Assumptions on State Capacity in the Austrian Lands of the Habsburg Empire, 1500–1800," *German History* 10 (1992): 39–61.

53. On the emergence of rank in Russian society, see John P. LeDonne, *Absolutism and Ruling Class: The Formation of the Russian Political Order, 1700–1825* (Oxford: Oxford University Press, 1991); on social organization and the impact of the Table of Ranks, see the classic article by Gregory Freeze, "The *Soslovie* (Estate) Paradigm in Russian Social History," *American Historical Review* 91 (1986): 11–36.

54. See Christopher Storrs, ed., *The Fiscal-Military State in Eighteenth-Century Europe: Essays in Honor of P.G.M. Dickson* (Surrey: Ashgate, 2009), 55–146.

55. On the pace of economic development in early modern Eastern Europe, see Thomas Munck, *Seventeenth-Century Europe: State, Conflict, and the Social Order in Europe, 1598–1700* (Houndmills: Palgrave Macmillan, 1989), 128–132. On Russia, see A. V. Demkin, *Gorodskoe predprinimatel'stvo v Rossii na rubezhe XVII i XVIII vekov* (Moscow: Institut istorii RAN, 2000), and N. V. Kozlova, *Rossiiskii absoliutizm i kupechestvo v XVIII veke* (Moscow: Arkheograficheskii tsentr, 1999). On state involvement in economic life in East-Central Europe, see, for example, the dated but still useful article by Hermann Freudenberger, "State Intervention as an Obstacle to Economic Growth in the Habsburg Monarchy," *Journal of Economic History* 27 (1967): 493–509. For an overview of Frederick's attempt to micromanage the Prussian economy, see W. O. Henderson, *Studies in the Economic Policy of Frederick the Great* (London: Frank Cass, 1963).

56. On eighteenth-century Berlin, see Robert R. Taylor, *Hohenzollern Berlin: Construction and Reconstruction* (London: P. D. Meany, 1985); on Vienna, see John P. Spielman, *The City and the Crown: Vienna and the Imperial Court, 1600–1740* (West Lafayette, Ind.: Purdue University Press, 1993), and Jeroen Duindam, *Vienna and Versailles: The Courts of Europe's Dynastic Rivals, 1550–1780* (Cambridge: Cambridge University Press, 2003). The literature on early modern St. Petersburg is vast; for an overview, see W. Bruce Lincoln, *Sunlight at Midnight: St. Petersburg and the Rise of Modern Russia* (New York: Basic Books, 2000), 17–104.

57. On provincial cities in early modern Eastern Europe, see Jaroslav Miller, *Urban Societies in East-Central Europe, 1500–1700* (Hampshire: Ashgate, 2008), and J. Michael Hittle, *The Service City: State and Townsmen in Russia, 1600–1800* (Cambridge, Mass.: Harvard University Press, 1979).

58. See Maria Bogucka, "Polish Towns between the Sixteenth and the Eighteenth Centuries," in Fedorowicz, *Republic of Nobles*, 135–153.

59. On the Petrine "revolution," see E. V. Anisimov, *The Reforms of Peter the Great: Progress through Coercion in Russia*, trans. John T. Alexander (Armonk, N.Y.: M. E. Sharpe, 1993), and James Cracraft, *The Revolution of Peter the Great* (Cambridge, Mass.: Harvard University Press, 2003).

60. The classic account is Marc Raeff, *The Well-Ordered Police State: Social and Institutional Change through Law in the Germanies and Russia, 1600–1800* (New Haven, Conn.: Yale University Press, 1983); but see also Andre Wakefield, *The Disordered Police State: German Cameralism as Science and Practice* (Chicago: University of Chicago Press, 2009).

61. See Richard S. Wortman, *Scenarios of Power: Myth and Ceremony in Russian Monarchy*, vol. 1 (Princeton, N.J.: Princeton University Press, 1994).

62. On Catherine's reign, see Isabel de Madariaga, *Russia in the Age of Catherine the Great* (London: Weidenfeld and Nicolson, 1982).

63. The quotation is from Andrzej Walicki, *A History of Russian Thought from the Enlightenment to Marxism*, trans. Hilda Andrews-Rusiecka (Stanford, Calif.: Stanford University Press, 1979), 34.

64. See Andrei Zorin, *Kormia dvuglavogo orla: literatura i gosudarstvennaia ideologiia v Rossii v poslednei treti XVIII-pervoi treti XIX veka* (Moscow: Novoe literaturnoe obozreniie, 2001), 31–156.

65. On Frederick II as an exemplar of "enlightened absolutism," see Eckhart Hellmuth, "Enlightenment and Government," in *The Enlightenment World*, ed. Martin Fitzpatrick et al. (New York: Routledge, 2004), 442–456.

66. See Derek Beales, *Enlightenment and Reform in Eighteenth-Century Europe* (London: I. B. Tauris, 2005).

67. Compare Karin Friedrich, *The Other Prussia: Royal Prussia, Poland and Liberty, 1569–1772* (Cambridge: Cambridge University Press, 2000), 189–216; David E. Fishman, *Russia's First Modern Jews: The Jews of Shklov* (New York: New York University Press,

1995), 46–100; and Larry Wolff, *The Idea of Galicia: History and Fantasy in Habsburg Political Culture* (Stanford, Calif.: Stanford University Press, 2010), 13–62.

68. See Zorin, *Kormia dvuglavogo orla*, 297–336.

69. These tensions contributed to the Decembrist revolt in 1825; but they were characteristic of pre-reform gentry culture in general. See Raeff, *Origins of the Russian Intelligentsia: The Eighteenth-Century Nobility* (New York: Harcourt Brace, 1966), and Yu. M. Lotman, *Besedy o russkoi kul'ture: byt i traditsii russkogo dvorianstva XVIII-nachalo XIX veka* (St. Petersburg: Iskusstvo, 1994).

70. See Nicholas V. Riasanovsky, *A Parting of the Ways: Government and the Educated Public in Russia, 1801–1855* (Oxford: Clarendon Press, 1976),

71. On the Nicholaevan origins of enlightened bureaucracy, see Richard S. Wortman, *The Development of Russian Legal Consciousness* (Chicago: University of Chicago Press, 1976), and W. Bruce Lincoln, *In the Vanguard of Reform: Russia's Enlightened Bureaucrats, 1825–1861* (DeKalb: Northern Illinois University Press, 1986).

72. Israel, *Democratic Enlightenment*, 938.

73. On the comparative politics of Atlantic revolutions, see Klooster, *Revolutions in the Atlantic World*, as well as Marcel Dorigny, *Révoltes et révolutions en Europe et aux Amériques (1773–1802)* (Paris: Belin, 2004), and *Rethinking the Atlantic World: Europe and America in the Age of Democratic Revolutions*, ed. Manuela Albertone and Antonino De Francesco (New York: Palgrave Macmillan, 2009). The classic account remains R. R. Palmer, *Age of the Democratic Revolution: A Political History of Europe and America, 1760–1800*, 2 vols. (Princeton, N.J.: Princeton University Press, 1969–1970).

74. Kant, "Perpetual Peace: A Philosophical Sketch (1795)," *Political Writings*, 112–113.

75. On Kant's conception of "public right," see "Perpetual Peace," 125–127; and "The Metaphysics of Morals," *Political Writings*, 136–137.

76. Kant, "What Is Enlightenment?" 60. Emphases in the original.

77. For the quotation, see Paul Guyer, *Kant* (London: Routledge, 2006), 302.

78. Heine, *The Romantic School and Other Essays*, ed. Jost Hermand and Robert C. Holub (New York: Continuum Publishing, 1985), 66–67.

79. The quotation refers to Kant's allusion to the French Revolution in "Perpetual Peace," 113.

80. Kant, "What Is Enlightenment" 63. Emphases in the original.

81. The quotation comes from the title of a famous essay by Ahad Ha'am (b. Asher Ginzberg), the founder of "spiritual Zionism." See "Slavery within Freedom," in *Selected Essays by Ahad Ha'am*, ed. and trans. Leon Simon (Philadelphia: Jewish Publication Society, 1962), 171–194.

82. See Gai Miron, "Beyn berlin lebagdad: heker toldot yehudei irak veetgar historiografiya meshulevet," *Zion* 71 (2006): 89–97, and Lital Levy, "Reorienting Hebrew Literary History: The View from the East," *Prooftexts* 29 (2009): 127–172.

CHAPTER 2 — BEYOND THE ENLIGHTENMENT

1. Jacob Raisin, *The Haskalah Movement in Russia* (Philadelphia: Jewish Publication Society, 1913).

2. See David Sorkin, "Early Haskalah," in *New Perspectives on the Haskalah*, ed. Shmuel Feiner and David Sorkin (Oxford: Littman Library of Jewish Civilization, 2001), 9–26.

3. James Schmidt, "Preface," in Schmidt, ed., *What Is Enlightenment? Eighteenth-Century Answers and Twentieth-Century Questions* (Berkeley: University of California Press, 1996), ix.

4. Steven M. Lowenstein, "The Shifting Boundary between Eastern and Western Jewry," *Jewish Social Studies* 4 (1997): 61.

5. Mordechai Breuer, *Jüdische Orthodoxie im Deutschen Reich, 1871–1918: Sozialgeschichte einer religiösen Minderheit* (Frankfurt am Main: Athenaeum, 1986), 48.

6. See Ivan T. Berend, *History Derailed: Central and Eastern Europe in the Long Nineteenth Century* (Berkeley: University of California Press, 2003), 41–88.

7. Ibid., 42.

8. Alfredo De Paz, "Innovation and Modernity," in *Romanticism*, ed. Marshall Brown, vol. 5, *The Cambridge History of Literary Criticism* (Cambridge: Cambridge University Press, 2000), 30.

9. Richard Crouter, "Introduction," in Friedrich Schleiermacher, *On Religion: Speeches to Its Cultural Despisers* (Cambridge: Cambridge University Press, 2003), xxviii.

10. For the quotations, see Uzi Shavit, "'Hahaskalah' mahi? levirur musag hahaskalah besifrut ha'ivrit," *Mehkerei yerushalayim besifrut 'ivrit* 12 (1990): 53.

11. Ibid., 62–67.

12. Ibid., 62–63.

13. Ibid., 69.

14. Ibid., 74.

15. Mendelssohn, "On the Question: What Is Enlightenment?" in Schmidt, *What Is Enlightenment?*, 53.

16. Shavit, "'Hahaskalah' mahi?" 76.

17. Ibid., 79.

18. See Frederick C. Beiser, "The Concept of *Bildung* in Early German Romanticism," in *The Romantic Imperative: The Concept of Early German Romanticism* (Cambridge, Mass.: Harvard University Press, 2003), 88–105.

19. Ibid., 93.

20. Ibid., 94.

21. Ben Knights, *The Idea of the Clerisy in the Nineteenth Century* (Cambridge: Cambridge University Press, 1978), 8.

22. Ibid., 13.

23. This is a phrase from Julien Benda's famous 1927 polemic, *The Treason of the Intellectuals*, trans. Richard Aldington (New Brunswick, N.J.: Transaction Books, 2007), xxix. Although Benda applied his description to intellectuals throughout history, it resonates particularly well with Romanticism; Benda himself was something of a Romantic who idealized the distinctive social position that he ascribed to the people whom he called *les clercs*. Culled from the romantic lexicon, the term obviously corresponds to the English construct of "clerisy."

24. Isaiah Berlin, *The Roots of Romanticism*, ed. Henry Hardy (Princeton, N.J.: Princeton University Press, 1999), 130–131.

25. A. W. Schlegel, cited in Bernard M. G. Reardon, *Religion in the Age of Romanticism: Studies in Early Nineteenth-Century Thought* (Cambridge: Cambridge University Press, 1985), 5.

26. Ethel Matala de Mazza, "Romantic Politics and Society," in *The Cambridge Companion to German Romanticism*, ed. Nicholas Saul (Cambridge: Cambridge University Press, 2009), 191–207, here, 204.

27. Gilles Deleuze and Félix Guattari, *Kafka: Toward a Minor Literature*, trans. Dana Polan (Minneapolis: University of Minnesota Press, 1986), 17.

28. Melissa Frazier, *Romantic Encounters: Writers, Readers and the Library for Reading* (Stanford, Calif.: Stanford University Press, 2007), 161–162.

29. The literature on the rise of romantic historicism is enormous. For an introduction to the topic, see Ann Rigney, *Imperfect Histories: The Elusive Past and the Legacy of Romantic Historicism* (Ithaca, N.Y.: Cornell University Press, 2001); John M. Ganim, *Medievalism and Orientalism: Three Essays on Literature, Architecture and Cultural Identity* (London: Palgrave Macmillan, 2008); and Stephen Bann, *The Clothing of Clio: A Study of the Representation of History in Nineteenth-Century Britain and France* (Cambridge: Cambridge University Press, 2011).

30. For an account of this tension, see Marilyn Butler, *Romantics, Rebels and Reactionaries: English Literature and Its Background, 1760–1830* (Oxford: Oxford University Press, 1981).

31. See, for example, George S. Williamson, *The Longing for Myth in Germany: Religion and Aesthetic Culture from Romanticism to Nietzsche* (Chicago: University of Chicago Press, 2004).

32. See Murray Roston, *Prophet and Poet: The Bible and the Growth of Romanticism* (London: Faber and Faber, 1965), and, more recently, Stephen Prickett, *Origins of Narrative: The Romantic Appropriation of the Bible* (Cambridge: Cambridge University Press, 1996).

33. Blanchot, "The Athenaeum," *Studies in Romanticism* 22 (Summer 1983): 163–172, here, 171.

34. For the Russian source, see Sarah Pratt, *Russian Metaphysical Romanticism: The Poetry of Tiutchev and Boratynskii* (Stanford, Calif.: Stanford University Press, 1984), 97.

35. Daniel J. Harrington, *Wisdom Texts from Qumran* (London: Taylor and Francis, 1996), 76. See also Lawrence Schiffman, *Reclaiming the Dead Sea Scrolls* (Philadelphia: Jewish Publication Society, 1994), 125.

36. For an example, see the *Sefer hamaskil,* a thirteenth-century work informed by the esoteric doctrines of Rhineland pietists and written by Solomon Simhah of Troyes, a descendant of Rashi. There is a discussion of this text in Ephraim Kanarfogel, *"Peering through the Lattices": Mystical, Magical, and Pietistic Dimensions in the Tosafist Period* (Detroit: Wayne State University Press, 2000), 239–241.

37. Moshe Hallamish, *An Introduction to Kabbalah* (Albany: State University of New York, 1999), 88. On the image of the maskil as divine "visionary," see Elliot R. Wolfson, *Through a Speculum That Shines: Vision and Imagination in Medieval Jewish Mysticism* (Princeton, N.J.: Princeton University Press, 1994), 378–389.

38. On the complicated relationship between rationality and mysticism in Luzzatto's thought, see Joëlle Hansel, "Hakirah vekabbalah bemishnat ramhal," *Da'at* 40 (1998): 99–108, esp. 101.

39. See Hansel, "Hakirah vekabbalah," 104–108, and her "'Shoresh ve'anafim': higayon vekabbalah behaguto shel haramhal," *Italia* 12 (1996): 47–51.

40. See the tendentious but still valuable summary in Daniel Ben-nahum, *Bema'aleh dorot: 'iyyunim besifrut hahaskalah* (Merhaviah: Sifriyat poa'lim, 1962), 127–131.

41. For a discussion of Luzzatto's "obsessive" iteration of the "call to reflection," see Uzi Shavit, "Le'olamah haidei ule'aklimah haruhani shel hadramah 'l'yesharim tehillah' shel ramhal," in *Shirah ve'ideologiah: letoldot hashirah ha'ivrit vehitpatehutah bameah ha-18 uvameah ha-19* (Tel Aviv: Am oved, 1987), 80–83.

42. See Shmuel Werses, "Dimuyav shel Rav Moshe Hayyim Luzzatto besifrut hahaskalah," *Hakitsah 'ami: sifrut hahaskalah be'idan modernizatsiah* (Jerusalem: Hebrew University, 2001), 3–24.

43. On Luzzatto's career as a messianic activist, see Elisheva Carlebach, *The Pursuit of Heresy: Rabbi Moses Hagiz and the Sabbatian Controversies* (New York: Columbia University Press, 1990), 161–255.

44. On the play, see Shavit, "Leolamah ha'idei," 56–98. On Luzzatto's mystical conception of marriage, see Isaiah Tishby, "The Messianic Ferment in Rabbi Moses Hayim Luzzatto's Group in the Lights of a Messianic Marriage Contract and Messianic Poems," in *Messianic Mysticism: Moses Hayim Luzzatto and the Padua School* (Oxford: Littman Library of Jewish Civilization, 2008), 190–222.

45. For the citations, see Martha Woodmansee, *The Author, Art, and the Market: Rereading the History of Aesthetics* (New York: Columbia University Press, 1994), 13–18.

46. On Shakespeare and the Romantic ideal of originality, see Jonathan Bate, *The Genius of Shakespeare* (Oxford: Oxford University Press, 1997).

47. Jonathan Karp, "The Aesthetic Difference: Moses Mendelssohn's *Kohelet musar* and the Inception of the Berlin Haskalah," in *Renewing the Past, Reconfiguring Jewish Culture from al-Andalus to the Haskalah,* ed. Ross Brann and Adam Sutcliffe (Philadelphia: University of Pennsylvania Press, 2004), 93–120, here, 99.

48. Ibid., 108.

49. Ibid., 110.

50. Compare M. H. Abrams, "Kant and the Theology of Art," *Notre Dame English Journal* 13 (1981): 75–106.

51. Schelling, *On University Studies,* ed. Norbert Guterman (Athens: Ohio University Press, 1966), 144.

52. Mendelssohn, *Jerusalem,* trans. Allan Arkush (Hanover, N.H.: University Press of New England, 1983), 102–103.

53. The quotation is from Alexander Altmann, *Moses Mendelssohn: A Biographical Study* (Tuscaloosa: University of Alabama Press, 1973), 545.

54. Ibid., 547.

55. Rousseau, *Emile, or On Education,* trans. Allan Bloom (New York: Basic Books, 1979), 321.

56. See the references to Gen. 26:32–33, 16:14, 18:1, and 21:46–48.

57. See Jacob Grimm, "Von der Poesie im Recht [1815]," *Kleinere Schriften,* 8 vols. (Berlin: Dümmerl, 1882), 4:153, 158–159, and *Deutsche Rechtsalterthümer,* 2 vols. (Darmstadt: Wissenschaftliche Buchgesellschaft, 1955), 1:179.

58. Savigny, *Of the Vocation of Our Age for Legislation and Jurisprudence* [1814], trans. Abraham Hayward (London: Littlewood, 1831), 67–69.

59. Mendelssohn, *Jerusalem,* 128. Emphasis in the original.

60. See the introduction to the *Biur,* cited in Altmann, *Moses Mendelssohn,* 369.

61. Woodmansee, *The Author, Art and the Market,* 90. See also Lucy Newlyn, *Reading, Writing and Romanticism: The Anxiety of Reception* (Oxford: Oxford University Press, 2000).

62. See Baumgarten, *Introduction to Old Yiddish Literature,* trans. Jerold C. Frakes (Oxford: Oxford University Press, 2005), and *Le people des livres: Les ouvrages populaires dans la société ashkénaze XVIe–XVIIIe siècle* (Paris: Albin Michel, 2010).

63. Cardoso, *Las excelencias de los Hebreos* (Amsterdam, 1679), cited in Yosef Hayim Yerushalmi, *From Spanish Court to Italian Ghetto* (Seattle: University of Washington Press, 1981), 375–376.

64. See Elchanan Reiner, "The Ashkenazi Elite at the Beginning of the Modern Era: Manuscript versus Printed Book," *Polin* 10 (1997): 85–98.

65. See Breuer, "Jüdische Religion und Kultur in den ländlichen Gemeinden 1600–1800," in *Jüdisches Leben auf dem Lande: Studien zur deutsch-jüdischen Geschichte*, ed. Monika Richard and Reinhard Rürup (Tübingen: Mohr Siebeck, 1997), 69–78.

66. For a different reading of the connection between the *Biur* and the *Tsene-rene*, see Naomi Seidman, *Faithful Renderings: Jewish-Christian Difference and the Politics of Translation* (Chicago: University of Chicago Press, 2006), 171.

67. The quotation is from Newlyn, *Reading, Writing and Romanticism*, xi.

68. See Wessely's letter, in *Hameasef* 1 (1784): 7–8.

69. On this tendency, see Michael C. Steinlauf, "Fear of Purim: Y. L. Peretz and the Canonization of the Yiddish Theater," *Jewish Social Studies* 1 (1995): 44–65.

70. See Feiner, "Haishah hayehudiyyah hamodernit: mikreh-mivhan beyehasei hahaskalah vehamodernah,"in *Sexuality and the Family in History: Collected Essays*, ed. Israel Bartal and Isaiah Gafni (Jerusalem: Zalman Shazar, 1998), 253–303.

71. Friedländer's letter to Aaron Halle-Wolfssohn (1799), in Leopold Stein, *Die Shrift des Lebens*, 2 vols. (Strassburg: J. Schneider, 1877), 2: 444–445, cited in Shmuel Feiner, *Jewish Enlightenment*, trans. Chaya Naor (Philadelphia: University of Pennsylvania Press, 2003), 320. Translation slightly altered.

72. See Mendelssohn, "Soll man der einreissenden Schwärmerey durch Satyre oder durch äussere Verbindung entgegenarbeiten?" *Berlinische Monatsschrift* 5 (February 1785): 133–137.

73. Saul, "Aesthetic Humanism (1790–1830)," in *The Cambridge History of German Literature*, ed. Helen Watanabe-O'Kelly (Cambridge: Cambridge University Press, 1997), 202–271. See also Littlejohns, "Crossing a Threshold: The Example of German Romanticism," in *Schwellen: Germanistische Erkundungen einer Metapher*, ed. Nicholas Saul et al. (Würzburg: Königshausen and Neumann, 1999), 152–163. On the relationship between "Weimar classicism" and the German Romantics, see T. J. Reed, "The 'Goethezeit' and Its Aftermath," in *Germany: A Companion to German Studies*, ed. Malcolm Pasley (London: Methuen, 1972), 493–553.

74. Saul, "Aesthetic Humanism," 205. Emphasis in the original.

CHAPTER 3 — HASKALAH AND HISTORY

1. Shmuel Feiner and David Sorkin, "Introduction," in *New Perspectives on the Haskalah* (London: Littman Library of Jewish Civilization, 2001), 1.

2. Jacob Katz, *Tradition and Crisis: Jewish Society at the End of the Middle Ages*, trans. Bernard Dov Cooperman (Syracuse: Syracuse University Press, 2000), 196.

3. Ibid., 220.

4. Ibid., 212.

5. Ibid., 215.

6. Ibid., 226–234.

7. Moshe Rosman, "Haskalah: A New Paradigm," *Jewish Quarterly Review* 97 (2007): 129.

8. Meyer, *The Origins of the Modern Jew: Jewish Identity and European Culture in Germany, 1749–1824* (Detroit: Wayne State University Press, 1967), 8–9.

9. Ibid., 8.

10. Ibid., 56.

11. Todd Endelman, *The Jews of Georgian England, 1714–1830: Tradition and Change in a Liberal Society* (Philadelphia: Jewish Publication Society, 1979), 7–8.

12. Ibid., 166.

13. Ibid., 272–273.

14. Ibid., 293.

15. Ibid., 8.

16. For examples, see Bill Williams, *The Making of Manchester Jewry, 1740–1875* (Manchester: Manchester University Press, 1985), William W. Hagen, *Germans, Poles, and Jews: The Nationality Conflict in the Prussian East, 1772–1914* (Chicago: University of Chicago Press, 1980), and, most recently, Till van Rahden, *Jews and Other Germans: Civil Society, Religious Diversity, and Urban Politics in Breslau, 1860–1925*, trans. Marcus Brainard (Madison: University of Wisconsin Press, 2008).

17. Salo Baron, "Ghetto and Emancipation," *Menorah Journal* 14 (1928): 515–526.

18. Ibid., 524.

19. For three outstanding examples, see Marsha L. Rozenblit, *The Jews of Vienna, 1867–1914: Assimilation and Identity* (Albany: State University of New York Press, 1983); Steven J. Zipperstein, *The Jews of Odessa: A Cultural History, 1794–1881* (Stanford, Calif.: Stanford University Press, 1986); and Paula E. Hyman, *The Emancipation of the Jews of Alsace: Acculturation and Tradition in the Nineteenth Century* (New Haven, Conn.: Yale University Press, 1991).

20. Jacob Katz, ed., *Toward Modernity: The European Jewish Model* (New Brunswick, NJ: Transaction Books, 1987), 1.

21. Hillel Kieval, "Caution's Progress: The Modernization of Jewish Life in Prague, 1780–1830," in ibid., 83.

22. Michael Silber, "The Historical Experience of German Jewry and Its Impact on the Haskalah and Reform in Hungary," in ibid., 115.

23. Lois Dubin, "Trieste and Berlin: The Italian Role in the Cultural Politics of the Haskalah," in ibid., 209.

24. See Jacob Katz, *Out of the Ghetto: The Social Background of Jewish Emancipation, 1770–1870* (Cambridge, Mass.: Harvard University Press, 1973), 65–70.

25. Israel Bartal, "'The Heavenly City of Germany' and Absolutism à la Mode d'Autriche: The Rise of the Haskalah in Galicia," in Katz, *Toward Modernity*, 33.

26. Michael Stanislawski, *Tsar Nicholas I and the Jews: The Transformation of Jewish Society in Russia, 1825–1855* (Philadelphia: Jewish Publication Society, 1983), 51.

27. Ibid., 108.

28. Ibid., 111.

29. Ibid., 120–121.

30. See Benjamin Nathans, *Beyond the Pale: The Jewish Encounter with Late Imperial Russia* (Berkeley: University of California Press, 2002), and Olga Litvak, *Conscription and the Search for Modern Russian Jewry* (Bloomington: Indiana University Press, 2006).

31. Michael Stanislawski, *For Whom Do I Toil? Judah Leib Gordon and the Crisis of Russian Jewry* (Oxford: Oxford University Press, 1988), 4.

32. Lois Dubin, *The Port Jews of Habsburg Trieste: Absolutist Politics and Enlightenment Culture* (Stanford, Calif.: Stanford University Press, 1999).

33. David Fishman, *Russia's First Modern Jews: The Jews of Shklov* (New York: New York University Press, 1995), 122.

34. Nancy Sinkoff, *Out of the Shtetl: Making Jews Modern in the Polish Borderlands* (Providence: Brown Judaic Studies, 2004), 83.

35. Ibid., 203.

36. Marcin Wodzinski, "Good Maskilim and Bad Assimilationists, or Toward a New Historiography of the Haskalah in Poland," *Jewish Social Studies* 10 (2004): 97.

37. Ibid., 107–108.

38. Ezra Mendelsohn, *Class Struggle in the Pale: The Formative Years of the Jewish Workers' Movement in Tsarist Russia* (Cambridge: Cambridge University Press, 1970).

39. Eli Lederhendler, *The Road to Modern Jewish Politics: Political Tradition and Political Reconstruction in the Jewish Community of Tsarist Russia* (Oxford: Oxford University Press, 1989), 155.

40. See Rachel Manekin, "Naftali Herz Homberg: hadmut vehadimui," *Zion* 71 (2006): 153–202, and Marcin Wodzinski, *Haskalah and Hasidism in the Kingdom of Poland: A History of Conflict*, trans. Sarah Cozens and Agniezska Mirowska (Oxford: Littman Library of Jewish Civilization, 2005).

41. This vision of the state anticipates the politics of renewal pursued by the architect of modern Israel, David Ben-Gurion: see Shlomo Aronson, *David Ben-Gurion and the Jewish Renaissance*, trans. Naftali Greenwood (Cambridge: Cambridge University Press, 2010).

42. Steven Lowenstein, *The Berlin Jewish Community: Enlightenment, Family and Crisis, 1770–1830* (Oxford: Oxford University Press, 1994), 8–9.

43. Ibid., 5.

44. Ibid., 191.

45. David Sorkin, "The Early Haskalah," in Feiner and Sorkin, *New Perspectives on the Haskalah*, 26. On the connection between Sorkin's reading of the Haskalah and German Jewish history, see his *Transformation of German Jewry, 1780–1840* (Oxford: Oxford University Press, 1987).

46. See David Sorkin, "From Context to Comparison: The German Haskalah and Reform Catholicism," *Tel Aviver Jahrbuch für deutsche Geschichte* 20 (1991): 23–58.

47. Shmuel Feiner, *The Jewish Enlightenment*, trans. Chaya Naor (Philadelphia: University of Pennsylvania Press, 2003), 342.

48. For a summary of this argument, see Shmuel Feiner, "The Pseudo-Enlightenment and the Question of Jewish Modernization," *Jewish Social Studies* 3 (1996): 62–88.

49. Feiner, *The Jewish Enlightenment*, 363.

50. Feiner, "Haishah hayehudiyah hamodernit: mikreh-mivhan beyahasei hahaskalah vehamodernah," in *Sexuality and the Family in History: Collected Essays*, ed. Israel Bartal and Isaiah Gafni (Jerusalem: Zalman Shazar, 1998), 269.

51. See Tova Cohen, *'The One Beloved, the Other Hated': Between Fiction and Reality in Haskalah Depictions of Women* [Heb.] (Jerusalem: Magnes Press, 2002).

52. See Eliyana Adler, *In Her Hands: The Education of Jewish Girls in Tsarist Russia* (Detroit: Wayne State University Press, 2011).

53. Naomi Seidman, *A Marriage Made in Heaven: The Sexual Politics of Hebrew and Yiddish* (Berkeley: University of California Press, 1997), 22.

54. Ibid., 23–24.

55. On the growth of Jewish secular literature in nineteenth-century Western Europe, see Michael Galchinsky, *The Origin of the Modern Jewish Woman Writer: Romance and Reform in Victorian England* (Detroit: Wayne State University Press, 1996); Maurice Samuels, *Inventing the Israelite: Jewish Fiction in Nineteenth-Century France* (Stanford, Calif.: Stanford University Press, 2009); and Jonathan Hess, *Middlebrow Literature and the Making of German-Jewish Identity* (Stanford, Calif.: Stanford University Press, 2010).

56. David Roskies, "Ayzik Meyer Dik: The Storyteller as Enlightened Maggid" [Heb.], *Khulyot* 1 (1993): 7–41.

57. Dan Miron, "Folklore and Antifolklore in the Yiddish Fiction of the Haskala," in *Studies in Jewish Folklore*, ed. Frank Talmage (Cambridge, Mass.: Association for Jewish Studies, 1980), 219–248, here, 233.

58. On the "neoclassical" aesthetic of Haskalah literature, see Dan Miron, *From Romance to the Novel: Studies in the Emergence of the Hebrew and Yiddish Novel in the Nineteenth Century* [Heb.] (Jerusalem: Mosad Bialik, 1979), 17–51.

59. Jeremy Dauber, "The City, Sacred and Profane: Between Hebrew and Yiddish in the Fiction of the Early Jewish Enlightenment," *Jewish Studies Quarterly* 12:1 (2005): 43–60.

60. Shimon Halkin, *Conventions and Crises in Hebrew Literature* [Heb.] (Jerusalem: Mosad Bialik, 1980), 44.

61. Amir Banbaji, *Mendele and the National Project* [Heb.] (Beer Sheva: Ben-Gurion University Press, 2010).

62. The quotation is from Emanuel Etkes, "Haskalah," in *YIVO Encyclopedia of Jews in Eastern Europe*, ed. Gershon Hundert, 2 vols. (New Haven, Conn.: Yale University Press, 2008), 1: 687.

CHAPTER 4 — HASKALAH AND MODERN JEWISH THOUGHT

1. Allan Arkush, "The Liberalism of Moses Mendelssohn," in *The Cambridge Companion to Modern Jewish Philosophy*, ed. Michael L. Morgan and Peter Eli Gordon (Cambridge: Cambridge University Press, 2007), 37.

2. Alexander Altmann, *Moses Mendelssohn: A Biographical Study* (Tuscaloosa: University of Alabama Press, 1973), 5.

3. Ibid., 552.

4. Ibid., 549–550.

5. Allan Arkush, *Moses Mendelssohn and the Enlightenment* (Albany: State University of New York Press, 1994), xiv.

6. David Sorkin, *Moses Mendelssohn and the Religious Enlightenment* (Berkeley: University of California Press, 1996), xxii.

7. Alexander Altmann, "Moses Mendelssohn's Concept of Judaism Re-examined," cited in Arkush, *Moses Mendelssohn*, xii.

8. Arkush, *Moses Mendelssohn*, xiv–xv.

9. Ibid., 260.

10. Ibid., 242.

11. Ibid., 283.

12. Arkush, "The Liberalism of Moses Mendelssohn," 37.

13. Sorkin, *Moses Mendelssohn*, xxiii.

14. See the well-known article by Ismar Schorsch, "The Myth of Sephardic Supremacy," in *From Text to Context: The Turn to History in Modern Judaism* (Hanover, N.H.: University Press of New England, 1994), 71–92.

15. David Sorkin, "From Context to Comparison: The German Haskalah and Reform Catholicism," *Tel Aviver Jahrbuch für deutsche Geschichte* 20 (1991): 27.

16. Sorkin, *Moses Mendelssohn*, xxiii.

17. Ibid., 8.

18. Ibid., 143.

19. Ibid., 136.

20. David Sorkin, "The Mendelssohn Myth and Its Method," *New German Critique* 77 (1999): 7–28.

21. Ibid., 27.

22. Ibid., 24–25.

23. Sorkin, "From Context to Comparison," 56. Sorkin has recently devoted an entire book to this argument; see *The Religious Enlightenment: Protestants, Jews, and Catholics from London to Vienna* (Princeton, N.J.: Princeton University Press, 2008).

24. For an example of this tendency in postmodern scholarship on the Enlightenment, informed not only by critical theory but also by the work of Michel Foucault along similar lines, see Dorinda Outram, *The Enlightenment* (Cambridge: Cambridge University Press, 2005).

25. Jacob Katz, "The German-Jewish Utopia of Social Emancipation," in *Studies of the Leo Baeck Institute*, ed. Max Kreutzberger (New York: Frederick Ungar, 1967), 59–80.

26. Daniel Boyarin, *Unheroic Conduct: The Rise of Heterosexuality and the Invention of the Jewish Man* (Berkeley: University of California Press, 1997), 333.

27. See Daniel Boyarin and Jonathan Boyarin, "Diaspora: Generation and the Ground of Jewish Identity," *Critical Inquiry* 19 (1993): 693–725.

28. The provocative image of the "fat rabbi" recurs throughout Daniel Boyarin's work; see his *Carnal Israel: Reading Sex in Talmudic Culture* (Berkeley: University of California Press, 1994), and, most recently, *Socrates and the Fat Rabbis* (Chicago: University of Chicago Press, 2009).

29. Boyarin, *Unheroic Conduct*, 267–268.

30. Sam Moyn, "German Jewry and the Question of Identity: Historiography and Theory," *Leo Baeck Institute Yearbook* 41 (1996): 308. See also Steven E. Aschheim, *Beyond the Border: The German-Jewish Legacy Abroad* (Princeton, N.J.: Princeton University Press, 2007), 81–119.

31. Aamir Mufti, *Enlightenment in the Colony: The Jewish Question and the Crisis of Post-Colonial Culture* (Princeton, N.J.: Princeton University Press, 2007), 42–43. Emphasis in the original.

32. Willi Goetschel, *Spinoza's Modernity: Mendelssohn, Lessing, and Heine* (Madison: University of Wisconsin Press, 2004), 148.

33. Jonathan Hess, *Germans, Jews, and the Claims of Modernity* (New Haven, Conn.: Yale University Press, 2002), 118. Emphasis in the original.

34. For a summary of the argument, see ibid., 17–18.

35. Nancy Sinkoff, "Benjamin Franklin in Jewish Eastern Europe: Cultural Appropriation in the Age of the Enlightenment," *Journal of the History of Ideas* 61.1 (2000): 151.

36. Shmuel Ettinger, "Yehudim betsavat hahaskalah," (1980), cited in Mordechai Zalkin, "Between the Humanists and Nationalists: Developments in the Study of the Jewish Enlightenment in the State of Israel" [Heb.], *Zion* 74 (2009): 177.

37. For the quotation, see Edward Breuer, *The Limits of Enlightenment: Jews, Germans, and the Eighteenth-Century Study of Scripture* (Cambridge, Mass.: Harvard University Press, 1996), 227.

38. Cited in Perez Sandler, *Mendelssohn's Edition of the Pentateuch* [Heb.], 2nd ed. (Jerusalem: Reuven Mas, 1984), 226.

39. Friedrich Schlegel, *Lucinde and the Fragments*, trans. Peter Firchow (Minneapolis: University of Minnesota Press, 1971), 147.

40. Uzi Shavit, "'Hahaskalah' mahi? levirur musag hahaskalah besifrut ha'ivrit," *Mehkerei yerushalayim besifrut 'ivrit* 12 (1990): 52.

CHAPTER 5 — EXILE

1. On the mythology of Exile as a response to pagan and Christian hegemony, see Chaim Milikowsky, "Notions of Exile, Subjugation, and Return in Rabbinic Literature," in *Exile: Old Testament, Jewish and Christian Conceptions*, ed. James M. Scott (Leiden: Brill, 1997), 265–296; and Israel Jacob Yuval, "Mitos hahaglayah min haaretz: zman yehudi vezman notsri," *Alpayim* 29 (2005): 9–25.

2. 4 Ezra 5:23, cited in Martin Goodman, *Rome and Jerusalem: The Clash of Ancient Civilizations* (New York: Vintage, 2007), 425.

3. Judah Halevi, *The Kuzari: An Argument for the Faith of Israel*, trans. Hartwig Hirschfeld (New York: Schocken, 1964), 294.

4. See Israel J. Yuval, *Two Nations in Your Womb: Perceptions of Jews and Christians in Late Antiquity and the Middle Ages*, trans. Barbara Harshav and Jonathan Chipman (Berkeley: University of California Press, 2006), 257–296.

5. Menahem Lorberbaum, "Medieval Jewish Political Thought," in *The Cambridge Companion to Medieval Jewish Philosophy*, ed. Daniel H. Frank and Oliver Leaman (Cambridge: Cambridge University Press, 2003), 176–200, here, 177.

6. Cited in Marc Saperstein, *Jewish Preaching, 1200–1800: An Anthology* (New Haven, Conn.: Yale University Press, 1989), 82.

7. Jeremy Cohen, *Sanctifying the Name of God: Jewish Martyrs and Jewish Memories of the First Crusade* (Philadelphia: University of Pennsylvania Press, 2004), 80.

8. On the difference between "systemic" and "occasional" violence, see David Nirenberg, *Communities of Violence: Persecution of Minorities in the Middle Ages* (Princeton, N.J.: Princeton University Press, 1996), 127–230.

9. Elisheva Baumgarten, *Mothers and Children: Jewish Family Life in Medieval Europe* (Princeton, N.J.: Princeton University Press, 2004), 12.

10. See Yosef Hayim Yerushalmi, "Exile and Expulsion in Jewish History," in *Crisis and Creativity in the Sephardic World, 1391–1648*, ed. Benjamin R. Gampel (New York: Columbia University Press, 1997), 3–22.

11. Ibid., 11.

12. On religion and the rise of modern state theory, see the classic account by Quentin Skinner, *The Foundation of Modern Political Thought*, vol. 2, *The Age of the Reformation* (Cambridge: Cambridge University Press, 1978).

13. On the theory and practice of religious toleration in early modern Europe, see Perez Zagorin, *How the Idea of Religious Toleration Came to the West* (Princeton, N.J.: Princeton University Press, 2003), and Benjamin J. Kaplan, *Divided by Faith: Religious Conflict and the Practice of Toleration in Early Modern Europe* (Cambridge, Mass.: Belknap, 2007).

14. See Benjamin Ravid, "A Tale of Three Cities and Their *Raison d'État*: Ancona, Venice, Livorno, and the Competition for Jewish Merchants in the Sixteenth Century," *Mediterranean Historical Review* 6 (1991): 138–162.

15. Adam Teller, "Jewish Literary Responses to the Events of 1648–1649 and the Creation of a Polish-Jewish Consciousness," in *Culture Front: Representing Jews in Eastern Europe*, ed. Benjamin Nathans and Gabriella Safran (Philadelphia: University of Pennsylvania Press, 2007), 27.

16. Ibid., 30.

17. Hobbes argued that political coercion wielded by an "absolute government" was the only way to counteract the "dissolute condition of masterless men" and to "tie their hands from rapine and revenge." See Perez Zagorin, *Hobbes and the Law of Nature* (Princeton, N.J.: Princeton University Press, 2009), 58.

18. On the ambiguous image of covenants in *Abyss of Despair*, see Mordechai Nadav, "The Jewish Community of Nemyriv in 1648: The Massacre and Loyalty Oath to the Cossacks," *Harvard Ukrainian Studies* 8 (1984): 380–387.

19. Gershon Hundert, *Jews in Poland-Lithuania in the Eighteenth Century: A Genealogy of Modernity* (Berkeley: University of California Press, 2004), 130.

20. Lawrence Fine, *Physician of the Soul, Healer of the Cosmos: Isaac Luria and His Kabbalistic Fellowship* (Stanford, Calif.: Stanford University Press, 2003), 312.

21. Hundert, *Jews in Poland-Lithuania*, 119–130.

22. The quotation is from Elisheva Carlebach, *The Pursuit of Heresy: Rabbi Moses Hagiz and the Sabbatian Controversies* (New York: Columbia University Press, 1990), 2.

23. See Marc David Baer, *The Dönme: Jewish Converts, Muslim Revolutionaries, and Secular Turks* (Stanford, Calif.: Stanford University Press, 2009), 1–24.

24. This is essentially the view of Moshe Idel. See his "'One from a Town, Two from a Clan'—The Diffusion of Lurianic Kabbalah and Sabbateanism: A Reexamination," *Jewish History* 7 (1993): 79–104.

25. See Scholem, "Tenu'at hashabtaut bepolin," *Beit yisrael befolin,* ed. Israel Halpern, 2 vols. (Jerusalem: Hamahlakah le'inyane hano'ar shel hahistadrut hatsiyonit, 1948–1954), 2:36–76.

26. Carlebach, *The Pursuit of Heresy,* 273.

27. See, for instance, Shmuel Ettinger, "Hapulmus emden-eybeschutz leorah shel hahistoriografiah hayehudit," *Kabbalah* 9 (2003): 329–392.

28. Carlebach, *The Pursuit of Heresy,* 9.

29. Ibid., 17.

30. Cited in Michael A. Meyer et al., ed., *German-Jewish History in Modern Times,* 4 vols. (New York: Columbia University Press, 1996), 1:238. For the source of Emden's biblical quotation, see Ezra 9:2. On Emden's views of his Jewish contemporaries' contact with Christians, see Blu Greenberg, "Rabbi Jacob Emden: The Views of an Enlightened Traditionalist on Christianity," *Judaism* 27 (1978): 351–363.

CHAPTER 6 — NEW CREATION

1. *The Memoirs of Ber of Bolechow,* ed. and trans. Mark Vishnitzer (London: Oxford University Press, 1922), 97–102.

2. Glückel provides one of the few characterizations of Jewish life in Berlin before the arrival of Mendelssohn; the marked absence of the city in contemporary Jewish literature is, in and of itself, a strong indication of obscurity. See *Glikl, zikhronot* [Heb. and Yid.], ed. and trans. Chava Turniansky (Jerusalem: Hebrew University Press, 2006), 386–400, here, 397.

3. On the image of early modern Poland as the "center of Torah," see Moshe Rosman, "Dimuyav shel beit-yisrael befolin k'merkaz torah aharei gzerot tah-tat," *Zion* 51 (1986): 435–448.

4. Naftali Herz Wessely, *Divrei shalom ve'emet* (Vienna: Anton Schmid, 1826), 10. This is the third edition of the text, originally published in Berlin in 1782.

5. Ibid., 8.

6. Ibid., 11.

7. Ibid., 22.

8. The quotation is from Joseph's own characterization of his new "religion of the state," cited in Gregory L. Freeze, *The Russian Levites: Parish Clergy in the Eighteenth Century* (Cambridge, Mass.: Harvard University Press, 1977), 13.

9. Wessely, *Divrei shalom ve'emet,* 13.

10. Ibid., 9.

11. Ibid.

12. Ibid., 15.

13. John G. Gager, *Reinventing Paul* (Oxford: Oxford University Press, 2000), 140.

14. The quotation is from Mark 1:15. But the idea did not originate in the New Testament; for the source in the Hebrew Bible, see Habbakuk 2:3, where the prophet refers to the "appointed time" of revelation.

15. Gager, *Reinventing Paul*, 124.

16. Ibid., 112.

17. Ibid., 141.

18. Martin Goodman, *Rome and Jerusalem: The Clash of Ancient Civilizations* (New York: Vintage, 2007), 520.

19. Deut. 30:1–3 JPS. Emphasis added.

20. Est. 9:29–32 JPS. Emphasis added. Translation slightly altered.

21. Landau's sermon was reprinted in 1886; for the citation, see Shmuel Feiner, *Haskalah and History: The Emergence of a Modern Jewish Awareness of the Past* [Heb.] (Jerusalem: Zalman Shazar, 1995), 70n27.

22. Ibid., 70.

23. Ibid., 71.

24. I am referring to the well-known tenet of ultra-Orthodox legal and cultural practice, "The Torah forbids innovation" (Heb. *Hadash asur min hatorah*, lit. "First fruits are prohibited according to biblical law"). This principle is attributed to R. Moses Sofer, the spiritual heir to Landau and Fleckeles. See Michael Silber, "The Emergence of Ultra-Orthodoxy: The Invention of a Tradition," in *The Uses of Tradition: Jewish Continuity in the Modern Era*, ed. Jack Wertheimer (New York: Jewish Theological Seminary, 1992), 23–84.

25. On modern ultra-orthodox separatism, see Silber, "The Emergence of Ultra-Orthodoxy," and "Alliance of the Hebrews, 1863–1875: The Diaspora Roots of an Ultra-Orthodox Proto-Zionist Utopia in Palestine," *Journal of Israeli History* 27 (2008): 119–147.

26. This is a point made by Shmuel Feiner; see *The Jewish Enlightenment*, trans. Chaya Naor (Philadelphia: University of Pennsylvania Press, 2004), 163.

27. Moses Mendelssohn, *Jerusalem, or on Religious Power and Judaism*, trans. Allan Arkush (Hanover, N.H.: University Press of New England, 1983), 95–96.

28. Moses Mendelssohn, *Phaedon, or the Death of Socrates* (1767), cited in Paul Hazard, *European Thought in the Eighteenth Century*, trans. J. Lewis May (Cleveland and New York: Meridian, 1963), 430.

29. Mendelssohn, *Jerusalem*, 42.

30. Ibid., 43.

31. Ibid., 97.

32. Ibid., 79.

33. For the quotation from Cranz's letter, see Alexander Altmann, *Moses Mendelssohn: A Biographical Study* (Tuscaloosa: University of Alabama Press, 1973), 507.

34. Moses Mendelssohn, "Reply to Lavater (1769)," in *The German-Jewish Dialogue: An Anthology of Literary Texts, 1749–1993*, ed. Ritchie Robertson (Oxford: Oxford University Press, 1999), 36–45, here, 41. Emphasis in the original.

35. Ibid., 41.

36. Ibid., 39. Emphasis in the original.

37. Mendelssohn introduced his own argument with references to Hobbes and Locke; see *Jerusalem*, 35–37. On the relationship between the politics of *Jerusalem* and Spinoza's *Theological-Political Treatise*, see Willi Goetschel, *Spinoza's Modernity: Mendelssohn, Lessing, and Heine* (Madison: University of Wisconsin Press, 2004), 159–169.

38. Mendelssohn, *Jerusalem*, 129–130.

39. Ibid., 77.

40. Ibid., 89–90.

41. On this point, see Allan Arkush, *Moses Mendelssohn and the Enlightenment* (Albany: State University of New York Press, 1994), 254–274.

42. Mendelssohn, *Jerusalem*, 98.

43. Ibid., 127. Emphasis in the original.

44. Ibid., 135.

45. Ibid.

CHAPTER 7 — FAITH

1. Cited in B. D. Weinryb, "Le-toldot RiVaL," *Tarbiz* 5 (1934): 204.

2. David G. Roskies, *A Bridge of Longing: The Lost Art of Yiddish Storytelling* (Cambridge, Mass.: Harvard University Press, 1995), 6.

3. Joseph Perl, *Revealer of Secrets*, trans. Dov Taylor (Boulder, Colo.: Westview Press, 1997), 272. For the Yiddish original, see Simhah Katz, "New Materials from the Perl Archive: Joseph Perl's Introduction to the Yiddish *Revealer of Secrets*" [Yid.], *YIVO Bleter* 13 (1938): 557–561, 566–575.

4. Perl, *Revealer of Secrets*, 53–54.

5. Ibid., 38.

6. Ibid., 68.

7. Ibid., 239.

8. Ibid., 33.

9. See Alyssa Quint, "Naked Truths: Avraham Goldfaden's *The Fanatic or the Two Kuni-Lemls*," in *Arguing the Modern Jewish Canon: Essays on Literature and Culture in Honor*

of Ruth R. Wisse, ed. Justin Cammy et al. (Cambridge, Mass.: Harvard University Press, 2008), 551–577.

10. On the fruitless maskilic struggle against the legalization of Hasidic prayer gatherings (Heb. *minyanim*) in Galicia, see Rachel Manekin, "Galician Haskalah and the Discourse on *Schwärmerei*." This important paper is forthcoming in a collection of essays about Jewish secularization to be published by the University of Pennsylvania Press. I am grateful to Dr. Manekin for sharing a draft with me.

11. For the quotations, see Shmuel Feiner, *Haskalah and History: The Emergence of a Modern Jewish Awareness of the Past* [Heb.] (Jerusalem: Zalman Shazar, 1995), 125–126.

12. Ibid., 128.

13. Ibid., 188.

14. Ibid., 109.

15. Ibid., 109.

16. Ismar Schorsch, "From Wolfenbüttel to *Wissenschaft*: The Divergent Paths of Isaak Markus Jost and Leopold Zunz," in *From Text to Context: The Turn to History in Modern Judaism* (Hanover, N.H.: University Press of New England, 1994), 242.

17. Reuven Michael, *I. M. Jost: Founder of Modern Jewish Historiography* [Heb.] (Jerusalem: Hebrew University, 1983), 67–68. For the original source, see Jost, *Geschichte der Israeliten seit der Zeit der Maccabaer bis auf unsere Tage*, 9 vols. (Berlin: Schlesingerische Buch und Musikhandlung, 1820–1828), 9:50–51.

18. "Moreh nevukhei hazman," in *The Writings of Nachman Krochmal* [Heb.], ed. Simon Rawidowicz (London: Ararat Publishing Society, 1961), 7–9.

19. Ibid., 292. On Krochmal's philosophy of Jewish law as a polemical response to Hegel's Christian triumphalism, see Jay M. Harris, *Nachman Krochmal: Guiding the Perplexed of the Modern Age* (New York: New York University Press, 1991), 44–102, here, 56.

20. Hindy Najman, "The Writing and Reception of Philo of Alexandria," in *Christianity in Jewish Terms*, ed. Tikvah Frymer-Kensky et al. (New York: Basic Books, 2002), 99–105.

21. Harris, *Nachman Krochmal: Guiding the Perplexed*, 137.

22. "Moreh nevukhei hazman," 40–41.

23. Harris, *Nachman Krochmal: Guiding the Perplexed*, 81.

24. "Moreh nevukhei hazman," 11.

25. Ibid., 15.

26. For the quotation, embedded in his thoughtful discussion of the rabbinic metaphor of the two paths, see Harris, *Nachman Krochmal: Guiding the Perplexed*, 24.

27. Ibid., 86.

28. Feiner, *Haskalah and History*, 104.

29. Ibid., 153.

30. "Mikhtav le'bik [1830]," *Hashahar* 4 (1873): 486.

CHAPTER 8 — PARADISE

1. Sh. J. Fuenn, *Kiryah ne'emanah* (Vilna: Isaac Funk, 1915), 148.

2. On the relationship between Vilna's traditional learned elite and the maskilic social ideal, see Mordechai Zalkin, *A New Dawn: The Jewish Enlightenment in the Russian Empire, Social Aspects* [Hebrew] (Jerusalem: Hebrew University Press, 2000).

3. Ibid., 34.

4. Czeslaw Milosz, *The History of Polish Literature* (Berkeley: University of California Press, 1969), 232.

5. See Mikhail Dolbilov, *Russkii krai, chuzhaia vera: etnokonfessional'naia politika imperii v Litve i Belorussii pri Aleksandre II* (Moscow: Novoe literaturnoe obozrenie, 2010).

6. Lev Levanda, *Goriachee vremia: roman iz poslednego pol'skogo vosstaniia* (St. Petersburg: A. E. Landau, 1875), 61. Emphasis in the original. The novel first appeared in serial form between 1871 and 1873, in the Russian-Jewish literary annual *Evreiskaia biblioteka*, edited by Landau, and subsequently reissued as an offprint.

7. See ChaeRan Y. Freeze, "The Politics of Love in Lev Levanda's *Turbulent Times*," in *Gender and Jewish History*, ed. Marion A. Kaplan and Deborah Dash Moore (Bloomington: Indiana University Press, 2011), 187–202.

8. Ibid., 201.

9. H. N. Shapira, *Toldot hasifrut ha'ivrit hahadashah* (Tel Aviv: Masada, 1967), 122.

10. For the citations, see Tova Cohen, *'One Beloved, the Other Hated': Between Fiction and Reality in Haskalah Depictions of Women* [Heb.] (Jerusalem: Hebrew University, 2002), 165.

11. On Mapu's competitive attitude to contemporary French novels in general and on his jealousy of Shulman in particular, see David Patterson, *Abraham Mapu: A Literary Study of the Creator of the Modern Hebrew Novel* (Ithaca, N.Y.: Cornell University Press, 1964), 102–104.

12. M. L. Lilienblum, *Autobiography* [Heb.], ed. Shlomo Breiman, 3 vols. (Jerusalem: Mosad Bialik, 1970), 1:131.

13. Abraham Mapu, *The Love of Zion and Other Writings*, trans. Joseph Marymount (London: Toby Press, 2006), 11.

14. Ibid., 12.

15. Ibid., 132–133, 152, 172.

16. On the mystical androgyny of the date palm, see Elliot R. Wolfson, *Language, Eros, Being: Kabbalistic Hermeneutics and Poetic Imagination* (New York: Fordham University Press, 2005), 311.

17. Mapu, *Love of Zion*, 142.

18. Ibid., 157.

19. Ibid., 24.

20. Ibid., 131.

21. Ibid., 43. Translation altered. For the original, see *Kol kitvei Avraham Mapu* (Tel Aviv: Dvir, 1955), 11.

22. For information about Eleazar Raschkow, see his obituary in *Ha-magid* 14.32 (August 1870): 9. See also Cohen, 'One Beloved, the Other Hated,' 45. Cohen misdates the work and attributes it to Alexander Süsskind Raschkow, a Hebrew poet from Prussian Poland who wrote several biblical dramas. Unfortunately, Cohen does not provide a source for her citation from the poem.

23. On the female readership of Mapu's work, see Iris Parush, *Reading Jewish Women: Marginality and Modernization in Nineteenth-Century Eastern European Society*, trans. Saadya Sternberg (Waltham, Mass.: Brandeis University Press, 2004), 216. Within two decades of publication, *Love of Zion* was translated into Yiddish, which secured its popularity among a more general class of Jewish readers; see Shmuel Werses, *Yiddisch [sic] Translations of Ahavat zion by Avraham Mapu* [Heb.] (Jerusalem: Akademon, 1989), 15–49.

24. On the formal "neoclassical" plot of *Love of Zion*, see Dan Miron, *From Romance to the Novel: Studies in the Emergence of the Hebrew and Yiddish Novel in the Nineteenth Century* [Heb.] (Jerusalem: Mosad Bialik, 1979), 17–53, esp. 24–26.

25. Mapu, *Love of Zion*, 266.

26. For the citation, see Shmuel Feiner, *Haskalah and History: The Emergence of a Modern Jewish Awareness of the Past* [Heb.] (Jerusalem: Zalman Shazar, 1995), 212.

27. Richard S. Wortman, *The Crisis of Russian Populism* (Cambridge: Cambridge University Press, 1967), 81.

28. There is only one complete English translation of "The Tip of the Yud." See Stanley Nash, "'Kotso shel yud' ('The Tip of the Yud')," *CCAR Journal* 53 (2006): 107–188, here, 174. Nash provides the Hebrew text alongside the English, hereafter cited as Gordon, "Kotso shel yud."

29. Nash, "'The Tip of the Yud,'" 165.

30. Compare Cohen, 'One Beloved, the Other Hated,' 291–300. Michael Stanislawski suggests that the poem is a parody but does not elaborate on the implications of his important correction of the conventional insistence on the poem's realism; see Stanislawski, *For Whom Do I Toil? Judah Leib Gordon and the Crisis of Russian Jewry* (Oxford: Oxford University Press, 1988), 127–128.

31. Nash, "'The Tip of the Yud,'" 120.

32. Ibid., 121.

33. Gordon, "Kotso shel yud," 125.

34. Nash, "'The Tip of the Yud,'" 133; the relevant talmudic passage is BT Hullin 70a.

35. For the full text of the poem in English translation, see *The Complete Poems of Heinrich Heine: A Modern English Version,* ed. and trans. Hal Draper (Boston: Suhrkamp/Insel, 1982), 580–583.

36. Nash, "'The Tip of the Yud,'" 155. Emphasis added.

37. Ibid., 157.

38. Ibid., 166.

39. See Stanislawski, *For Whom Do I Toil?* 127.

40. Nash, "'The Tip of the Yud,'" 176.

41. Gordon, "Kotso shel yud," 178.

42. Elliot R. Wolfson, "Circumcision, Vision of God and Textual Interpretation," in *Circle in the Square: Studies in the Use of Gender in Kabbalistic Symbolism* (Albany: State University of New York Press, 1995), 41–42.

43. Nash, "'The Tip of the Yud,'" 183.

44. Ibid., 186.

45. Tova Cohen and Shmuel Feiner, *Voice of a Hebrew Maiden: Women's Writings of the Nineteenth-Century Haskalah Movement* [Heb.] (Tel Aviv: Hakibbutz Hameuchad, 2006), 130.

46. Dan Miron, "Rediscovering Haskalah Poetry," *Prooftexts* 1 (1981): 303.

47. Ibid., 304.

48. For the quotation from "The God Apollo," see Heine, *Complete Poems,* 580.

49. Roland Barthes, "The Death of the Author," in *Modern Criticism and Theory: A Reader,* ed. David Lodge (London: Longman, 1988), 172.

CHAPTER 9 — FALL

1. Isaac-Baer Levinsohn, *Di hefker-velt* (Warsaw: David Sova, 1903), 32.

2. Isaac-Baer Levinsohn, *Yalkut ribal* (Warsaw: A. Ginz, 1878), 72.

3. The quotation is from Thomas Carlyle, *Sartor Resartus* [1830] (Oxford: Oxford University Press, 2008), 141.

4. The quotation is from Zelig Kalmanovich, *Yosef perls yidishe ksovim* (Vilna, 1937), cited in Ken Frieden, "Joseph Perl's Escape from Biblical Epigonism through Parody of Hasidic Writing," *AJS Review* 29.2 (2005): 277.

5. For the source of the quotation, see Friedrich Schlegel, *Lucinde and the Fragments,* trans. Peter Firchow (Minneapolis: University of Minnesota Press, 1971), 148.

6. See Shmuel Werses, "Yad yamin dohah, smol mekarevet: 'al yahasam shel sofrei hahaskalah lelashon yidish," in *Awake, My People: Hebrew Literature in the Age of Modernization* [Heb.] (Jerusalem: Magnes Press, 2001), 252.

7. Saul Ginzburg, "New Material Regarding Israel Aksenfeld," *YIVO Annual of Jewish Social Studies* 5 (1950): 174–175.

8. Israel Aksenfeld, "The Headband [sic]," in *Shtetl: A Creative Anthology of Jewish Life in Eastern Europe*, ed. and trans. Joachim Neugroschel (New York: Richard Marek, 1979), 107.

9. Ibid., 108.

10. For a striking example, see the figure of Aaron Lustig, in G[rigorii] Bogrov, "Poimannik," *Evreiskaia biblioteka* 4 (1874): 1–100.

11. Arnold J. Band, "The Bratslav Theory of the Sacred Tale," in *Nahman of Bratslav: The Tales* (New York: Paulist Press, 1978), 37.

12. Aksenfeld, "The Headband," 114. Translation slightly altered. For the original, see Yisroel Axenfeld [sic], *Dos shterntikhl un der ershter yidisher rekrut* (Buenos Aires: Literatur-gezelshaft bay YiVO in Argentine, 1971), 112.

13. See the charter of the OPE, cited in Brian Horowitz, *Jewish Philanthropy and Enlightenment in Late-Tsarist Russia* (Seattle: University of Washington Press, 2009), 32.

14. Cited in Shmuel Feiner, *Haskalah and History: The Emergence of a Modern Jewish Awareness of the Past* [Heb.] (Jerusalem: Zalman Shazar, 1995), 378–379.

15. For the early versions of *The Little Man* and *Fishke the Lame* in English translation, see Ken Frieden, ed., *Classic Yiddish Stories of S. Y. Abramovitsh, Sholem Aleichem, and I. L. Peretz* (Syracuse: Syracuse University Press, 2004), 3–54.

16. Compare Cathy Popkin, "Distended Discourse: Gogol, Jean Paul, and the Poetics of Elaboration," in *Essays on Gogol: Logos and the Russian Word*, ed. Susanne Fusso and Priscilla Meyer (Evanston, Ill.: Northwestern University Press, 1992), 185–199, here, 194.

17. S. Y. Abramovitsh, "The Brief Travels of Benjamin III," trans. Hillel Halkin, in *Tales of Mendele the Bookpeddler*, ed. Dan Miron and Ken Frieden (New York: Schocken, 1996), 361–362. Translation altered; for the Yiddish original, see Abramovitsh, "Masoes binyomin hashlishi," in *Ale verk fun Mendele Moykher-sforim*, 17 vols. (Warsaw: Ferlag Mendele, 1911–1913), 10:81.

18. Mendele Moykher-Sforim, "Fishke the Lame," trans. Gerald Stillman, in *The Three Great Classic Writers of Modern Yiddish Literature*, ed. Marvin Zuckerman et al., 3 vols. (Malibu, Calif.: Joseph Simon/Pangloss Press, 1991), 1:172–173. Translation altered. For the Yiddish original, see Abramovitsh, "Fishke der krumer," *Ale verk*, 11:6–7.

19. Abramovitsh, "Benjamin III," 378. Translation slightly altered.

20. Ibid., 380. Translation slightly altered.

21. Ibid., 319.

22. Ibid., 383.

23. Friedrich Schlegel, *Philosophische Vorlesungen aus den Jahren 1804 bis 1806*, cited in Anne K. Mellor, *English Romantic Irony* (Cambridge, Mass.: Harvard University Press, 1980), 27.

24. Abramovitsh, "Benjamin III," 384.

25. Ibid., 389. Translation altered; for the original see, Abramovitsh, "Masoes," 117.

26. Friedrich Schlegel, "On the Aesthetic Value of Greek Comedy" (1794), cited in Raymond M. Immerwahr, *The Esthetic Intent of Tieck's Fantastic Comedy* (St. Louis: Washington University Press, 1953), 22.

27. Moses Mendelssohn, *Jerusalem; or, On Religious Power and Judaism*, trans. Allan Arkush (Hanover, N.H.: University Press of New England, 1983), 127–128.

28. Sh. J. Abramovitsh, *The Wishing Ring*, trans. Michael Wex (Syracuse: Syracuse University Press, 2003), 1.

29. Ibid., 12.

30. Ibid., 1–2.

31. *Two Essays: Naïve and Sentimental Poetry and On the Sublime*, trans. Julius A. Elias (New York: Frederick Ungar, 1979), 154.

CHAPTER 10 — THE END OF ENLIGHTENMENT

1. Cited in Abraham P. Socher, *The Radical Enlightenment of Solomon Maimon: Judaism, Heresy and Philosophy* (Stanford, Calif.: Stanford University Press, 2006), 109. I have altered Socher's translation slightly; for Moritz's original introduction to the volume, see *Salomon Maimons Lebensgeschichte*, ed. Zwi Batscha (Frankfurt am Main: Jüdischer Verlag, 1995), 7–8.

2. Heinrich Graetz, cited in Socher, *Radical Enlightenment*, 5.

3. Shmuel Feiner, *The Origins of Jewish Secularization in Eighteenth-Century Europe*, trans. Chaya Naor (Philadelphia: University of Pennsylvania Press, 2011), 4.

4. Ibid., 24–25.

5. Socher, *Radical Enlightenment*, 8.

6. Ibid., 113.

7. Ibid., 163.

8. Ibid.

9. Ibid., 9.

10. Ibid., 36.

11. Maimon, *Autobiography*, trans. J. Clark Murray (Urbana: University of Illinois Press, 2001), 6. This widely available paperback is a reprint of an English translation of *Lebensgeschichte* that was first published in 1888. It leaves out most of the philosophy and, for the most part, fails to reproduce Maimon's self-deprecating humor. I cite it here

for the sake of the reader's convenience; a more accurate and complete translation remains a desideratum.

12. Ibid., 21.

13. Ibid., 43.

14. This passage appears in the introduction to the second part of the book; see *Lebensgeschichte*, 146. The entire section is missing from the English *Autobiography*, which does not retain the structure of the original and divides the entire text into chapters.

15. Gen. 12:1–2 JPS.

16. Maimon, *Autobiography*, 31.

17. Ibid., 89.

18. Ibid., 49–50.

19. Ibid., 106–107.

20. Ibid., 206.

21. Ibid., 194.

22. Ibid., 143.

23. Ibid., 122.

24. Ibid., 129–130.

25. Ibid., 189.

26. Ibid., 205.

27. Ibid., 209.

28. Ibid., 218–219.

29. Ibid., 219–220.

30. Ibid., 236–237.

31. Ibid., 241.

32. Ibid., 258.

33. Ibid., 264.

34. Ibid., 282.

35. The English edition condenses the final chapter and omits the list of articles entirely; see the original ending, in *Lebensgeschichte*, 206–212.

36. Socher, *Radical Enlightenment*, 102.

Index

Abramovich, Sh. J., 63–64, 164–180
The Abridged Travels of Benjamin III (Abramovich), 167–180
Abyss of Despair (Hanover), 84–86
Adorno, Theodor, 71
Aksenfeld, Israel, 158–161
Alexander I, 57, 132
Alexander II, 16, 20–22, 56, 132, 137, 161, 166, 174
Altmann, Alexander, 36, 65–66
Amnon and Tamar (Raschkow), 144
Anton Reiser (Moritz), 183
Aramaic (language), 148–150
Arendt, Hannah, 72
Arkush, Allan, 65–68, 70
Ascher, Saul, 8
Ashkenaz, 24, 42, 68. *See also* Eastern Europe; Jewishness and Judaism; *specific cities and intellectuals*
assimilation, 54–55, 58–59, 61, 70–72, 136. *See also* secularization
Atlanticist perspective (on Enlightenment), 9, 11–12, 16–17, 25, 192n25

Balzac, Honoré de, 25
Banbaji, Amir, 63
Baron, Salo, 53, 193n38
Bartal, Israel, 55
Barzilay, Isaac, 193n38
Baumgarten, Jean, 40
Benda, Julien, 199n23
Bendavid, Lazarus, 8
Ben-Gurion, David, 204n41
Ben Solomon, R. Elijah, 131–135
Ben Yehoshua, Shlomo, 182–185, 187–191
Berdichevskii, M. J., 75–76
Berend, Ivan, 25
Berlin, 14, 19–23, 50, 53, 59, 77, 92–93, 185–191
Berlin, Saul, 104–105, 122
Ber of Bolechow, 89
Bible, the, 31, 34, 39, 42
Bick, Jacob Samuel, 123, 129–130
Bildung (concept). *See* education (concept)
Biur (Mendelssohn), 39, 41–43, 76, 96
Blanchot, Maurice, 31

Bloch, Samson, 123
Bogrov, Grigorii, 163–164
Boyarin, Daniel, 72–73, 77
Byron, George Gordon, Lord, 135–136

Cardoso, Isaac, 40, 43
Catherine the Great, 15–16, 91
Catholicism: comparative studies of, 11, 53, 60; Habsburg empire and, 13; Iberian, 10–11; as political dimension, 83–84, 89–92, 98, 100, 134, 172
Chmielnicki war, 84, 89
Christianity. *See* Catholicism; Jewishness and Judaism; Protestantism; Russian Orthodoxy
citizenship (concept), 67, 74, 91, 95, 129, 166, 172–177
City of Faith (Fuenn), 131–135, 146
Cohen, Jeremy, 83
Cohen, Tova, 61
Coleridge, Samuel Taylor, 31
colonialism: early modern Europe and, 9–10; Haskalah and, 55–56, 71–74; Jewish outsider status and, 91–115, 129–130, 152, 161, 187; Romanticism and, 30. *See also* postcolonial thought
Confessions (Rousseau), 8
Cranz, August Friedrich, 107, 109–110
Crime and Punishment (Dostoevsky), 165
Crimean War, 171
critical theory, 71–72, 207n24, 215n30
Czartoryski, Adam, 57

Darwin, Charles, 174
Dauber, Jeremy, 62
Decembrist revolt, 16, 197n69
de'Rossi, Azariah, 85
Descartes, René, 5
Dialectic of Enlightenment (Adorno and Horkheimer), 71
diasporas: Exile as concept and, 81–88; Haskalah and, 57, 72; Huguenot, 9; Pauline interpretation of, 98–99. *See also* Haskalah; Jewishness and Judaism
Dictionary (Johnson), 6

221

Diderot, Denis, 6, 15
Dik, Ayzik Meyer, 62, 157
Discourse on Inequality or second *Discourse* (Rousseau), 4
Dostoevsky, F. M., 165
double-consciousness, 161
Dubin, Lois, 56, 58

Eastern Europe: Enlightenment rationalism and, 12–13, 46; in Haskalah scholarship, 181–191; Haskalah's restriction to, 22–23, 54; Jewish emancipation in, 20–21, 84–85, 90–91; modernity and, 23–24, 54; Romanticism and Enlightenment in, 24–25; shtetls of, 167–172, 174–176, 180; Yiddish and, 157, 167–180
education (concept), 27–29, 32–36, 104, 106, 161–165
Emile (Rousseau), 37
Encyclopédie (Diderot), 6
Endelman, Todd, 51–52
England, 9, 11–12
Enlightenment (European movement): absolutism and, 12–17, 21, 55–57, 101–103, 106–112, 131–135, 146, 162–163, 209n17; Atlanticist view of, 9–12, 16, 25, 192n25; chronology of, 3–4; critiques of, 70–77, 181; Haskalah's mistranslation and, 3, 23–24, 26, 46; historical context of, 9–11; materialism and, 10, 29, 120, 125, 127, 161, 164, 179; Mendelssohn and, 65–71; modernity and, 50–51; rationalism and, 4–8, 24–26, 50, 66, 140, 164–167, 170, 212n37; revolution and, 15–18; Sephardim and, 10–11; social contract theory and, 17–18, 37, 178
Erik, Max, 26
Ettinger, Shmuel, 76
Euchel, Isaac, 120–121
Eugene Onegin (Pushkin), 154–155
excommunication, 11, 109–110, 112
Exile (concept), 81–89, 92, 122, 140, 147. *See also* diasporas
experience (in Haskalah thinking), 66

Feiner, Shmuel, 60–61, 76–77, 181–182, 186
First Fruits of the Times (Jeiteles), 121
Fishke the Lame (Abramovich), 167–170, 180
Fishman, David, 56–58
Fleckeles, R. Ezekiel, 103–104, 211n24
Foucault, Michel, 207n24
Frankfurt School, 71–72
Frederick II, 15, 19, 59, 91

Freeze, ChaeRan, 135
French Revolution, 3–4, 9, 15–16, 18, 28–30, 130
Friedländer, David, 44–45
Frivolity and Hypocrisy (Halle-Wolfssohn), 120
Fuenn, Sh. J., 131–135, 146

Galicia (Eastern Europe), 23–24, 54–58, 91, 94, 96, 100, 121–129, 146
Gans, David, 85
Gaon, the, 131–135
Gates of Zion (Hanover), 86
Gelehrter, 18–19, 27–28, 177
gender: language and, 148–150, 152–53, 157; maskilim's view of, 43–44, 61, 135–156, 174–178; reading and, 39–40, 42–43, 155–156; Russian politics and, 162
ghettos, 53, 60, 84
glasnost, 162
Glorious Revolution, 9
Glückel of Hameln, 93, 221n2
"The God Apollo" (Heine), 151
Goethe, Johann Wolfgang von, 20, 25, 45
Goldfaden, Abraham, 120
Goldish, Matt, 194n41
Gordon, David, 165
Gordon, Judah Leib, 56, 137, 147–156
Graetz, Heinrich, 68
Great Reforms, 21–22, 56, 136, 146, 148, 161–163, 170–177
Grimm, Jacob, 38
Guide for the Perplexed (Maimonides), 27, 68, 186–187
Guide for the Perplexed of Our Time (Krochmal), 8, 125–130
The Guilt of Samaria (Mapu), 137

Habsburg dynasty, 12–13, 15, 42, 55–56, 91–95, 98. *See also specific dynasts*
Hakohen, Shalom, 144
Halevi, Judah, 81
Halkin, Shimon, 62
Halle-Wolfssohn, Aaron, 120
Hameasef (journal), 43
Hanover, Nathan, 84–86, 90–91
Hasidim: in Jewish fiction, 115–121, 123–130, 159–161; Jewish tradition and, 49–50, 123; maskilim's view of, 32, 43, 57, 62, 123–124, 126, 129–135, 146, 157; messianic tensions in, 86–88; practices and beliefs of, 114–115; rabbinic authority and, 69
Haskalah: *Bildung* and, 27–28, 30–36, 106, 159–161, 164; chronology of, 8; definitions

of, 26–28, 33; in Eastern Europe, 22–23, 54, 167–180; European enlightenment and, 3, 9–17, 23, 32, 37–46, 50, 55, 58, 65–77; exegetical work and, 39, 41–43; Exile and, 81–89, 140, 147; Frankfurt School and, 71–73; gender and, 43–45, 135–156, 176–178; German, 24–25, 45–46, 65–66, 68–69; Hasidic Judaism and, 43, 113–121, 131–135, 157, 159–161; Jewish emancipation and, 21–23, 55–57, 59, 192n16; liberalism and, 65–67; literary elements of, 60–64, 82, 93–112, 115–140, 157–158, 166–180; Mendelssohn's thinking and, 65–71; messianic tensions in, 86–112, 122, 160, 167, 175, 185; modernity and, 50–54, 115–130; Romanticism and, 25, 29–34, 81, 102; Rousseau and Kant and, 8; scholarship on, 23–46, 49–53, 55–65, 74–76, 181–191; secularization and, 49, 56, 58, 72; temporality and, 94–97, 101, 104–107, 122–126, 168, 172, 180; translation issues and, 8–9, 22, 24, 46, 76; as transnational phenomenon, 24–25, 54–59

Hebrew (language), 43, 45, 136–138, 152–153, 158, 163, 183–184

Hegel, Georg Wilhelm Friedrich, 30, 125, 127, 179, 190

Heine, Heinrich, 20, 125, 151, 154

Herder, Johann Gottfried, 31

Herz, Marcus, 8

Herzl, Theodor, 74

Hess, Jonathan, 74

Hobbes, Thomas, 19, 209n17, 212n37

Hoffmann, E.T.A., 117

Hohenzollern dynasty, 12, 91–93. *See also* specific dynasts

Holocaust, 72

Holy Roman Empire, 12, 98

Horkheimer, Max, 71

hypocrisy, 8, 113–121, 123–126

Ibn Ezra, Abraham, 45, 70

Ibn Verga, Solomon, 85

In the Heat of Time (Levanda), 134–136

Islam, 82–83, 86

Israel, Jonathan, 9, 11

Jeiteles, Judah, 121–123

Jerusalem (Mendelssohn), 36–39, 65–71, 74, 77, 105, 107–110, 112, 127, 178–179

Jewishness and Judaism: aesthetics and, 32–33, 35–36, 43; anti-Jewish sentiment and, 89–90; Ashkenazi, 24, 42; blood libel and, 67, 90; double-consciousness, 161;

education (*Bildung*) and, 27, 29, 159–161; enlightenment's translation and, 3–4, 8–9, 23–24, 46; excommunication and, 109–110, 112; exegetical work and, 39–41, 43; Exile and, 81–89, 122, 140, 147; gender and, 43–45, 135–156, 162, 174, 176–178; guilt and, 81–83; Hasidim and, 43, 113–115, 146, 159–161; Holocaust and, 72; interactions with other religions of, 82–84, 86, 94–100, 107–109, 112, 164, 172; languages and, 157, 183–184; laws and, 10, 36–39, 41, 50, 52, 73–74, 84, 107, 109–112, 125, 127–128, 151–152, 178–179; Mendelssohn's thinking and, 65–71; messianic rhetoric and, 86–112, 122, 160, 167, 175; modernity and, 26, 34, 50–52, 60, 62, 70–71, 74–76, 97, 113–115, 162–163; mysticism and, 86–87; nationalism and, 21–22, 26, 54, 57–58, 63–64, 72, 74–75, 134–135, 204n41; Orthodoxy and, 72, 105, 147, 211n24; Pauline writings and, 98–100; pogroms and, 21; political emancipation and, 21–23, 56–59, 101, 106–115, 127–135, 152, 166–177; postmodernism and, 72; rationality and, 66, 68, 70, 75–76, 98; secularization and, 26, 28, 43, 49, 52–53, 56, 65–67, 70, 84, 89, 146, 161, 163–164, 174–176, 182; Sephardim and, 10–11, 40, 68, 193n38, 194n41; shtetls and, 167–172, 174–176; temporality and, 94–97, 101, 104–107, 122–126, 168, 172, 180; Yiddish and, 41–42, 44, 60–63, 157–158, 160, 164

The Jews of Georgian England (Endelman), 51–52

Johnson, Samuel, 6

Joseph, Heimann, 184

Joseph II, 15, 91, 93–96, 98–99, 101, 103, 112, 146

Jost, Isaac Markus, 124, 128–129

Journal of Practical Psychology, 183

Der Judenstaat (Herzl), 74

Kabbalah, 32, 68, 86–87, 137, 186, 188

Kalmanovich, Zelig, 158

Kant, Immanuel: aesthetics and, 35; critical project of, 4–9, 24–26, 28, 176–177, 181, 190; on freedom, 18–21, 140, 161; Haskalah thinking and, 27, 66, 130, 189–190; social contract theory and, 17–18

Karp, Jonathan, 35–36

Kater Murr (Hoffmann), 117

Katz, Jacob, 49–55, 59, 72–73, 75–76

khappers (term), 170–174

Kieval, Hillel, 54–55

Klausner, Joseph, 26
Kohelet musar (journal), 35–36, 69
Krochmal, Nahman, 8, 124–130, 179
The Kuzari (Halevi), 81

Landau, Ezekiel, 103–105, 211n24
Lavater, Johann Kaspar, 107
Lederhendler, Eli, 57–58
Lefin, Mendel, 57
Leibniz, Gottfried, 23, 31
Lessing, Gotthold Ephraim, 30
Levanda, Lev, 134–136, 163–164
Levinsohn, Isaac-Baer, 114, 157–158, 160
The Life History of Solomon Maimon (Maimon), 181–191
Light of the Eyes (de'Rossi), 85
Lilienblum, M. L., 137
literature: Bible as, 31, 34; gender and sexuality and, 139–157; Haskalah's definition and, 33; Jewish fiction writing and, 115–121, 124–130, 157–161, 163–164, 166–180; maskilim styles and tropes and, 93–112; Romanticism and, 28–33. *See also specific authors and works*
Littlejohns, Richard, 45
The Little Man (Abramovich), 167
Locke, John, 67, 109, 212n37
Love of Zion (Mapu), 136–146, 153, 215n23
Lowenstein, Steven, 24, 58–59
Luria, Isaac, 86
Lutheranism, 13
Luzzatto, Moshe Hayyim, 32–34
Luzzatto, Samuel David, 129

Maimon, Solomon, 8, 27–28, 32, 181–191
Maimonides, 27, 45, 68, 70, 76, 183–184, 190
Manekin, Rachel, 58
Mapu, Abraham, 136–147, 153, 155, 215n23
Maria Theresa (empress), 91
Marx, Karl, 8, 26
maskilim: *Bildung* and, 27–28, 32–36; definitions of, 32; in Eastern Europe, 54–58, 61–62, 113–116, 157; European enlightenment and, 55; exegetical work and, 39, 41–43; Frankfurt School critiques and, 71–73; gender and, 43–45; Jewish reception of, 31, 43, 60–61; Kant and Rousseau and, 8–9, 21, 66; language of renewal and, 74–77, 89–112, 160, 166–168, 185; mysticism and, 87–88; rabbinic authority and, 33, 103–105, 111–112, 147–149, 184, 186; relation to aristocracy, 17, 84–85, 113–115, 132–133, 146–147, 162; secularization and, 26, 52, 54, 56, 60–61, 164; translations of, 3; women and, 43–44, 61, 135–156, 174–178
materialism, 8, 10, 29, 120, 125, 127, 161, 164, 179
Mendele and the National Project (Banbaji), 63–64
Mendelsohn, Ezra, 57
Mendelssohn, Moses: assimilation and, 59, 188; *Bildung* concept and, 28, 106, 164; *Biur*, 39–43, 76, 96; Enlightenment and Romanticism's relation to, 34–46, 212n37; founder status of, 24–25, 27, 34, 65, 68, 92, 121–122; gender and, 43–45; Haskalah scholarship and, 54, 65; *Jerusalem*, 36–39, 65–71, 74, 77, 105, 107–110, 112, 127, 178–179; Jewish law and, 106–109, 111–112, 178–179; maskilim's definition and, 32; rabbinic repudiations of, 104–105, 109; secularization and, 73–75; social contract theory and, 38–39; temporality and, 96, 106–107
Meyer, Michael, 50–51, 54
Mickiewicz, Adam, 133
Milosz, Czeslaw, 133
Miron, Dan, 62
modernity: Eastern Europe and, 23–24, 49, 181–191; Hasidic responses to, 113–115; Jewish fiction writing and, 115–130; Polish literary movements and, 131–135; Romanticism and, 26, 105–108; secularization and, 49–51, 54, 58, 60, 62, 70, 74–76, 113–115, 121, 146, 161; Wessely and, 97
Mondshein, Zelig, 124
morality, 4, 18–19, 31, 35–36, 58, 124–130, 187
Morgulis, Menashe, 169–170, 175
Moritz, Karl Philipp, 181–191
Moses Mendelssohn and the Religious Enlightenment (Sorkin), 68–70
Mufti, Aamir, 74

The Nag (Abramovich), 165, 170, 173
Nahman, R., of Bratslav, 158–159
Napoleonic Wars, 16, 24, 28, 59, 132, 158
Nathan of Gaza, 86
Newton, Isaac, 31, 122
Nicholas I, 16, 55–56, 133, 146, 162, 166, 170–174
Nieto, David, 12
Nietzsche, Friedrich, 75

OPE (Society for the Education of the Jews in Russia), 162–164, 166, 173
orientalism, 31
Origins of the Modern Jew (Meyer), 50

Pale of Settlement, 25, 55, 57, 157, 161, 164–165, 173
Paul, Saint, 97–102
Perl, Joseph, 57, 115–121, 125, 155, 157–158, 160
"Perpetual Peace" (Kant), 17, 21
Peter the Great, 13–14, 16
Philo, 125
Polish-Lithuanian Commonwealth: colonial practices in, 89–112; enlightened absolutism and, 15, 17, 84, 90–91, 101–103, 106–113, 131–135; government of, 13; Jewish tradition and, 49–50, 56–58, 84–85, 104, 131–135, 157; literary movements in, 131–135; political boundaries of, 89; socioeconomic reconstruction in, 113–115
Pope, Alexander, 122
positivism, 8, 71, 164–167, 170
postcolonial thought, 70–71, 73–74
postmodernism, 72, 207n24
Potemkin, G. A., 57
Prague, 54, 185
The Preacher (journal), 165
Protestantism, 10, 53, 60, 83–84
Prussia: enlightened absolutism and, 12, 15, 42; Haskalah's origins and, 25, 181–191; Lutheranism in, 13
Pugachev rebellion, 15
Pushkin, Alexander, 154–155

rabbinic authority: dissident status of, 73; exegetical work and, 33, 41, 43; Exile question and, 81–83; Hasidim and, 69; Jewish literature and, 41–42, 103; literary representations of, 131–135; maskilim as threat to, 60, 87–88, 96, 103–105, 111–112; secularization and, 49
Rabinovich, Osip, 163–164
Rapoport, Solomon Judah, 129–130
Raschkow, Eleazar, 144
rationalism, 24–25, 66–70, 98, 120–121, 128–129, 140, 164–170, 212n37
reading, 40–43, 155–156
Reb Henokh or What's to Be Done? (Euchel), 120
Reformation, 83–84
Renan, Ernest, 31
Revealer of Secrets (Perl), 115–121, 155, 157–158, 160
Richardson, Samuel, 154–155
Romancero (Heine), 151
Romanov dynasty, 12–14, 91. *See also specific dynasts*
Romanticism: definitions of, 25–26; German, 28; Hasidim and, 114–115;

Haskalah's connections to, 25, 27–30, 32–46, 56, 76–77, 81, 102; Kant and, 28–29; literature and, 35, 157–158; wholeness and, 29–31. *See also* Haskalah; Jewishness and Judaism; *specific thinkers*
Roskies, David, 62
Rousseau, J. J., 4, 7–8, 18, 25, 29, 37–38, 58
Rubin, Solomon, 123
Ruderman, David, 11–12
Russia: enlightened absolutism and, 12–17, 20–22, 91, 146, 167–172; Haskalah in, 23–25, 54–57; Jewish emancipation and, 21–23, 56–57, 131–136, 160–163, 166, 168–173, 176–177; pogroms in, 21
Russian Orthodoxy, 13, 17, 89, 134, 172
Russo-Turkish War, 171–172

Sabbatian movement, 86–88, 104
Saul, Nicholas, 45
Savigny, Friedrich Carl von, 38
Schelling, Friedrich, 36
Schiller, Friedrich, 25, 28, 30–31, 35, 45, 180
Schlegel, Friedrich, 76
Scientific Revolution, 3–4
Scott, Walter, 30
Secrets of Paris (Sue), 137
secularization: Frankfurt School and, 71–72; Hasidic Judaism and, 120; Haskalah and, 26, 43, 49–50, 52–54, 56, 58–60, 62; Jewish modernity and, 59–62, 70–71, 74–77, 84, 89, 163–164, 174–176, 182; Kant and, 28; literary tastes and, 61–62; Mendelssohn's thought and, 70; messianic politics and, 95
Seidman, Naomi, 61–62
Sephardim, 10–11, 40, 68–69, 193n38, 194n41. *See also* Exile (concept); Jewishness and Judaism; *specific thinkers*
Shakespeare, William, 35
Shapira, H. N., 136–137
Shavit, Uzi, 26–28, 76
Shear, Adam, 193n38
Shelley, Percy Bysshe, 30
Shoot of David (Gans), 85
shtetls, 167–172, 174–176, 180
Shulman, Kalman, 137
Silber, Michael, 55
Simhah, Solomon, 200n36
Sinkoff, Nancy, 56
Sins of Youth (Lilienblum), 137
"Sketches from the Talmudic Era" (Morgulis), 168
Smolenskin, Peretz, 130
Socher, Abe, 182–184, 190

social contract theory, 11, 17–18, 30, 37–39, 84, 111, 178, 209n17, 212n37
Society for the Education of the Jews in Russia (OPE), 162–164, 166, 173
Sofer, R. Moses, 211n24
Songs of Splendor (Wessely), 97
Sorkin, David, 60, 66, 68–70, 77
Spinoza, Baruch, 5–9, 66, 83, 99, 107–109, 188, 190, 192n16
Staff of Judah (Ibn Verga), 85
Stanislawski, Michael, 55–56, 215n30
Stern, Betsalel, 146
St. Petersburg, 14, 57, 157, 164
Sue, Eugène, 25, 137

Teller, Adam, 84
temporality, 95–98, 101, 104–107, 122–126, 168, 172, 180
Terror, the, 16, 28–29, 130
"The Tip of the Yud" (Gordon), 137, 147–156, 215n28
Toleranzpatent (public policy), 91–94, 96, 98–101, 106, 112
Toward Modernity (Katz), 54–55
Tradition and Crisis (Katz), 49, 51–52, 59
translation, 3, 8–9, 22–26, 46, 76
The Treason of the Intellectuals (Benda), 199n23
Trivellato, Francesca, 11
Tsar Nicholas I and the Jews (Stanislawski), 55
Tugendhold, Jacob, 114

Ukraine, 84–85

Venevitinov, D. V., 32
Vienna, 14
Vilna, 131–135, 157, 160
The Vineyard (journal), 131
Voltaire, François Marie Arouet de, 15

Wars of Religion, 84
Wessely, Naftali Herz, 27, 32, 43, 92–112, 121, 125–126, 146, 180
"What Is Enlightenment?" (Kant), 6–7, 18
The Wimple (Aksenfeld), 159–161
The Wishing Ring (Abramovich), 167, 180
Wodzinski, Marcin, 56, 58
Wolf, Sheyna, 156
Wolff, Christian, 23, 28
women: in Haskalah literature, 134–156; maskilim's view of, 43–44, 61; reading and, 39–40, 42–43, 155–156; Russian reforms and, 162
Words of Peace and Truth (Wessely), 27, 92–96, 98, 101–103, 105, 107, 112, 121

Yiddish (language), 24, 41–44, 61–63, 157–164, 215n23

Zionism, 21–22, 26, 54–58, 63–64, 72–75, 134–135, 204n41
Zorich, Semion, 57
Zvi, Sabbatai, 86, 95

About the Author

OLGA LITVAK is an associate professor and Michael and Lisa Leffell Chair in Modern Jewish History at Clark University. She is the author of *Conscription and the Search for Modern Russian Jewry* (Indiana University Press, 2006).

www.ingramcontent.com/pod-product-compliance
Lightning Source LLC
Chambersburg PA
CBHW020647300426
44112CB00007B/270